TAKING LEAVE

TAKING LEAVE

a novel by

Roger Hubank

 THE ERNEST PRESS

Published by The Ernest Press
© Roger Hubank 2004

ISBN 0 948153 75 X

Type-set in 11 on 15 point Goudy by Stanningley Serif
Printed by St Edmundsbury Press

Acknowledgements

I am grateful to A.P. Watt Ltd, on behalf of Michael B
Yeats, for permission to quote a line from W.B. Yeats's 'He
wishes for the Cloths of Heaven'. The quotation from
'Poetry of Departures' by Philip Larkin is reprinted from
The Less Deceived by permission of The Marvell Press,
England and Australia.

Other quotations include lines from Philip Larkin's 'Mr
Bleaney'(*The Whitsun Weddings*, Faber & Faber. 1964);
William Empson's 'Aubade' (*The Gathering Storm*, Faber &
Faber. 1940); W.H. Auden's 'Missing' (*Collected Shorter
Poems 1930–1944*, Faber & Faber. 1950); Marianne
Moore's 'Poetry' (*American Poetry*, ed. Donald Hall, Faber
& Faber. 1969); and Raymond Queneau's 'Si tu
t'imagines'. Every effort has been made to contact the
copyright holders, and the author will be happy to correct
mistakes and omissions in future editions.

I would also like to express my thanks to Dave Beamish,
for invaluable advice, to Chris Fitzhugh and John
Kendrick, for help with the proofs, and to Nick Howarth,
of the Derby Mountain Rescue team.

For Michael,
with whom all this began
so long ago.

Autumn

'It is too late to start
For destinations not of the heart.'

Philip Larkin

ONE

Moor House. The man switched off the engine. Sat back. This was it, then.

Wind rattled dead leaves under the gate. Flickered up more leaves against the dry stone wall. Gravel. A rough lawn. More wall. A stand of trees. Then the open moor. Dead bracken and bleached tussocky grass scrambling past rocks and boulders up to the plantation.

He felt the exhilaration of his drive evaporating fast. It left a chill behind.

Running, rather than arriving, had obsessed him all afternoon as he drove north. Buoyant at the leap he'd taken. Exuberant. At hedges, fields, flashing past. Oh, to get away..

Once across the Cheshire plain, he crossed the border. Derbyshire, the sign said. Then on through Chapel, Slackhall, rounding the zig-zags, letting the Rover race down the Winnats into Castleton, past caves and caverns, lines from the Larkin poem singing in his head:

He chucked up everything
And just cleared off.

Just then Win Hill slid aside. He saw again the dark line of the Derwent moors. Then, in mid-distance, he caught sight of the great grey headland high above Bamford, and felt the old clutch of excitement. Yes, that was the wall to set one's back against.

Heart leaping, he'd swung left at the Marquis and roared on up through the village, singing, exulting. Hardman's exit from the Halls of Death.

Truth was, the literature he'd helped deconstruct was flaking badly. Chunks flying off and rattling in his head. *Yeah, it seemed the best thing to be up and go.* The thought of October coming round again, of another year, filled him with panic. He had to get away. He'd picked up the phone the moment he saw the let in the Guardian. Sent a cheque the same day. Thank God, he thought, for money.

He looked doubtfully at his new home. Its face of bleak, grey cladding. A square stone house, sideways to the track. The track ran on up the dale. Two huge trees hung over a gable end. A house standing in another century. Dour, it looked. And damp. The windows, though, were handsome. Each with its grooved, stone surround. There was a name for them, he remembered. Windows like that. It spoke of taste, proportion. And that grave front door with its stone pilasters, its pediment. The key, massive and black, lay on the seat beside him.

A flurry of wind whipped up the leaves again as he stepped on to the track. The man shivered. He lifted his bag, then slammed back the boot.

The iron gate had stuck in its worn groove. He had to lift it free. A bird watched from stunted beech twigs beside a wall. He went on past a solitary rose-bush, crunching over the stiff gravel.

He pushed the heavy key into the lock. *It's a bit on the stiff side*, said the postmistress who'd given him the key. *Gi'e it a good bang.*

He turned key and handle together, and put his shoulder to the door. It opened to him with a groan.

He looked round. White walls. A long rectangular hall. Fine wide staircase to one side. Rush matting. A floor of dark, wooden blocks. His heels rang against them as he moved about. Door left. Locked. Must be the other, empty half of the house. Door on the right. He opened it. Too gloomy to see much. A high ceiling. Shapes of chairs. A sofa. A wide stone hearth. Something massive in one corner. A further door, half-open. Under the window the leaden daylight lit on a long black table. Black, high-backed chairs set round as if, it struck him darkly, for the Reading of the Will. A sour fug of stale smoke filled the room.

He fastened back a loose shutter, drew down an upper sash.

Across the valley the dark mass of Kinder loomed under the last grey light. Something sailed past the window. Owl? Bat?

He turned, and bumped round the table. Things struck his knees. Cautiously he felt his way, contoured round a sofa, traversed a chimney breast. Chair. Another table. A switch, ah.

The small lamp caught the nearest chair in a pool of light. The rest flung back in shadow. Something looming turned out to be a dresser as black and massive as the table. The light glinted on worn brass locks and handles. It struck a chilly gleam. Black oak, he thought. Six feet high at least. Carved. Crenellated. With doors, drawers, serpentine columns. Under a frieze, topped by a kind of balustrade, a deep shelf sheltered a family of grimy plates.

In front of the huge, empty grate stood an electric fire. The man plugged it in. Its meagre glow did little to cheer the spirit.

But the kitchen comforted. Clean, too, he thought with relief. A neon strip lit up a long narrow room filled with familiar things. Electric cooker. Gleaming taps. A sink of stainless steel. He opened drawers filled with new cutlery. Things for frying, poking, ladling, hung from a wall.

The sight of his shopping list, propped against a teapot, brought to mind the note waiting for his wife. Still ten days or so before she got back from the States. Though Elizabeth's response was not difficult to guess. *I simply can't imagine why you're doing this. It's beyond me..* In a cupboard the tins he'd ordered. Milk in the fridge. Cold cooked chicken. There was a freezer too, he remembered, in the washhouse. A red light glowed beside a switch. That looked promising. He turned on a tap: water gushed, getting hotter. He turned it off.

Whistling now, he opened a further door and stepped back into the hall. Found a switch, saw his bag at the entrance, darkness beyond the open door. He banged the door shut, picked up his bag and climbed the dogleg stair past old oil paintings of nineteenth century gents. Farmers with long, lugubrious faces. Sharp-faced, foxy country lawyers.

A landing. Door off. More doors at the end. But a further flight of stairs surprised. A room in the roof? He went up to see.

An attic. He stood a moment in the close, musty space under the roof. Plenty of room, though. A skylight. Bunk beds. A box of battered toys. Yes, for the summer holiday kids.

He came down again to the landing. Under an arched window, an old dower chest. Really old. Panels decayed in places. Ah, extra blankets.

He opened the other door into a vast Spartan bedroom. Bare boards. A strip of carpet. Old-fashioned bedstead. Brass, by the look of it. Must be worth a bit, he thought, a bed like that. An air of decayed grandeur hung over the panelled walls, the spacious window with its white shutters, its curtains of rough, undyed wool that slid on rings along a massive cornice pole.

He unpacked his bag, tossing shirts, towels, toilet bag on to the bed. A folding photograph frame slid on to the floor. He bent down to retrieve it, stood it on the bedside table, staring at his wife's face. *It's beyond me..* That voice, its note of weary exasperation, echoed in his head:

"There's a great deal that's beyond you," he ground out, as he unpacked the rest of his clothes. Though Elizabeth, he reflected sourly, never let that stand in her way.

There it was again, that welling up of bile. The sourness that poisoned everything. Over the years he'd said many things he'd regretted. But they stayed said. Suddenly he felt depressed again. As if he'd turned a corner to find himself back where he'd started. Or else his malaise had gone ahead of him, to greet him here in this strange house of musty rooms, and massive funerary furniture.

He tumbled the last items from the bottom of his bag, a few socks, pants, a woollen sweater. It was like unpacking in a tomb.

To begin with he slept badly. At home, even in bed at night, he was used to light, noise. He had forgotten what darkness was. Here, even with the curtains open, no light entered the room. He lay in the strange bed staring up into the darkness, illuminated by flashes of a world he'd turned his back on. Presumably his resignation had been announced. He imagined Seton sitting at the long table littered with agendas, minutes, timetables, lists of students.. *God, he was so sick of words.*

By day he roamed restlessly from room to room. He wished now he hadn't left his mobile phone behind. It had been an impulsive gesture. A deliberate burning of his boats. He wanted no messages. No voice mail. He especially didn't want to be called by Seton. Now, he found himself longing for contact. He thought of his colleagues, reassembling over coffee in the common room. He embarked on imaginary confrontations as, one after another, they pleaded with him to reconsider. But the nervous craving for argument, for justification, found, in this silent house, no foil, no response.

It began to rain. He stood at a window watching the rain filling Blackden Clough. Ragged clouds, like smoke from a disaster, were driving over the Kinder plateau. His mood of dereliction deepened. He heard the wind stirring, troubling the trees above the gable, moaning in the chimney pots, telling him this was a mistake. The absence of his wife, whom he suddenly and ridiculously missed, fell on him like a hammer-stroke.

Then a great weight of weariness broke loose and swamped everything. The next few days passed in a torpor. Meals provided almost his only purposeful activity, while his sleep was so profound it might have been drugged.

One morning he woke to the drumming of a dense downpouring. He looked out over Blackden to see the moor, a vague immensity, all but blotted out by curtains of rain. The wind raged, hurling the rain against the windows, battering about the house, a double insulation, isolating him from a world he'd left behind.

It rained all day. Untroubled, now he'd emerged from that flood of sleep, he moved about over the stone flags, in the quiet spaces of the house. Or stood at a window, watching the milky rush of a brook in spate where the clough had become a torrent bed. He saw a Landrover coming down the track. He didn't wonder where it had come from. Where it was going. He felt no interest in its occupant. It was peaceful and comforting, with the wind thrashing the trees above the gable, the rain flooding from the gutters, to select from his box of books, and read, and watch the flame flickering over a fire of logs.

Towards evening the storm receded, leaving in its wake a stillness, a silence broken only by a lorry passing on the Snake. He looked up from his book to stare at the sky, a swathe of sullen fire dying over the Kinder plateau, filled with a tranquillity that was wordless.

Behind the house, across a cobbled yard, a stile set in a stone wall gave on to a sparse copse. Beyond the copse, the hillside rose steeply to the plantation. One evening he climbed the hill behind the house. It was almost dusk. Already lamps were glimmering down in the Woodlands valley. Up ahead, the dark mass of the plantation loomed against the sky. He sat on a rock to take stock of his surroundings. Far up the dale, dwindling between forested fellsides, the lights of a lonely farm. Beyond that, all visibility petered out eventually amid the wilderness of Bleaklow.

That night he sat down to his supper as the moon rose over Kinder. The fire crackled in the grate. The room smelt faintly of woodsmoke. He ate his meal in solitary peace and silence. It was enough.

After he'd cleared away the remains of his meal, and washed the dishes, he unfolded the map to see what manner of place it was. That lonely farm. It was well-called. Dalehead. His eye followed a mile or more of track to a huddle of buildings. A stand of trees. A stream, issuing from a clough, curling round and down to the river. The contour lines pressing together, pressing in. Beyond, the wastes of Bleaklow stretching away.

Most mornings he chopped logs. There was a mound of timber, covered by a tarpaulin, heaped against the wall, and spilling over into the copse. Untrimmed, most of it. Still green and damp. He found an axe in the washhouse. Blunt, rusty, but it served well enough. He sent it crashing through the wood, scattering bark, beetles, sent spiders scurrying away.

More than once the axe struck sparks as he missed, flashing back at him from the stones. He leaped back, swearing. But he enjoyed it. Swinging the axe in the fresh air. Raised a sweat, too. Strenuous. He soon stripped off in the sun. Was breathing hard, heart pounding.

He stacked the cut wood in the washhouse. It got to him, though. This labour. He ached for days.

Then followed a spell of settled weather, days when the dale was washed in a slanting October light. He saw a boy once, walking up the track towards the farm, and wondered who he was. Mostly, though, he did nothing but soak up the light. He would take his tea-tray, and sit in a sunny angle of the outhouse wall while the shadows lengthened over the cobbles. The university, its rites and formulas, had no sway here. To be out of all that was a great blessing. Freed from all that, he found himself released into a space that seemed endlessly open.

A car went by remotely on the Snake. The wind stirred the boughs above the gable. Or there would pour suddenly from some unseen bird a song of such piercing sweetness, he couldn't but raise his head from his book simply to attend. There were things he could have done, places he might have gone to. Instead, he yielded to the fullness of the moment, which was too good to miss: the clarity of light dappling the copse; a buzzard soaring over the Woodlands; a late butterfly sunning itself on the washhouse wall.

So he remained immersed in the immediate, luminous reality that was the afternoon. Solitude, it seemed, could be a home-coming.

The days passed, and Hardman settled in his house. He seemed to fill out in its space and silence. He slept well. And when he woke, whether to rain, or to light streaming in at the window, it was no longer with that sinking feeling, that quailing at the prospect of another day.

No demands were made upon his nervous energy. No *Good mornings* where no goodness was. No poisonous conversations over coffee. At a stroke, it seemed, he'd put off that load. Sometimes, pausing in the cobbled yard, or sitting on the wall under the airy, autumn trees, it actually felt like that: a putting-off of straps and weights, after the long, uphill trudge. The flexing of cramped limbs.

Sometimes, though, he couldn't help wondering how his resignation had been received. He had no way of knowing. Phone-calls would have gone unanswered. Letters unread. Seton didn't know where he was. No doubt *he* would have put it down to a sudden nervous breakdown, an explanation which his colleagues would find no difficulty in accepting. *Elizabeth*, he could hear them saying, *has been papering over the cracks in Anthony for years.* That brought back, with a rush, the spilt wine darkening the carpet, the shocked hush, his own voice, high-pitched, hysterical: *Don't anyone come near me..*

Looking back now, he was appalled. He couldn't think what had come over him. It was as if some shadowy stranger had suddenly erupted, bursting out from below. No matter. Let them think what they liked. Life, he was discovering, was most real where most simple. Cooking, washing up, seeing to the fire, keeping the place clean, seemed to him as much as he needed to be doing, at least for the time being. He saw little of his neighbours. Once or twice, hearing an engine noise, he looked out to see the battered Landrover bumping along the track. Or else he might spot the boy trudging along the track.

Often his eye was drawn to the flank of Kinder Scout, looming out of the south. He went out one morning. Misty. A bite of autumn in the air. But with a hint of brightness to come. He crossed the track, slipping down through sparse, stunted oaks to the river, where a silver birch clung in a tangle of roots to the bank. Then on, by stile and gate and footbridge over the Ashop, to join the bridle road which crosses the low end of a spur of hills coming down from Kinder Scout.

On the brow of the hill above Upper Ashop he stopped to look back. He was now at an angle above the valley which, on the right, ran down to Ladybower, under a high green ridge which ended at Crook Hill. A low October light lay over the northern moors. Just below, the Snake road wound up the pass on its way to Glossop. Before him lay the wooded mouth of the dale. He picked out Moor House, and the Rover, a Dinky toy pulled in beside the wall, with Hey Ridge above, over the hill from a huddle of grey stone that must be the barns and sheds of Heathy Lea. Eastwards, beyond Slip Wood, where Birchenlee doubled over suddenly into the dale, the tumbled stones of an ancient rockslide. To the north, empty, bare, lay Bleaklow. Under that sloping light the dark moor resembled a hazy upland desert: a baked, brown waste of shadowy folds and glowing copper hollows.

You'd never dream, he thought, of a human habitation in the middle of all that. Of men making a living. Yet Dalehead was hidden there.

Turning aside, he plodded slowly up the bridle road. Now, away to his right, he could see the craggy edge of Crookstone Knoll coming and going in the mist eddying over Kinderscout. Here the Roman road ran down to Hope. Crossing a wall, he began the climb up to the ridge, winding between stone walls and little fields where the cropped pasture gradually gave place to coarse bents and sedges. Soon he was on the open heathery moor, plodding up through bilberry and heather, buffeted by the breeze which haunts the summit of Win Hill, with the rocky pike now in view. From the summit he looked down into the deep defile of Ladybower, and its rivers, the Derwent, overhung by its craggy edges, the Ashop, winding into the heart of the Peak. To the north lay more sheets of water, between rugged hills draped by woods. Eastwards, beyond green heights, the long dark line of Derwent Edge, stretching away to Lost Lad.

Infinitely distant, now, the shocked faces, the spilt wine darkening the carpet. For years he had been struggling to keep an even keel. Now at last he had fallen off the wire. But none of that mattered. Only this new dimension of existence mattered. The reflection left him with a sense, if not of something settled, then at least of something begun. Only when he thought of Elizabeth, his uneasiness returned.

One evening he went down to the pub. A thin mist was lifting off Ladybower. Hemmed in by the hills, it clung to the gloomy ranks of spruce on the flanks of Win Will, hanging sullenly over the narrow strip of river land, that raw damp that soon chills to the bone.

A lamp fixed to a wall spilled a bleak, wet light over the sign. Bridge Inn. Hardman hesitated. Strange places made him nervous. At last he pushed open the door. Found himself in a wide, open passage. Part of a large room, dimly lit. Dark wood added to the gloom. A low partition partly screened an inner area of small heavy tables, straight-backed chairs. An upholstered bench ran round half-panelled walls which were lit by little fancy lanterns, and hung with horse brasses, odds and ends of copper, bits of fancy brass. Hardman caught a glimpse of card players: a puffy-faced woman with ashy hair, eyes screwed up against the smoke from her cigarette; the hollow side of a man's face, unshaven, under a railwayman's peaked cap.

"You've done it again," he said disgustedly.

The woman looked confused.

"You've let 'im in now," the railwayman went on. "He's throwin' away on them."

Somewhere out of sight an unseen hand tossed a card on to the table.

"That's it," said the railwayman bitterly. "We shan't stop him now."

Early yet. Not many in. Hardman moved forward towards the bar, set in a recess at one side of the room. A figure leant there, squat, barrel-chested, in conversation with just such another blunt, balding, thick-necked column of a man the other side of the bar. Tweedledum, it might have been, and Tweedledee.

"We took 'im on for a day's fencin'," he was saying. "Well, three stakes an 'e were buggered. Aye. Three stakes – and that were th' end o' t' story. He couldna lift t' bloody hammer."

He glanced casually at the newcomer.

Hardman nodded uneasily.

"Yes, young man?"

He looked up into shrewd, pale eyes. His eye fell on the pump, a name he remembered.

"Pint of Stones," he said, hoping that was right.

"Pint o' Stones," repeated the landlord, reaching for a glass.

The beer came up golden, frothing. Rich. Nutty. It was good.

Hardman set down the pint.

"Good stuff!" he said.

The landlord counted coins out of the till, slid the change back across the bar, and turned to resume his conversation.

Hardman, ill-at-ease, put a coin into the collection box on the bar. Derwent Mountain Rescue Team, it said on the side. Then, at a loss, suddenly plunged in.

"You wouldn't happen to know," he began, acutely aware of his own voice, "you wouldn't happen to know who farms up at Dalehead?"

Surprised, the two men glanced at him. He was so totally an outsider, one whose voice, manner, excluded him so thoroughly from their concern, it was as if Hardman, having ceased to exist, had suddenly reappeared.

"Dalehead?" said the younger man, shooting a hard, sideways stare.

The landlord had been polishing a pint pot. Now his cloth circled the glass slowly, mechanically, like something running down.

"That'll be Mr Ashe. He's up at Dalehead."

"Aye, owd Tom."

The stranger, rattled, cast about for words.

"Is he.. er.. approachable," he began uncertainly.

The landlord looked at him sharply.

"He'll not take his gun to you if that's what you mean. Why?"

Hardman wasn't used to bluntness.

"Oh, nothing sinister," he chuckled, trapped into just the sort of plummy laugh he loathed. "It's just that I'm a new neighbour of his. I'm renting the house over the hill from him."

The two men were still staring.

"Moor House," he added.

The landlord grunted.

"Aye. Well it's Mr. Ashe you want."

He turned back to his polishing, interest quelled as quickly as it had arisen.

Hardman drank the rest of his beer quickly without enjoyment, and left the pub.

*

So, gradually, he entered into this deeply folded land of humps and hollows, of narrow dales and looming hills. He looked long at earth and sky, trying to understand what he was doing here.

One day he parked the Rover in a grassy space at the foot of a long steep lane. He was glad no one was about. He must look a sight. A relic from an earlier age. Scarlet stockings. Icelandic sweater, out at the elbow. Tattered moleskin breeches. Mountain boots stiff now with disuse. Most of his friends had worn these. Eggers. Or Frendos. Thirty pounds he'd paid for them long ago at Snell's, in Chamonix.

Over the wall, then..

He lifted an awkward boot, swung a thigh astride, slithered down. A stone toppled off behind him. He stopped to put it back.

The wind stirred suddenly, ran on through the thin stand of trees beyond the wall. Somewhere, sharp, distinct, a dog began to bark. He tramped uneasily through the sparse, autumn copse. Twigs crackled under foot. Here and there bleached bones scattered about. A skull goggled at him under leaves. He looked up through high, skeletal domes. A bright afternoon. Sharp, though. A sun more for colour. It lit up the grey stone, the dried apricot bracken. Gave air a sparkle. He came out from the trees. Started up steep bracken.

Hardman was trespassing. Years had passed but he knew enough to know that. They were always strictly preserved, the moors above Bamford. To the sense of space around him, the freshness of things, it gave an added *frisson* of excitement. Of the illicit.

He walked in the way he remembered. Flatfooted, rolling the thigh to lengthen the stride. A slow, steady plod. But the boots felt heavy. Sinewy strands of bracken caught at his ankle, legged him down. He scrambled up abrupt banks, only to slip back as the soft peat slid. Not long, and his calves strained at every stride.

Christ, a rest would be nice. A look at the view. Too soon, though. Heart pounding, he plodded on. Came at last, thankfully, to a shoulder where easier land began

Fresh up here. He felt the wind buffeting. Sweat chilling the nape of his neck. He stopped a moment to catch his breath. Glanced back.

Already the sparse wood, the road, were far below. Smoke drifted over the Hope valley between green humpbacked hills. Across the valley, above its dark plantation, the summit of Win Hill. Once, years ago on Derwent Edge, he'd watched a pennant of snow crystals streaming from that summit cone, trailing all afternoon across the sky. Head on to the gale he went that day, struggling upward through a foot of fresh snow, crouching between boulders to eat his bread and cheese while the sleet shot in at every cranny.

Exposed now, high on the hill, Hardman kept a wary eye for keepers. *I do not approve*, he meant to say, *of the private ownership of moorland*. But feared a rough, abusive man.

He tramped now, with crunch and crackle of bracken, broken twigs, dried oak leaves, in a belt of relict oaks. Iron black. Swept uphill by centuries of wind. Steep under the trees. Low branches scraped at his scalp. One, rotten, broke as he blundered into it. He fell awkwardly, sprawled a moment, panting, heart pounding, sticky and sweating. A coppery taste filled his mouth. He spat disgustedly.

Boulders next. He picked his way, stepping gingerly, wary of a slip.

Then, among the spillage of millstone grit, he came upon

three great wheels propped on blocks. All the edges east of the Derwent are littered with these stones. Great six-foot wheels. Massive two-foot grinders. Some square-hubbed. Others blank, unfinished. Abandoned long ago.

Hardman slogged past without a second glance. Though worth stopping for. Those wheels. Two hundred years of rain have pitted the dressed stone, heather sprouts in the hollows of the hubs, but if you look closely you can still see marks of the chisel. The stones become contemporary, the family that squatted here, day-in, day-out, rain or shine, hard hands gripping the hammers, chip-chip-chipping the grindstones for the forges of Abbeydale, over the moor.

A grim job, dry-grinding. Astride the wooden horse, face to the wheel. Grim. Breathless at twenty. Knackered on the slightest hill. Coughing up the metal dust in balls. Dead at thirty. Grind the steel wet, you lived a little longer. Hard drinkers, they say, lived longest. They stayed off work the most.

Hardman, breathing heavy, sat a moment. Marvellous. Win Hill still hogging the foreground. But he could see beyond it now. The sun lighting on broadbacked Derbyshire hills patchy with mist. A black buffalo hump stuck up somewhere above Castleton must be Mam Tor. The sun sparkled on Ladybower. Shadows picked out the arches of the bridge that carried the Glossop road to its long haul over the Snake. Smoke drifted from Eyre's cement works. A white dust falling there. A land of quarried hills, mined, riddled with shafts and tunnels.

It might boom, he fancied. The land here. Like a drum. If you could beat it.

All he heard, though, was the drone of a lorry climbing the Snake. Somewhere a cock crowed. Stiff-legged, Hardman got to his feet. A minute more brought him up beneath steep, curving walls.

They face west. The gritstone edges. Sharp at dawn, with the sun behind them, they throw up a long black silhouette, blocky, capped with squares and oblongs. Then, as the sun climbs higher, a network of dark lines picks out the vertical joints that form the angular corners, the cracks and pockets that will take a jammed fist or a boot. Where sun touches a face or buttress the smoky grit turns a faint, grey, honey colour. By mid-afternoon the solid rock seems a study in black shadow and slabs of golden light.

They hurt, the gritstone edges. Yet submit oneself to their action, and they may do something in the way of grinding and polishing.

Bamford Edge stretches more than a mile: outcrops, isolated buttresses, steep, heathery moor between. But the great headland that one sees at a distance, Great Tor, towering over the Derwent Valley, extends for less than a hundred yards. For a hundred-and-fifty years there has been no right of access here. Not since the common land was enclosed. Hardman, though, is looking for privacy. There are, he remembers, a collection of easy chimneys, of antiquarian interest, such as might suit an aging crag-rat emerging from retirement. Though years have passed he has flogged up this hill nursing a secret hope, less hope than expectation, that he might still *climb* something.

Does it matter, he asks himself. Childish, in a man of his age. But for him it matters.

One look here is enough. In this steep, unrelenting place. Wandering slowly, gazing like a man patrolling a street that seems familiar, searching for a house he can no longer find, he follows a dusty path that will bring him steeply up to the terrace below the upper tier. For the edge is split at mid-height by a layer of softer shale, ground down to a runnel of sandy debris and heathery boulders that separates two tiers of steep rock.

Dominating the upper tier is a long high front of overhanging rock. The thick, upper layer, displaced eight feet or so, hangs like a roof over the cracked, slabby face. You can see the shadow of that roof from the main road half a mile away. At its base a huge, curving flake has split off from the rock. Hardman has scrambled in behind that flake. Has wriggled up left. A moment, and his head pops up ten feet higher, at a narrow bilberry ledge. Hardman, wedged safely in behind the flake, works out a theoretical ascent. A move here, a move there..

A faded sling, jammed under the roof, hints at the struggle. He looks along the ledge, narrow, sloping, to his left. A silver birch gleams at the further end. There is a chimney there, above the tree: a black gap, maybe twenty feet, with, halfway up, a chockstone.

Hardman squints at the chimney. Well, he can see how to do it – hands on the chockstone, smear with the feet, one arm reaching deeper..

Suddenly, on impulse, he pulls himself up and out from the flake and begins to edge his way along the ledge, stretches, *stretches*.. grasps, at last, the tree.

Now he surveys the chimney. Narrow. Not steep, though. The chockstone just out of reach. He'll need to thrutch a bit to get to it.

A man wedged in that chimney, engaged in strenuous pushing-down to raise the body – his downward glance would plunge past the ledge and the ten feet or so of rock beneath it – past the sloping terrace – over the drop of the lower tier and down to the steep hillside sixty or seventy feet below.

It is a characteristic of the climbing here at Bamford. This sense of exposure. You feel it on almost every route. It has to do with the foreshortening perspective, and the steepness of the ground below. Climbers get used to it. But this man is gripped. Has hooked an arm over the chockstone – a sharp edge there to which he clings gratefully – but finds all upward progress blocked now by the stone to which that arm is clamped. His head is pressed against it. He is so squeezed into the rock, his left arm, deep inside the chimney, virtually immobilised. Cautiously he ducks his head out from under the stone, leans out, frees the left arm and reaches up with it, but can do no more than jam a hand between the side wall and the sloping surface of the chockstone – now finds himself half-in, half-out of the chimney, stranded, clinging desperately.

He must come out of the chimney altogether. Get his feet out on to the rounded walls and step up (it isn't steep), trusting the friction of the grit. It is the only way. He knows it. Yet he clings, sweating, to his stone. Feels the grit grinding into his knuckles. Even thinks of lowering himself back into the chimney. Would give *anything* now to get back between those walls, but is terrified that if he lets go of the chockstone he'll fall backwards. Which is quite likely. It would require a cool head now to get back under that stone.

There is really only one way for him to go. Yet seconds tick away, and there he sticks, knowing – not long now, either – that his grip on the stone will slacken, that he must make the move.

Suddenly, an all-or-nothing haul on the arms, boots scuttling up – and Hardman heaves his top half over the chockstone. A strenuous wriggle – and he's safe between the walls, gasping, shaking with relief.

Moments later he'd climbed stiffly out at the top. He was still shaking, intermittently. Sheer panic had carried him over that chockstone. He might just as easily have fallen. Fitness? It had nothing to do with fitness. Most men of his age were capable of scrambling up a thing like that. Time was when he'd have stepped up a thing like that without a second thought. Yes – climbed it carrying a sac, en route to a bigger cliff.

No, it was something he once had. Presumed, stupidly, he still possessed. Gone now.

Dusk was falling as he came down to the road. A blue haze gathering in nearer folds of fields and woods. Trees in the west seemed drawn with a fine point against the sky. Pale lemon, the sky. It glimmered with a pallid sheen on Ladybower. Already lights were dotted here and there: on Shatton Moor, at Thornhill across the river, down in Bamford. Win Hill grew in inky bulk as he clumped down.

A stillness filled the valley, a hush in which sounds carry; a bird's cry, the bleating of a lamb, the drone of a lorry, its lights tracking the Snake. There was a time when he'd sunk happily into that hush. At dusk. Tired, content, coming off the hill.

He came down now, spent, disconsolate, knees aching from the jarring, downhill jolt, a ridiculous figure who had no business here.

A mood of weary dejection settled about him as he drove back up the Snake. His body had never lied to him. His mind had, but not his body. What had he come here for? What did he expect? The grit, he should have known, destroys all pretences.

He drove past the Woodlands chapel thinking longingly of his solitary refuge, now, as he rounded the bend below Gillot Hey, a grey shape looming against the hill. He thought he could make out what looked like a thin column of smoke rising vertically above the trees.

He crossed the bridge. Trees loomed closer. Somewhere above he thought he saw a light.

Alarmed, he got out of the car to open the gate. Yes – as the house came into view – yes, definitely. A dim light moving somewhere beyond the window. There was someone in the house.

*

It was firelight Hardman saw from the car. That glimmer beyond the window. Bright flames leaping from logs piled in the grate. Then the car, pulled off the track.

"Liz?"

The firelight flared and glimmered, catching in flashes her eyes, her face, the hammered silver stars in her ears, where she sat back in the winged chair, unmoving, her gaze fixed on him.

"I must get these bloody boots off," he said awkwardly. Grimacing, he dropped to one knee. Began unlacing. "How did you get in?"

"Through the door," she said quietly.

He enquired after her trip to the States.

"How was Northwestern Pacific?"

"Wonderful, as usual."

"And Leo?"

"He sends his regards."

He tossed the boots one by one into a corner.

"Why couldn't you have told me?" she asked at last.

"You weren't there," he said, his voice muffled, as he tugged the sweater over his head. An evasion, of course. He could have rung her. But she would have doled out her usual draught of icy medicine.

"Why?"

He tossed the sweater after the boots, and sank wearily into the chair opposite.

"I told you." He'd been through all this in his letter.

"Five lines, I think it was."

Reaching down, she produced the incriminating note from her bag, and holding it to the firelight, began to read in a flat, expressionless voice.

I have to get away. I really feel I need a change of scene for a while. I've written to Seton to tell him I'm not going back. I can't really say much more than that. I'll be in touch when you get back.

"I've had enough," he said shortly. "I don't know who I am any more."

"So you've come here in search of your lost self!"

It was no more than he expected. Yet he felt it. It came sharp.

"I suppose this is all about your fracas with Davenport."

"You've heard about that."

"Well, what did you expect? Hardly a thing you could hope to keep quiet. Bashing an external examiner."

He winced, caressing a bruised toe.

"It's such a fuss about nothing," she went on. "You all had far too much to drink, as you invariably do on these occasions. Some fool said something to upset you, and you took a swing at him. Rather ineffectually, from what I've heard."

"It's just too ridiculous for words," she went on exasperatedly. "I mean, it's not as if anyone took it terribly seriously. It's not as if you bashed a student. So why on earth resign? If you feel you need a rest why not just ask for a term off? You've never had one."

"No," he said. "It's best as it is. Seton wanted me out anyway."

"Oh, nonsense. *Nonsense!*" Her brisk voice again. "You're imagining it."

"It's nothing to do with the department, is it?" she said quietly, leaving him to pick up the implication: *It's to do with us.*

"I just needed to find a quiet, isolated place where no one knows me."

"You want to disappear."

"No. It's not that." He knew what would follow, if he allowed that.

"I have to be.." – conscious now he was clutching at straws – "..I have to become something I *ought* to be, something I feel is right for me."

She raised her head, directing at him the kind of keen-eyed look she might have aimed at one of her clients.

"And what's that?"

It was Elizabeth's gift to put her finger unerringly on painful places, while bringing no relief.

"What are you doing here, Anthony? What do you want?"

"Perhaps what I want," he burst out, "is just to be a man. Not an academic, not a husband, not a subject of the Queen, but a mere man. A non-categorized man. A man plain and simple. Man as a starting point. No, it doesn't require me to take to the hills. This is just my way of doing it. But no doubt you'll soon chop that down to size."

He sucked his knuckles. The grazes on his hand were smarting.

There was, he thought, a time when he'd rejoiced in that bare condition. A man of flesh and bones, who rejoiced to feel the sun on his back. Who shivered in the cold and wet.

"Let's have some tea," she said eventually.

She went off to the kitchen. Distantly he heard the tap turned, a rush of water drumming into the kettle, the clink of cups.

"Do you want anything to eat?" she called.

He didn't answer.

When Elizabeth came in again with tea and toast on a tray, she found him staring into the fire.

She put the tray down on the hearth, knelt down beside him, and leant across to switch on the lamp. Its yellow light fell in a little pool around them.

"What have you done to your hand?" She'd noticed the grazes, the dried blood. "Let me see."

"Oh, it's nothing," he told her absently. "It's just the grit."

For a while they sat, but scarcely together, watching the ashy logs sink and crumble in the fire. There was a time when he would have sunk down at her side, his head in her lap. He remembered, as if in another life, the touch of her fingers stirring gently against his neck. Or she would take a brush from her bag, and brush his head with slow, caressing strokes. He used to love the pressure of her hand, resting on his thigh as he drove, or passing across his back as they went together into some strange place.

"You know, Roger's very concerned about you," she said suddenly. "He wants you to take some study leave."

She took an envelope from her bag. Then, as he made no move to take it, she sighed, and put it back.

"Running away won't solve anything."

"I'm not running away. I'm simply heading in the opposite direction from the rest of you."

She looked at him wonderingly.

"Aren't you lonely?"

"I'm not lonely here." Suddenly, he was acutely conscious of their separation.

"What's the use of going into all this?" he said wearily. "I must get cleaned up."

She seemed to soften.

"You're really upset, aren't you," she said gently. "Look. Take Roger's offer. Come home with me. Let me look after you."

It might have been compelling once. But 'home', when he pictured it, resolved itself into a bleak image of her Friday night encounter sessions: that doleful procession of lame beggars who presented themselves for cleansing. There was something chilling about the way Elizabeth slid in among those bruised and bleeding psyches. The thought of himself numbered among her clients was more than he could stomach.

He shook his head.

"Look. I just know this is the way I have to be living now. Maybe not forever, maybe not next term even, but now."

Still jet-lagged from her flight, she was too tired to drive back.

"You have the bed," he said. "I'll sleep down here."

Sighing, she went upstairs, only to reappear some minutes later.

"How on earth," she began brightly, "are you going to live for a year with that bathroom?"

But he was not to be won over.

"Oh, for God's sake, Anthony. Come to bed." Getting no response, she sighed and left him to it.

Towards two o'clock he got up to go to the lavatory, wincing at the pain of bruised toes and chafed, swollen ankles. His whole body felt abused: his grazed hands sweaty and stinging, his calves, thighs, the muscles of his upper arms and chest, aching at every turn. Stiffly, groping up the stairs, he felt his way to the bathroom and switched on the light. The glare of orange walls hurt his eyes. He pissed, and pulled the chain, recoiling at the massive clank of iron, the gurgling of enormous sluices, the rush and roar of water. Then he felt his way through the darkness to the bedroom.

He sank back wearily, settling his aching limbs in the bed beside her. His wife never stirred. Close though it was, the centre of that spreading warmth, he kept his own cold flesh from contact with her body. Was anxious not to wake her. Sleepless himself, he lay a long time, hearing the soft rise and fall of her breathing, grieving for their life unlived together.

She left as abruptly as she'd arrived.

"I've put Roger's letter on the sideboard," she said tersely. "At least answer it."

"You don't have to go now," he said.

"Oh," she added, "I almost forgot." Rooting through her bag, she fetched out his mobile phone. "I brought you this. In case you need it."

She threw open the front door. Pale sunlight, filtering through mist, lit up a green, lichenous wall. A distant lamb called somewhere in the dale.

She walked on ahead down the path.

As she was unlocking the car door a piercing whistle came from somewhere over the hill. Moments later a dog shot out from the mist, and came racing down the slope. Then a man's voice, distant, yet distinct: "Come back 'ere, yer daft bogger."

"You can understand this, Liz," he faltered, "if you want to."

But she was already on her way, the BMW slipping softly, slowly down the track.

It was designed for easy disengagements, their life together.

*

Unable to settle, he prowled restlessly about the house, plunged once more into the numb misery that was his marriage. Phrases from the breakfast table still stinging in his mind. *Deeply troubling*, she'd called it. *Regressive.. narcissistic.. a flight from reality*. The truth was she was in no mind to listen.

He tried to immerse himself in simple things. He raked over the embers, swept the hearth, then set about the breakfast dishes. Yet the comfort he found in these solitary tasks was missing now. He stood in the kitchen, waiting for the kettle to boil, seeing again the BMW slipping away from him. The memory triggered a sudden spasm of panic. He was back at the top of Central Gully, preparing to tackle the cornice – only the cornice, astonishingly, began to recede. Then, as the avalanche gathered pace, he'd realised what was slipping away was *him*, sinking with the snow, sinking faster and faster, bouncing off the walls of the gully, battered, flung this way and that, somersaulting down six hundred feet to the snows below.

He'd got away with it. But only just.

That's it, she said, at his bedside. *No more*.

She was pregnant. She lost the baby. So that was that. He sold his gear, and never climbed again.

He stared bitterly at the jet of steam spouting from the kettle. One moment you're starring in your own movie, and all the time real life is waiting in the wings to fuck you up.

Only the blow had fallen on her, not him.

He took up Seton's letter from the sideboard. It had a long, official look. He turned it over. Saw the crest, the franking stamp. Suddenly he felt himself drawn back into his old malaise. He couldn't rest. He had to get out of the house.

Driving without purpose he came at length, since the road took him there, to a junction with a narrow, winding lane that seemed in keeping with his wayward mood. It led steeply uphill, climbing a tongue of high land, an outlier of Bamford Moor. Below, behind, the roofs of Hathersage fell away into the Derwent valley.

After a mile or more, he came to a corner of dark pines, where the lane turned abruptly right to run along the open moor, tussock and tawny bracken rising to a long craggy wall of rock, coming and going in the eddying mist. Stanage. Years since he'd seen it. His mind went back to summer mornings, the dawn haze lifting off the rock: Stanage in winter under a thin skither of snow; cold, leaden, whipped by wind, against a lowering sky.

Away, now, to his right a green coniferous wood, picked out in a shaft of sunlight. A white track wound out of the wood. Beyond the wood, by steep green banks, the pale sun glinted on a wall. A house, seen through trees. North Lees, he remembered. Jane Eyre's Thornfield Hall. He drove on past the plantation, past the start of the track down to the Hall.

The moorland road he remembered had been widened, the grass verge replaced with a hard standing. He pulled in a little way apart from a solitary Citroen, and started up the flagged path that led to the Edge. She went climbing a few times. Affected to enjoy it. Certainly she enjoyed being chatted up by the lads. The Elizabeth of those days would have felt slighted if they'd ignored her. Until the time came when she was unable to conceal her boredom while watching him perform his party piece on this or that particular bit of rock. *It's simply a hobby, Anthony. Like gardening. Or model trains. It doesn't make you superior to ordinary mortals. Why can't you see that?*

After a while the flags gave place to a well-worn track climbing through the bracken. So, breathing hard, he came up at last to the rocks that rimmed the edge of the moor, and halted, gazing up at tilted slabs, buttresses, cracks, corners, that had the half-familiarity of places known once, now long neglected.

He wandered on, winding in and out among the boulders, following the foot of the crag. At length he came on a great slab of rock propped under an overhanging roof. He gazed at the oddly-shaped sequence of holds, a question mark of scratches, greased by the sweat of countless fingers, polished by innumerable toes. A long succession of men and women, at one particular moment of their lives, had passed this way. And so had he. Yes, tiptoed, catlike, over this very slab.

He first set eyes on it one summer afternoon, thirty years before. Invisible larks were singing. A lad in a white shirt stood on top of the overhang, coiling a rope. *I'll bring you up, if you like..* One of those Sheffield lads who'd strutted across pipes spiky with wire, plunged into sludgy rivers contemptuous of tin cans, broken bottles, chemical foam. Brian Jackson might have been born and bred to climb on grit. Of the world he came from, backyards up entries, walls bristling with jagged glass, fences that in summer stank of creosote and piss, he'd known nothing. While he was teaching, Jacko earned a living crawling in and out of boilers, hauling cast iron pipes about. He lived for the weekends. For the hills.

He reached out wonderingly, felt the coarse grit catch at his fingers, but they were far off, those days, their echoes faint, distant.

Thus preoccupied, he drifted on along the undulating path that follows the edge. A little way, and he saw a man standing below the rock. This man stood in a little bay, under the jutting angle of a crag, surveying a succession of stony bulges that hung like swags of drapery, one above the other, abutting a blank wall.

It was Mississippi Buttress. The man was studying it intently. He was moving up it in his mind. Hardman felt a quiver of excitement. He remembered it as one of the old gritstone classics, steep and exposed. To climb it roped, protected, was one thing. But this man was alone.

Suddenly, in a movement odd and yet familiar, he bent to lean against the rock and wiped the sole of each boot with the palm of his hand. Then he began to climb: easily at first, up the corner, then a long, upward step, the right leg snaking out to bridge across the groove, and so up, among that hanging drapery of stone.

He climbed with the grace and discipline of a dancer, each movement measured, his body flowing through the pattern of the dance. Solitary, indifferent to his separation, he seemed to belong in his self-chosen space, a man at home in his life, a life nobody else could live. A toe on a wrinkle, fingers doubled in a crack, were enough to lift him to a fresh position. Yet progress seemed less a matter for toes and fingers, than of ongoing negotiations, head raised enquiringly, a continuous dialogue with the rock. Or else an equilibrium of forces, step by step, man and stone.

Unhurried, always at ease, though less and less substantial as he was swallowed up in the mist that hung about the upper buttress, he might have finished with regret. So it seemed to the man watching. Regret. Not thankful. Sweating. *Thank God for that..*

Hardman, too, felt regret. He had never been that good. Yet he'd known something of it once. The freedom that came with that delight.

The man came down afterwards to collect his sac. A man perhaps in his early thirties. Humorous, bony face. He spotted the watcher in the rocks. Nodded a greeting.

"Nice day." Though mists were drifting. A raw chill investing the cracks and corners.

And wandered on, still gazing upwards.

Hardman, too, wandered on. The act he'd just witnessed held meaning, value, only for the man who'd climbed. It did not relate to others. He knew that. Yet it was still that being he yearned after. Beyond what he was now.

The mist seemed to thicken as he roamed further. Somewhere ahead, below, a vague gauzy outline signalled the plantation. He wandered on, gazing up at the edge, racking his memory for half-forgotten names. Eventually he found himself below a high rectangular wall, its upper half split by a prominent vertical flake. He had a sense of standing at a threshold, hesitating between past and present, or else it was the present time of something past, knowing that beyond the wall he would find a recess, and in the wall of the recess a gaping groove, and in the groove an overhanging crack. And high in the crack, on that day of blistering heat, a sweating youth in torn moleskins, salt stinging his eyes. And the speckled rope looping down. And, lifting out of the crack as the rope rose, the last of his runners, sliding down to chink against the rest.

He stared up at the crack bulging between the jaws of the corner, sensing the emptiness below, around, the death creeping into his fingers, the sky a searing blue as he strained towards it.

That same night, hugely, joyously alive, laughing, joking with his peers. Foolish, incompetent young Anthony Hardman.

Dead now. Nothing survived. Not the body, filled with the strength and exuberance of youth. Not his hopes, dreams. Nothing. Only a name.

Yet perhaps, for some still living, he remained forever that young man who'd got the wind up that day on Tower Crack. *Do you remember the time Tony Hardman.. God, he was gripped. I was gripped just watching..*

He became aware of eddyings around him. Filaments of mist brushed against his face. Then, through a whispy thinning, a patch of blue appeared. The mist, as if gathered up in a giant hand, was rolling back. He could see fifty, a hundred yards down the hill. And started off, plunging downhill towards the plantation, plunging through hip-high bracken.

On the edge the climbing man, finishing *Martello Buttress*, might just have caught a glimpse of movement as the dark trees swallowed Hardman. His gaze, though, was upward. While the man below struggled through a swampy interior of dank branches, massive mossy blocks, rotten boughs all but submerged in undergrowth, searching for the spot where he used to camp – struggled to light a fire..

It *must* be here. Yet he couldn't find it.

And stumbled through that gloomy wood driven by a re-gret so sharp, so potent, it brought back tangs, tastes – woodsmoke, tea drunk from polythene mugs, the peppery taste of a particular pork pie he favoured..

So vivid. Like something present in the wood, something to which he might stretch out his hand. Yet gone for ever.

So time began again for Hardman, as he drove back up the Snake. In its wake, the dust which he'd stirred up, settled again. A gift was gone which nothing could restore.

What was it, a man's life? You got up, you fell down. You got up, you fell down. You got up, over and over again.

The day had turned softly bright as he turned up the track to the house. A pale sun lit up the tawny bracken of the hill-side, leaving coves of shadow in the folds of the moor.

The stale smell of woodsmoke greeted him as he threw open the door. He felt he was back where he'd started. Stepping into an echoing, empty house.

He found her cardigan where it had fallen behind a chair. A faint perfume assailed him as he raised it to his face. He felt ashamed now of his hasty note. Yes, of course she was entitled to a proper explanation. A reasoned account of his behaviour.

"A few months away, that's all I need," he muttered as he pottered about his kitchen. There had to be a way of saying what he felt, of making it seem, if not acceptable, at least the necessary thing it seemed to him. This retreat in the hills.

He made himself a pot of tea, and brought it back to the fire, where the sight of the dead ashes did nothing to lift his spirits. His mobile phone lay where she'd left it, on the table next to Seton's letter. For a while he sipped the hot tea, eyeing the phone. At last, he picked it up, and rang her number.

Cool, professional, his wife's voice greeted him with impersonal courtesy.

I'm sorry I can't take your call. Please leave me a message.

He rang off.

Yet, as he set about preparing his evening meal, that voice continued to resonate, arousing stabs of discomfort: *What are you doing here.. What do you want..*

What was wrong with him? Always the sense of something missing. Always travelling in the wrong direction, diverted into ways that were not *his* way. Always the conviction he should be somewhere else, living the real life which he thought might be there, or ought to be there. Then the failure of courage, the gradual dissipation of desire, that ever-increasing sourness, sense of lostness, swept along by the current of a world he knew could never be his world.

And this last year, when he felt as if he'd fallen through the void, and hit rock bottom, crushed beyond the reach of any hope.

Later that night, as he washed his dishes in the kitchen, he heard a scratching at the back door. He opened the door to find a dog. A collie, by the look of it.

It raised its head and whined, its amber eyes fixed on the man.

Hardman ran some water in a bowl. Set it down. The dog drank gratefully, splashing water over the flags.

He wondered if it was hungry. What did you feed a dog? Poking about in his cupboard, he came across a tin of stew. He forked the contents on to a plate. The collie wolfed it down in seconds, then fell to licking up the gravy.

Very likely the dog he'd seen that morning. The dog from over the hill. What to do with it? Should he turn it loose? Leave it to make its own way back? He knew nothing of dogs.

In the end he shut it in the washhouse. He would take it back in the morning.

TWO

Nobody loves Bleaklow. All who get on it are glad to get off.

So wrote the author of a popular walkers' guide. Tommy Ashe, though, had lived there for as long as he could remember. He loved it because it was his home. All he knew and cared for, his family, the dale that gave them a living, lay enclosed in the dark moor. The boy roamed it winter and summer. He knew it in all weathers but the worst.

He lived more than a mile from the Snake road. In the dale on dark winter nights he could see, far-off in the south-west, a faint ring of light, vast and indeterminate, the reflection of countless lamps. Northwards, though, only the stars wheeled above the black miles of empty moor.

No road crosses Bleaklow. Topographically, it is a desert: a dark hinterland of peat hags, scored with a maze of groughs, steep-sided craters in the peat, flooded after heavy rain, filled with snow in winter. Wherever you go on Bleaklow you are never far from water. It roars down the winding, ever-narrowing V-shaped cloughs that cut ravine-like into the moor. It seeps continually from the peat, oozing, eroding. Sometimes whole banks tear, and slither down the steep clough sides. In winter icicles like organ pipes hang from the splintering river shales. Yet somewhere will persist the drip or trickle of water, still visible even under ice, a succession of tiny insects scuttling over stone. It is one of the few winter sounds. Water. And the wind, buffeting clumps of hair-grass and cotton-sedge.

When his grandad took down the book from the shelf and read that bit where the fearful man grabbed the little lad on the gaunt marsh – the man who shivered and hugged himself and wished he were a frog or an eel – it was on Bleaklow that the boy imagined it, with grey rain-smoke drifting over the dark plantation. The flat, winding river was his own river Dale. And the terrible young man who had a secret way of getting at a boy – at his liver and lights – was linked in his imagination with bloody caverns in the carcasses of lambs a fox had ripped, or a crow picked at.

His grandad read slowly, licking a thick forefinger to turn each page and marking each important bit with a *look*, head-lowered, over thick-rimmed glasses. He wore 'em just for reading. He took 'em off to look at folk.

"I reckon most folk look better a bit blurred," he'd say with a sly wink.

The boy kept watch on all comers to the dale. Weekend walkers, picking their way slowly above the river: he would hear their clatter, the strange voices, watch the brightly coloured jackets passing within yards, yet they never spotted him, hidden in a clough. Sometimes, when they were too far off to hear, he still spotted them, across the moor. Maybe grouse gave them away – *go.. go.. go.. go back! go back!* Or movement. On the moor nothing moved like a man. If only they kept still! He'd learnt that early. To keep quiet and still. Sometimes he stalked them, bent low, flitting from clough to clough. He could race over slopes that had grown men gasping.

Maybe they were Harald Finehair's men. Often, hidden high above the river in Guttery Clough, or Glittering Clough far down the dale, he kept watch for King Harald's killers. Watched for the longship, prowling up the fjord to attack the farm. He'd never laid eyes on Harald Finehair. But he knew from the story what he looked like. *Blond was his hair: bright his cheeks: grim as a snake's were his glowing eyes.* Dalehead still held out against him. But the king wanted all the land. So the boy kept watch, where the river swung past a flat, grassy bay by a ruined fold, a small green oasis that the sheep kept cropped. Then, as the dragon prow nosed round the steep bank side, down he'd come, screeching, weapon swinging, down on the ruined fold.

Grouse whirled away, calling their warning: *look.. look.. look-out.. look-out!*

But the king's men were surprised and slain in the lonely bay.

The boy inhabited a world not to be found on any map. A world of thresholds. His soul was lit by openings and closings. The light that emanated from this boy held that world in a primal clarity. Sometimes the light threw open caverns in the shadows of the moor. Sometimes it fell so as to illuminate the separate being even of stones. On dark days, though, the moor seemed closed against him. Its silence seemed to conceal a brooding presence. Something wholly other, over and against himself. It humbled him in a way he could not pronounce.

Once, at the Crookstones, he'd come across a lone man in grey, old-fashioned breeches and grey, flecked sweater. At his side a tall, tapering sac. He sat motionless. Still as a hawk on a rock. As the boy drew closer a tanned face turned towards him, expressionless. Eyes, set at infinity, shifted an instant, then slid back to the horizon. The leather face gave no greeting. The boy hurried past without a word.

A while after, he turned to look back, and saw the man still sitting there, by the grey edge of rock against the sky. Had he come for someone? Was he waiting for someone? Yet all around, as far as the eye could travel, was nothing human: no road, no barn. Just that figure. Still visible across half a mile of moor. Cold, empty, the sky seemed then, the sweep of moor desolate, forbidding.

Below the bridge that carried the Snake road, where the Dale river ran into the Ashop, a silver birch clung to the bank in a tangle of grey-green, lichenous roots. The river had washed out a cave behind them just big enough for a boy to crawl in. Hidden there he saw a figure going up into the dale.

Five hundred yards along the track to Dalehead was the

field barn. The boy wriggled out from his cave, doubled back along the river bed, and began to run, slanting up through the in-by land between the river and the track. Gasping, heart pounding, he got to it – was in through the door, burrowed into the hay there, waiting, watching, a full half minute before the man came into view.

Though aching from the previous day, Hardman tramped up the track, relishing the wind in the trees, the mellow, autumn sun, gazing down at the winding river, its trampled bays where cattle drank, the grassy banks and hollows of the intake land higher up, cropped, dotted with grazing ewes, with barns, and swelling knolls smothered in bracken.

Secured with a length of rope, the dog trotted at his side.

The track climbed steadily along the side of the dale. A line of bent black thorn trees straggled beside it, bowed down-hill, as if blown by the wind. Lambs lay along the track, tucked in under the banks. Black faces turned to the man as he passed. Spotted cattle dotted here and there in the dale. A fresh wind piling up the clouds.

A barn appeared at a bend. Here and there, lopped from the thorns, lay spindly branches he had to step across.

The barn drew nearer. He saw a face – boy, girl, he couldn't tell – small, pale, against the dark opening of the loft. A child was watching him. He felt a pang of sympathy. Went on stiffly past the barn.

All the way along the track lay branches lopped from the thorns. Large, some of them. Fresh cut, too. Moments later he came across the labourer at work. A squat figure in a black, tattered coat, legs apart, grunting as he swung the long-handled billhook.

A collie, grey with age, lay across the track. Hardman was conscious of a rheumy eye slid in his direction. Deep in the creature's throat began a warning growl.

"Good morning," he called out brightly.

The boy watched them, his grandad and the stranger. They shook hands, the old man wiping his first on his thigh. They talked awhile. His grandad looked at his watch. Then they went off together up the track towards the house..

It was dinner time, near enough. His dad was fencing in Ferny Clough. He went off at a run to meet him, climbing the steep bank above the track, towards the dark plantation.

To reach the trees took him no more than seconds.

Swallows first greeted Hardman at Dalehead. As the old man opened a gate they took off in a body, dipping over the yard, and dropping back on the gable. It was, he saw, an old-fashioned farm, with none of the modern buildings, the big sheds and lean-to's of Heathy Lea. Traditional stone-built barns and sheep-pens, grouped around a cobbled yard.

Hardman waited while the old man saw to the dog.

"He'd 'a come back on his own, y' know," he said again, as he fastened a stable door.

A small house. Smaller than he'd imagined. Windows, two up, two down. A white front door, opening on a scrap of garden. Michaelmas daisies. A gate in a low stone wall.

Then the yard became a track again, dipping down to the right, slipping round the house and running down beside a stream. Above the stream, a stand of great trees, oak, sycamore, towering over the green slates of the roof.

Mingling with the roar of water, the bleating of lambs. Blackfaced, like the lambs along the track, they thronged a maze of small enclosures flanking the barns.

"They look healthy." It was something to say.

"Aye," said Mr. Ashe. "They're ready for off."

"To market?"

"No, no. We winter 'em over on Longshaw. It's milder there. Same sort of pasture as they get here, d'you see – only it's milder there. We bring 'em back in t' spring."

Hardman thought of the bleak fields of Longshaw. Milder!

"If we were to put 'em on green grass for t' winter," the old man went on, "it wouldn't do for 'em. They wouldn't settle when we turned 'em out. They'd wander about."

Hardman followed the old man round the side of the house, under gold and yellow boughs, to a roar of water falling from Ferny Clough. Above the house the steep valley side was thick with trees: a blanket of larch, unbroken but for the deep scar of the clough, rolling down the dale as far as the eye could follow. Two or three hundred feet below, the Dale river ran through the shales and pebbles of the valley floor.

They went in at a deep stone porch to an infant howling, followed by a woman's shriek, shrill, ugly. The howls burst out again, an octave higher.

Hardman felt acutely uncomfortable. It was the last thing he wanted. This plunge into other people's lives. He wished to God he hadn't come.

But the old man had lifted the latch on the back door. Hardman followed, plunging into a miasma of swampy air. Fetid, clinging, it mingled with a fug of cooking, lapping the wide, dark kitchen like a sea. Clothes everywhere: draped over chairs, overflowing from baskets, piled in heaps on the stone floor. Toys, little shoes, a red Wellington, things scattered everywhere. An infant with red tufts of hair was clamped in a high chair chewing a carrot. Another squatted on its pot. A third crawled from under a table. It wore a dirty bib: DINNER, embroidered under a duck with a yellow bill. Its wet, blue eyes gazed up wonderingly at Hardman.

"They've driven me mad this morning," she burst out. Fair hair she hadn't time to bother with, drawn back tightly in an ugly bun, left the round face exposed. Still flushed.

"Oh.." Flustered, she forced a smile for the visitor, who smiled back at the worn, still pretty face, with its snub nose, its whisps of fair hair escaping.

"Have you come to look at the barn?"

"The barn? No, no. I brought back your dog."

"I live at Moor House," he began to explain..

"Aye," said the old man shortly. "Come through, will you. Shall you mek a pot o' tea," he called back.

He led the way into a low-ceilinged room. Wide as the kitchen, with strange low doors, like cupboards, opening off. Walls two feet thick, at least. Low windows, like little deep-set eyes. Worn chairs. A big bureau cluttered with papers. A long clock ticked in a corner.

"Sit yourself down," said Mr Ashe.

Hardman's eye ran to the shelves of books. A long run of Dickens. Nineteenth century, by the look of them. On a small table beside a shabby armchair lay a fat blue volume. A warrior figure stamped on the spine, sword raised over a horned helmet. *Myths & Legends of the Vikings.*

"May I have a look?"

The old man was taking off his boots.

"Oh, that," he grunted. "That's a book I'm reading to the lad."

Hardman turned back the cover. Inside was an inscription, written in a stiff, Victorian hand. *To Thos. William Ashe: for Bible Study.*

"A strange prize," he said, "for Bible Study."

A black boot clattered on to the tiled hearth.

"Aye," said the old man drily. "That were my mother's doing. Full o' surprises, she were. I expect she picked it up at a jumble."

Mr. Ashe caressed his toes with a calloused hand.

"I remember once," he went on, "she might have tipped up a pail or summat in t' dairy, I don't know rightly what it was now, but she were that put out. "What have I done to deserve that," she said. "I say my prayers every night." She wouldn't say 'em for a week after, she were that put out. "Dear, oh dear," my father said. "He will be upset.""

The old man reached under his chair, came out with a pair of tattered slippers.

"We get all sorts come here, you know," he went on, bending over a cupboard beside the fireplace. "Ministers, students, all sorts."

He lifted out a small, squat volume, bound in dark cloth, laid it on the table, open at the frontispiece.

"Now then," he said, with evident pride. "Look there."

There, indeed, above the design on the frontispiece, was the signature: *J.Wesley*, the *J'* and *W* joined together, and a date, 1783. The brown ink faded. The hand, neat, looping, might have been that of a child, or an old man.

"We don't rightly know to this day whether or not he left it in the barn," said the old man slyly. "My grandfather allus used to say it were his great-great-grandfather's bible, and that Wesley signed it for him before he left. He stayed the night here, you know."

There was a knock, then, at the door. It was Mrs. Ashe with the tea. She set down the tray to a fresh burst of wailing through the open door.

"They've been driving me wild this morning," she said, with a rueful smile. "Have you got any?" She was younger than he'd first thought. Not much more than thirty.

Hardman shook his head.

"Aren't you the lucky one?" she said dryly. Then, with Derbyshire directness: "Does your wife go out to work?"

An image of Elizabeth sprang to mind: earnest, pale, unsmiling, she seemed an unlikely presence in this place. What was he to say? She was a shrink, a psychotherapist, visiting professor at Northwestern Pacific, grand inquisitor of souls..

"She works with children," he said shortly. It was easier than the truth.

"Jack'll be back directly," she said. "They'll be having their dinners then. You'll stop and have some?" It was an assumption rather than a question.

"Well.." Hardman hesitated, remembering that kitchen, the infant on its pot.

"There's plenty made." She was looking at him, the offer hanging there. It seemed churlish to refuse.

"Well, thank you," he said. "I don't usually eat lunch."

If she thought that strange, she was too polite to show it. Hardman steeled himself. Yet he went in to find the floor washed, the clutter swept away. They sat down together in a clean, well-ordered room.

It was shepherd's pie. Full of meat, with chopped, fresh vegetables, tomatoes, carrots.

Mrs. Ashe sat stitching in a low-backed chair.

"What about you?" asked Hardman, alarmed he'd taken hers.

"Oh, I have mine with the children," she told him cheerfully.

He sat next to the husband. Older than her. Red, wiry hair. Pale lashes. Bony face. Clearly the father of the infant brood. Though the boy's hair was black. Lank and black as the old man's.

"Come to see the barn, have you?"

"No, no," said the old man. "He brought Gyp back."

"He turned up last night at my back door."

"Oh, aye? He'd 'a brought himself back, y' know."

The boy ate with an avidity that was odd to watch, bent forward, chewing, his gaze fixed on his food. His eyes scarcely left it, except for flickering glances, sidelong, furtive, looks a cat makes if it eats with other cats. Long after the plate was empty he was still scraping up tiny fragments with careful sweeps of his knife, scraping them on to his fork.

"Is there something special about the barn?" asked Hardman, to fill a silence.

"It was a hideout for outlaws," said the red-haired man with a grin.

"It was nothing of the sort," Mrs Ashe rebuked. "The old Nonconformists used to hold their meetings there. In the olden days. When it was against the law."

When would that have been, Hardman wondered. Bunyan's time? The Act of Uniformity? Three hundred years ago, at least.

"Were they ever caught?" he asked.

"They were," said the old man. "So they say." He ate with head erect, staring straight ahead, chewing slowly with a loose, rolling jaw.

After lunch they went to see the barn, the visitor clutching a basin of fresh farm eggs pressed on him by Mrs Ashe. The boy dragged along behind. Not with them. And yet a presence. Small, slight, in jeans and ragged sweater. Quick eyes in the hollow face. Nine.. ten.. Older, maybe, than he looked.

A lank cat slid out from under a door.

"Tip! Tip!" he called. But the cat had slipped away.

The old man unlocked a small door in the barn wall.

"She's had kittens," the boy said, to no one in particular.

But Hardman had already stepped across the threshold. Stepped into the gloom.

"Not much to see," said the old man. His voice echoed slightly.

A dim light came in high up at a gable end. A handrail followed wooden steps up to a loft.

"He were over eighty, y' know," said the old man. "When he preached here."

The visitor look round at limewashed walls. A stone floor, swept bare. What happened here, he wondered. But for him it was a space empty of content.

"Folk still come every year for the service," the old man went on. "They used to come miles. Set out before dawn, some on 'em. Same folk, year after year. Us lads used to sit in that corner, there. Where some o' th' owd religious fellers used to

get. *AMEN*, they used to call out. *HALLELUJAH!* Aye. Amen
Corner we used to call it."

Hardman smiled. For him it was a famous pitch in Langdale.
Amen Corner. Part of *'B' Route*. You said a prayer before you
battled up it. He was moved by the strange correspondence: the
lads gathered in the corner, old men stirred, alive. Though it
was probably no more than comfortable assent. The 'hear-hear'
of back-benchers. Whatever it was, he never heard it. Not in
his lectures. A-MEN, brother.. HALLELUJAH!

"We used to put rushes on t' floor, set out the planks. Tres-
tle table up front. Mother 'ud be baking for days. Pies. Cakes.
Big piece o' beef. Boiled ham. We had to feed 'em, you see.
They'd come miles, some on 'em. Oh aye."

The cool air was filled with a sweet hay smell. It reminded
the visitor of apples. Winter apples, stored in a box room long ago.

Something fluttered in the rafters.

"Aye, it were a real red letter day, the Lovefeast."

"Well – I'm very grateful," began Hardman. He felt at a
loss. Could think of nothing else to say. Then he noticed the
boy, hanging back beyond the door.

"Could you show me the kittens?" he asked, smiling.

And could have bitten off his tongue. As the boy dropped
his head, the rats' tails flopping down across his face. The next
moment he was gone – sudden as that.

Hardman saw, framed in the space he left, the yard beyond
the door, the low stone wall, the mauve heads of Michaelmas
daisies.

"I expect he's shy," he said.

"Shy!" said Mr Ashe. "Aye, he is that."

He banged the door to behind them. Locked it.

"Aye, he's a winter lamb, that one," added the old man darkly.

One day, after a wet blustery morning, the wind dropped,
the clouds lifted, and the tenant of Moor House went out into

the blue, freshly-laundered air. He felt freer now, walking in the dale.

Most days, it seemed, he caught sight of one or other of the Ashes. Jack Ashe on his quad bike, dogs perched at the back. Or it might be Mrs Ashe, waving as she drove past in the Land-rover to pick up the boy from the school bus. Sometimes the boy was on his own, a small, solitary figure trudging back along the track.

The blue sky beamed back at him from puddles of rain as Hardman made his way up to the farm. He was taking back the basin to Mrs Ashe. At the last bend before the farm he heard the revving of an engine. Had to step aside for a big Four x Four. Caught a glimpse of sheepskin. A pinkish face. Then the heavy car ploughed past.

Old Mr. Ashe was closing the yard gate. The grey collie, tail drooping, hung at his heel. At the sight of Hardman it uttered a low growl.

"Ne'er mind 'er" said Mr. Ashe, swinging the gate open again.

"Fancy car," said Hardman.

"A new generation cometh," said the old man sententiously, banging back the gate, "and the old passeth away," he slipped a loop of cord over the post, "but the landlord endureth for ever."

And grinned at Hardman, uncovering stumpy, yellow teeth. Hardman looked away along the track.

"Was that the landlord?"

"Him? No!" The old man was scornful. "That were his dog."

He led the way over to an enclosure, the dog loitering along behind. Evidently the old man had something else he wanted to show off.

"Now then," he said. "Just look at that."

That was a thick-necked, stocky ram, bought in from Mossy Lea.

Together they leant over the dry-stone wall as the old man pointed out the things to look for when buying in a tup. A good male head. Strong shoulders. Not too long a back, but a good, long side.

"You don't breed your own, then?" asked Hardman, who knew no better.

"No, no," said the old man, shocked. "Oh, *no*. That wouldn't do at all." And tried, as simply as he could, to convey some notion of the fluid, organic thing that was the Dalehead flock: the buying-in of fresh blood-stock, the suiting of tups to ewes, the struggle to maintain a constant equilibrium between his animals and their meagre living on the harsh, high moors.

"It's mekkin' the best of what we've got. D'you see?" He spoke slowly, consideringly, his eyes never straying from his new acquisition, dwelling on it with deep satisfaction.

"We've to breed a ewe that can live off what we've got. It'd be no use bringin' Hathersage sheep up here."

Hardman watched it following the ewes around, head raised, lip curled as it sniffed the odour of a ewe in season. A cold-blooded business it seemed to him. Tupping. Brief. Functional. A few quick thrusts, then on to the next.

Yet even tups, he saw, went diligently about their business.

Elizabeth's question continued to resonate: *What are you doing here?* Was it really the department he was running from? Or the non-life he shared with her? Maybe the truth was that something inexplicable had drawn him here. Perhaps the most he should hope for wasn't so much answers to satisfy the intellect, as moments of harmony for the heart.

So he began to spend his days among the hills again. He was lucky with the weather. Sharp, smoky dawns gave place to mellow days ripe as autumn apples. He drove from place to place, the Rover swishing along empty lanes. Each day he experienced the same strange metamorphosis. It began acutely.

Stiff. Aching. Boots chafing the swollen ankles. Breathless. That coppery taste again. Heart pounding on the uphill grind. Terrain, angle, alien. Rain, too, when it fell. He hated getting wet. All of which was a kind of not belonging. Yet, within an hour or two, it had become integral. As muscles stretched. Stained hands, smelling of earth, grasped at roots, took hold of stone. He had become a man of flesh and bones again.

He bought some new gear, new boots, a climbing guide. He visited a dozen different dales, climbing the steep hillsides, gazing down on lonely farms. And felt better, he told himself, than he'd felt in years. Lungs, legs were improving. Stiff in the morning, yet not so he couldn't walk it off.

Every morning he tapped the barometer hanging in the hall, himself a piece of the wet, the dry, the battering wind that echoed in his ears on blustery hills.

Bolder now, he walked moors and edges, silent for hours at a time. It suited now. This solitary life. Silence seemed to pick out an inner landscape where days flowed into one another. Here time seemed of a different measure. Here, the sun declared, and the folded land, was peace and permanence: hills stained with the tawny light of late October, the woods with their yellow rags of leaves, mist after sunrise, hanging over the wet pasture.

He missed Elizabeth. At Slippery Stones, on the little bridge, a dry wind rippled back the grass above the stream, and it swept over him – how much he missed her. Solitude had made him feel more keenly the emptiness they shared, even at the cost of pain. Yet he had to be alone. Exposed alone, to whatever was going to happen. Whatever it was, he knew obscurely, it could only happen to him on his own.

There were times, though, when he could have cried for happiness. He felt he had come home again. Taken possession of something he should never have let go. On Back Tor, with the hills of Howden rising to the north and the Derwent moors, wild and lonely, dropping away, the cairn of Lost Lad pointing to the sky, he was so stretched in spirit he could not have said precisely what it was that flourished so, as he strode home; something that seemed to range the sweeping slopes of head-high bracken, buried itself in wild, wooded cloughs, rejoicing in things not so much seen as felt.

He strode back, his heart leaping. Was it a deception? All this? He didn't know. *Wait and see*, he told himself. *Wait and see.*

One wet afternoon, as he arrived back at the house, Hardman saw the boy trudging home, the hood of his parka pulled up against the drizzle. He waved, called out, would have given him a lift. But the boy wouldn't look, much less return his greeting.

It must be, he thought, an isolated life. Only the twins to play with. No friends of his own age. What was it the old man called him?

That night, in the pub, he asked George, the landlord, what it meant.

"A winter lamb? One born before its time. They don't usually survive."

At the *Bridge* they were more willing, now, to talk in front of him. Not that anyone made it his business to include Hardman in anything. But after a week or two of reticence, conversation began to resume its casual, unimpeded flow.

Dalehead, it seemed, was a poor farm. It made little and it paid little.

"Even round here most folk have got a lambing shed, or a suckler shed," said a red-faced man with slicked-back hair.

"Owd Tom's too set in his ways for lambing sheds," said Malcolm, a burly youth who helped out now and then behind the bar.

"Too tight, more like."

"They're like a lot of folk," sighed the red-faced man. "They couldn't mek do wi'out the subsidy."

"It never were much of a livin', Norman, even in th' owd days," put in the railwayman, whose name was Monty.

"It's her I feel sorry for. I don't know how she sticks it."

That was the landlady. Beryl. Polisher, Hardman wondered, of all that fancy brass? For sure, no lover of the wild.

"Every time I see that raggedy lad of hers with his arse hanging out.."

"Maybe she likes it," ventured Hardman. Some impulse, obstinate, irrational, urged him to speak out for those who chose to live up lonely dales. Though he'd no reason to suppose anything of Mrs. Ashe. He didn't know her.

"Well, some people might," he added uneasily. For every eye was on him. Christ: he'd put his foot in it again.

"Like it?" The landlady's incredulity was scathing. "Stuck up there? She bloody *loathes* it."

George stirred behind the *Star*. Rustled the paper. He didn't care for this.

"Aye. Well. That's their business," he said shortly.

Hardman let it drop.

*

At Dalehead tupping was in full swing. Every day for a week Jack Ashe had been bringing down his ewes, sending his dogs to quarter the moor, fetching them down a few dozen at a time.

There are no walls on Bleaklow, no boundary fences, yet Jack Ashe knew where to find his sheep. A ewe generally keeps to its beat. They have an instinct for it. 'Hefting' they call it, in the north. A turned-out lamb returns instinctively to its home ground, the bleak stretch of moorland where it was born. In March, though, when the sedge moss begins to spread over the peat hags, the hardier ewes, those left to lamb on the hill, go out across the moor for the first good feed of the year. In summer it is a prized grass, a single stalk with a round white flower bell, that draws them up to the high ground above the Snake. That is the best time for a ewe: sheared in June, then turned-out to graze with its lamb. They gather it in assiduously, the good grass, reaping it with that rolling, sidelong motion of the jaw, alone with their lambs, and the larks and pipits.

Now, after their weeks of peace, they were alert again. Nervous, heads erect, at distant barking of the dogs.

Jack Ashe worked a pair of dogs. *An owd 'un to learn a young 'un.* Bob, his top dog, still, at ten, a good strong runner. It needed a good strong dog to work those groughs and gullies, a dog that knew its ground, and how to work on its own, out of sight or sound of the man. Together they covered the moor from the River Westend to Doctor's Gate, and as far north as Bleaklow Head, bringing the flock down in fits and starts.

At the end of a week he began to work the steep banks above the dale bottom, whistling his dogs up through the trees and cloughs.

"Bark 'em out! Bark 'em out!" he bellowed through cupped hands.

He'd no time for a silent dog. One that worked with its eye. It needed a good barker to fetch Bleaklow sheep from cover.

Already the dale bore the faded look of the dying year, a baked, brown aspect of withered bracken, the stunted oaks, stripped down to their last yellow rags, growing gaunter with each wind. The small, companionable birds were gone now from the eaves above the bedroom window. Their domed nests like little silent tombs stuck to the wall. Ellen Ashe missed the birds, the skim of wings, the low, guttural warbling that had greeted her as she came and went. She dreaded the long, dark months ahead.

Yet each year at this time, the Ashes brought their ewes down to the tups with a sense of an unfailing cycle, a rhythm vital as a beating heart. On bleak February days when scarcely a green thing showed in the dale, when nothing was that wasn't blackened, shrunken, or encased in ice, Jack Ashe's gaze would dwell on his in-lamb ewes, each one a warm, dark, secret centre of the life to come. They were his deepest pleasure. His animals. He knew each one. Whenever he bought a beast he spent what time he could getting to know it. In winter, after he'd battled up the dale with hay he'd often stop at the top fold to squat by a ewe, murmuring to it as it munched its feed. He never had arguments with animals. He never came away hurt.

Now he watched the black dots darting here and there on the bank, and the white dots gusting down, swirled down in fits and starts to the inby-land above the river. Coming down to the tups.

Jack Ashe ran a shrewd eye over the living. Just as, up on the moor, he had identified the dead. The buzz of flies, a sweet stench in a gully where a ewe had sickened and died, or fallen down a rocky clough – such things summoned him and he went heavily to his inspection. There were, too, green watery morasses where sheep, plunging up to the belly, could not get out: were trapped there, floundering about until they died. Jack Ashe would stir each fleece for signs of dye. If a skull was horned he hooked it up with his crook to look for a mark.

Some days the boy went with him. There were times when he seemed subdued, silenced by what confronted them on the moor: and though he was not as a rule given to instruction Jack Ashe, with a dim adult sense of a child's imagination o'erinformed, would feel the need to set the lad to rights.

"No", he might say, as they gazed together at a greenish mess of bones and fleece, "there's nowt in nature survives wi'out a struggle." Something of the sort. Phlegmatic. Kindly meant. It was what his work had taught him.

If Tommy Ashe was awestruck, though, it was not at the sight of putrefaction. He'd gazed often enough at that stark fact. Caught up in the flux of life, the boy was still mystified by the business of living in this universe. He was not yet wholly humanized, not quite centred in himself.

That summer he'd crept up close to a curlew. He'd often watched them mounting high in the air, as if climbing an invisible ladder, then spreading their wings and sailing in to land on the moor, long beaks curving, legs a-trailing. He'd mark the spot, then set off, patient, stealthy, but never had he got so close before. He watched it. A brown bird on a rock. Saw the curved beak open. Gazed at the slender throat, the strange soft cry that bubbled there, the strange *life*, and felt for the first time the edges of an unentered space, outside, beyond himself. As if the world he knew, the world of farms and men, had suddenly become transparent.

All things, man or beast, his grandad told him, lived according to the nature that was in them. So it seemed to the boy. And all the natures met in one great rhythm that went far beyond his understanding. Flocks of peewits, returning to the moor to breed, that came as one of the first signs of spring. Then the curlews, travelling by night. Sometimes, lying in bed, he heard them calling to one another as they passed overhead. In April lambs were born. And so were fox-cubs. "I've never understood," his grandad used to say, "why Almighty God made lambs to be born when he did. It's as if he made 'em on purpose to feed foxes." Then sheep were sheared, and hay made, and ewes dried off, and then the time began for shows and fairs. Then it was gathering time again.

That summer, though, high up on Fairbrook Naze, on a day's gathering his dad had given to Mr. Clarkson, he'd looked northward, beyond Longdendale, right over to Black Hill many miles off. He saw the brown Pennines stretching away, and lost himself in the vastness of creation, the numberless of its creatures. He couldn't contain all that was given. It was a mystery his mind would never fathom.

Sometimes, coming home from school in winter, coming back along the track with the light almost gone, he'd look back at the high, jagged line of Kinder, with Seal Edge and the Seal

Stones, and the great neb of Fairbrook sharp, distinct against
the sky. Blood-red, sometimes. In snow, blood-red: deepening,
darkening, with a swollen, copper sun dipping down. Somewhere a ewe might call, a thin small sound in the freezing air.
Its lonely note would enter his heart, and he would linger on
the track, conscious of his singularity, filled with a yearning to
throw off his separation, to dissolve, merge, with all he saw
around him, one with all.

No such imaginings troubled Jack Ashe. He went out each
day, and it was solidly there, his working life set down in a landscape from which he took a satisfaction as substantial as it was
solitary, a narrative in which nothing was ever lost or forgotten.

When bad weather threatened and the Dalehead sheep
came down in their hundreds, winding their way down to the
shelter of the dale, he would watch them, still with a certain
awe, a vague sense of something willed.

"Funny," he'd say, "how they seem to know."

"Aye, they can smell it," the old man replied.

Long before any human they saw it coming, the bad
weather, and they came down to the dale, hundreds of them,
dotted in threes and fours all over the banks and hollows. They
knew where to go, and Jack Ashe knew where to look for them.
They could stick it out under snow a week, a fortnight even,
until he got to them.

But it was six years since the last bad winter. And since
the Ashes rarely kept a ewe beyond its fourth year the Dalehead
flock had never known the Arctic grip of a hard winter. Sometimes this worried the younger man. He'd turn it over slowly,
while there formed in his mind, vague and menacing, images of
a vast disaster.

"Do you reckon they'd know what to do?" he'd asked uneasily, more than once.

But the old man remained unmoved. As if it was in the
nature of things for men to suffer a disaster once in their lives.

And he was right. Jack Ashe knew it.

He was just old enough to remember the winter he grew up. It had begun as a game, a wonder world with snow piled so high you could jump into it off the rocks. For three months he never went to school. And the yard and the farm kitchen seemed always full of men who'd come to rescue the sheep. A thousand sheep were lost that winter in the Woodlands valley. Tom Ashe lost half his flock.

At first it had seemed no worse than any other winter. He covered the regular leeward banks, scanning the filled-in hollows for a telltale depression. Dug out two or three shovelfuls. Thanked the Lord when he caught the glint of bright eyes in the gloom.

But the weather grew worse. Each day found Tom Ashe floundering through thick, fresh snow hauling his sheep to small islands of higher ground. They huddled together in little groups on the iron earth. There was no food for them. Tom Ashe carried hay up to the hillocks, but the wind swept it away.

As the days passed he began to dig out the dead. Where there were several gathered together, the smaller, weaker ewes had been crushed and trampled underfoot. Many, left exhausted on the barren windswept hillocks, died anyway. And still it went on snowing. Sheep dug out one day would be buried again by morning. Tom Ashe would go despairingly to dig them out again.

It snowed through February and March. The fresh snow froze hard each night. More men came to help carry weakened sheep down to the barns. It wasn't possible to take them all. Tom Ashe had to choose. Had he to make sure of his stronger ewes, and the lambs they carried? Should he leave the weakest? They might die anyway. He knew that. Yet if he thought they had a chance he sent them down.

Jack Ashe had been a boy of eight. After the first week or two of snow he was kept indoors. As the scale of the disaster grew he was kept away from the man.

"Just keep out your dad's road," his mam told him. She meant it for the best.

But each night the lad's shocked gaze ran back to the snow-plastered man who stamped into the farm kitchen, grey-faced and speechless.

He was needed now to help feed the stricken ewes. They thronged the big Lovefeast barn, many with long strips of wool hanging from emaciated flanks, wool they'd chewed at in their hunger. Huddled together, not caring to move away, or look even, at the boy who moved among them. Some died within a day or two. Others, who refused to eat, died later.

The dead were hauled out, and carted off in the tractor shovel. The stench of the burning, the reek of black, oily smoke, hung over the dale for weeks.

"I'll not forget it." Jack Ashe would say, as he told the tale. "Till the day I die I'll not forget it."

Now he ran the farm. "It's enough," the old man said, when he turned seventy. "Three score-year-and-ten. It's enough for any man." Though it irked the son. To have, yet not to have the farm. Yet he was glad the old man was there: honoured him, in his dour way, as he might have honoured a protective presence hanging over the dale, a promise that one can endure the worst that happens, and still survive.

The old man still picked out the tups. For he knew his sheep. He knew the pedigree of every one. Which tup to put to a ewe. Sometimes he tried to get the boy to pick out a likely couple. *White faces to black 'uns*, he told him. *Bright coats to slack 'uns*. For the boy was always with them; his grandad or his dad.

"You'll keep an eye on him," warned Ellen Ashe. With three little ones to cope with as well as a farmhouse she'd little time to spare for a boy of his age, and it made her anxious.

Oh, he'll be all right, they told her.

But while they worked he generally wandered off. And

they were men. They didn't bother much what a lad got up to as long as he didn't bother them. Only they wouldn't let him roam after dark.

Sometimes, towards nightfall, the old man grew morose, restless.

"I think I'll just step out for a bit," he'd say. And take his stick. It was as if the darkness drew him.

It irritated Ellen Ashe.

"He'll break his neck out there, I shouldn't wonder, one of these nights."

"He just likes to take a last look round, that's all," said Jack Ashe, unperturbed.

The boy would think of him going slowly up the steep bankside, between the stands of larches, under the moon. *Where was he going? What did he do up there?* He thought of his grandad standing silently between the dark trees, hearing the cries of owls, sniffing the darkness, and the soft wind over the dale.

But they would never let him go.

"Not at night," his mam insisted.

"You're not going," said his dad flatly. And that was that

Sometimes the old man put in his own dissuader, in tones as mocking as they were cautionary. Sullen, the boy ignored him. Secretly he was stirred, troubled, by the sly, insinuating voice.

"You don't want to go out on them there moors at night, lad. They *crawl.*"

THREE

One day Hardman visited the limestone country west of the Derwent. He drove under arching boughs that span the long straight road out of Calver, cutting across a soft, green, shallow bowl, with here and there the ribs of hills showing through. From Hassop he went by Great Longstone to Monsal Head, where the Wye swings abruptly westward in its bed five hundred feet below, descending the gorge to Upperdale and Cressbrook Mill.

Above the mill the road climbs steeply between wooded slopes. At a bend where it winds up and over the hill to Litton, a narrow lane slips down between the trees to Ravensdale. Where the lane ends, a row of cottages. Woods all around.

Here he stopped the car, and gazed up at what he'd come to see. Facing westward, across the narrow dale, a huge bastion of vegetated limestone thrusts forward from the steep hillside, towering above the cottages. It was, he remembered, a crag for long sunny evenings. A sweat box on a blazing afternoon. It brought back all the menaces of limestone; its angles, reassuring from below, rearing up alarmingly at closer quarters, its constraining bulges, the moves awkward, reachy, the pitches that went on and on, the sun's glare bouncing off white walls, the long, sweaty tension, perched on tiny stances, shifting his weight from foot to foot, the relief of climbing again; all these terrors and excitements burned again through his veins.

He left the car and set off for the crag, threading a squeezer stile in the stone wall, then by stepping stones in the dry river bed. A path zig-zagging up through the shady wood, then steep, lung-bursting steps climbing into sunlight, and so to a thorny bush at the foot of the crag. A climber belaying there, beside a jagged crack in the flaky wall, head craning upward. Double ropes dropping down. Right of an overhang, feet splayed across a niche, a young man was looking for a connection with the rock above. Hardman was never a rock star. Nor had he climbed with rock stars. But he had in former days ventured himself here, in this steep place where, even now, this young man was tensed, looking for the move.

To the left of the thorny bush a narrow path wound away in the grass below the crag. This time he'd brought a guide-book, a lavish compendium of climbs, complete with glossy photographs, more fitting for a bookshelf than the back pocket of a pair of breeches. Book in hand, he followed the path past famous climbs, *Mephistopheles*, *Medusa*, whose names reminded of encounters in another life.

He crossed a stile in a wire fence, and followed the path up the hillside. Below a steep wall, beside a straggling rose bush, another team were studying two parallel cracks high on the crag. Intent, gazing upward, they were oblivious of his presence as he passed by, a few feet away. He had stood so, studying the route, just such a keen-eyed young man with a coil of rope around his shoulders, knowing nothing of age, the chill that lay in store, untroubled by such questions as who he was, what he lived for.

A few yards further on he came upon a slippery corner – yes, that was *Tria*, he had been up there, his right foot stretching for that shiny flake on the right wall. Then through a cave, pausing beneath a steep flake he'd once laid siege to for a whole summer. *Gymnic*. No need to look in the book. The route was the same. He was the one who'd changed.

He raised a hand to the opening move, hooking his fingers as if to lay off a flake, and saw then that he was standing in the present time of what was past. If those days seemed to live for him now it was because they had been transformed by memory. Something had happened here, the significance of which could only be grasped now. Why? Because of the different person he'd become.

He went on past less distinguished rock, passing under a prominent rock tower. Then, just before the last low outcrop, an earthy trod wound precariously, as he knew it would, above a wide gully amid trees and bushes.

So Hardman came once more to the top of Raven Crag. Here was a high tableland of green, gently swelling pasture, criss-crossed by mile upon mile of dry stone walls where it was always summer, seemingly, the grass starry with flowers. Right under him lay the tiny row of cottages, with the wooded hillside crowding in beyond, and the little meadow, falling away to the woods and the dry river bed. Here and there, hammered into the turf, the iron posts he must have used for belaying.

So the man continued to sit on the level, close-cropped turf in a white glare of limestone, the air filled with the hot scents of pollen, caught up in a tangle in which climbs opened out of climbs, and days flowed into one another, back to the beginning.

Oh, if only it could begin all over again.. But that time was past. You had to be nineteen, twenty, to live that life.

Then, as if summoned from some deep, the youth himself materialized in thin air, whooping with delight as he hauled out on the finishing jugs of *Ploy*.

"How-do!" he gasped, on seeing Hardman.

Then, hauling in the rope, he went with lit face to fix the belay. For that moment he was limitless. For him freedom was everywhere: everywhere was freedom. The older man thought of him flowing up that exposed top wall, wholly focused on those tiny fingery holds, a young man confronting the crag, meeting it with his whole life.

Ah, we have all known them. Those afternoons when the rock was gripping, and we were bold. Immortal moments.

Suddenly the doors were open. Days long gone came back upon him. The hiding places of his youth and strength swung open. He was himself swinging up the flakes on *Dover's Wall*, revelling in the thuggish moves across the overhangs. Or he was mingling with the hordes in Dovedale on that Bank Holiday long ago, wading the river, thrashing a path through the nettles to get at *Snakes Alive*.

A sudden influx of joy at the transcendent moments he had lived swept over him. He might have been made drunk suddenly by an efflorescence of life that came at him out of the treetops opposite, and from the meadow lit by the tawny light. The sky bubbled with clouds. The wind caught his throat.

I shall remember, he thought tipsily, this place: that row of doll's house roofs, that patchwork of gardens. He got tears in his eyes from looking at it.

November mists were gathering as he drove home, in-filling the dales, investing the headlands, draining the land of all familiarity; trees, tongues of scree, a belt of crags, isolated in the gauzy uncertainty of mist. Another country, it might have been, at once very earthly and other worldly.

He was still not quite himself. He felt as if he'd been somehow jolted out of kilter, or else into some new alignment, and that contact with this other self was healing. At the same time he was acutely conscious of the futility of nostalgia. Renewal, he saw, couldn't be found in the past, only in the present.

Even so, he continued to be bowled over, swept away, by the bitter-sweetness of those days. He felt, with an infallible intuition which swelled and illumined his heart, that he had come home to his deepest belonging, to the place where he should stay, at least for the time being, where he might salvage whatever life was left in him.

The car park was empty when he pulled into the *Bridge*, the bar deserted but for a handful of early evening drinkers. The burly Malcolm was behind the bar, working his day off. He was on the phone, wholly engrossed in whatever he was hearing.

He looked up as Hardman reached the bar.

"Did you know?" he said, his face still registering shock. "Owd Tom Ashe is dead."

*

He'd been walling up at the top pen. Every afternoon that week he'd worked up there. It niggled him, that pen. Two miles or more up the dale, it was rarely used now. Yet for generations Dalehead sheep had sheltered there each winter. After every blizzard they'd find a dozen or more packed in behind the tumbled stones. The old man would think to himself, *One o' these days I'll do summat about that pen.* He remembered it as it used to be. A good stout pen. It niggled him, whenever he thought of that.

"We should never ha' let it go like that," he grumbled.

"Oh, leave it be," Jack Ashe told him. "What do you want to go breaking your back doing that for?"

"Aye, well, I'd like to see it put to rights before I go."

At first he took the boy to help. The grey collie loped along behind.

"First thing," he told the lad, "is get your footings right."

He checked the foundations, working out measurements on the back of an old envelope with the stub of pencil he carried in his coat.

For a while the boy watched as the wall took shape. But he soon grew bored. He wasn't interested in walling. Instead, he looked for the hardest way across the stream, and teetered over it on small, wide-spaced stones, then scrambled up the steep bank, and into the rocky notch of Hesleden Clough. He looked down, a long way down, at the old man and the collie, little shrunken figures in the green bay by the stream, then set off alone across the moor.

The old man worked on placidly, laying his stones. He worked slowly, binding both faces of the walls at intervals with longer, flatter 'through' stones, blocking with 'fillers' the gaps between. He left few gaps inside his walls. He worked that way, slowly, painstakingly, because it was the only way he knew to build a wall. At the end of the week he'd restored not quite half the pen.

That last afternoon he'd stayed on late to put a crest of capstones on top of the finished section of the walls. He set 'em 'cock-and-hen', as he called it. One-down, one-up. Like a castle wall. It was almost dark when he turned to go. The end of a raw autumn day. The thin drizzle, in which he'd worked all afternoon, coming on sharp.

"Now then, Meg," he said.

He set off, well content with his work. The grey collie loped along behind.

He'd reached a point where the dale widens, almost within sight of the farm, when he first felt queer. Faint. Dizzy. A dryness in his throat and mouth.

He put out a hand on the plantation fence to steady himself, then went on uphill, slowly, away from the river, feeling his way slowly along the fence, conscious of rain pattering in the plantation, of moist, earthy, forest air.

At each tightening in his chest, he had to stop.

He began to doubt whether he'd make it as far as the farm. Gasping at the pain, halting every step or two, he got at last to the stile at the plantation end.

Ponderously, he lifted a leaden foot up on to the stile, but as he placed his hands on the wooden posts, the lights of Dalehead reeled away.

They'll have to fetch me, he thought, bewildered. *I s'll have to send for 'em to fetch me.*

He remembered the pencil in his coat. The old envelope.

Unseeing, in the blackness he scrawled on the scrap of paper – stuffed it under the collie's collar.

"Geroff home, Meg," he whispered, against the pain across his chest. "Geroff home."

But the collie waited. He gasped at her to go. But the collie waited, brushing the sodden tussocks with low sweeps of its tail. Whistles, it knew. Shouts. Even the quieter voice. But that gasping from the throat meant nothing. Puzzled, it waited, eyes fixed on the face, sunk now into that dark, wet corner between the stile and the plantation fence. It *knew* this place was not a place to settle in. Several times it skipped through the stile, then trotted back again to the man. It pawed at the man's coat, whining uneasily, a low submissive whining that pleaded for instruction. It wanted to be off. But it couldn't go without command. It wouldn't go without the man.

It was some time before they missed him at Dalehead. Before they thought to look.

"I'm sure he's not been in," said Mrs. Ashe.

They searched the barns, the dairy, even clumped up the wooden steps to look in the lofts.

In the stable, excited by the bustle above them, the dogs began a frantic barking. It was dark now. A fresh, gusty wind was blowing in the dale that set the yard light swaying on its wire.

It was the boy, back from school, who first picked out, amid the dogs' racket, the distant yelping of the collie. He told his dad. Jack Ashe listened – then started off at a run. But the boy flew ahead of him, splashing through the stream behind the house. He seemed to skim through the darkness as the hill fell away below him. Jack Ashe saw him dimly, flying down the black void of the dale.

When he arrived the collie dashed at him, barking, then backed away. The boy squeezed through the stile and dropped to the ground.

"Grandad," he gasped. "Grandad."

There was no response. Unused, whimpering, he clutched at the old man's coat.

Then, in seconds, he heard a soft, wet thudding as his father crashed down the hill behind him.

Jack Ashe dropped to his knees beside the boy.

"Quick!" he gasped. "Tell your mam to ring the Clarksons.. tell 'em your grandad's been took bad. Hey – an' tell her ring for t' doctor. Look sharp. Run!"

The boy needed no bidding. He raced back up the bank, staggering, stumbling over the tussocks, his heart bursting – skidded on the wet stones of the stream – fell heavily on his back.

Soaking wet, he gasped out his message at the kitchen door.

It took the Clarksons less than ten minutes to get up the dale. Maurice Clarkson, and two of his sons.

"We s'll have to get a door," he said.

The boy watched them as they lifted the larder door from its hinges.

"By, it's heavy, is this," young Clarkson gasped. He'd the whole weight of it against his fingers.

"What about some corrugated iron," said his brother. "Have you got a bit?"

The boy looked at his mam, her face dazed, uncertain. He was about to offer, but Maurice Clarkson wouldn't wait.

"No. We've not time," he said. "This'll have to do."

The boy took the big torch from the back of the kitchen door, and shone them down the hill.

The old man was laid flat on the ground when they arrived. His coat was open, and Jack Ashe crouched above his chest. He looked up into the pallid glare of the torch, the rain streaming from his bony face, his red hair blackened, plastered down.

"I think he's gone," he cried, in a voice strange and terrible to the boy.

He shone the torch for them as they lifted the old man on to the door, shivering, his shocked eyes fastened on the gaping mouth, the face ghastly under its stubble. The collie circled, whining softly, hindering this way and that, getting under the men's feet as they slipped and struggled to lift their burden. Young Clarkson stumbled – let slip his corner – the boy saw his grand-dad's hand slip loosely down.

Jack Ashe lashed his boot at the collie: "Gerrout, yer bug-ger! Go on!"

Yelping, it leaped aside – then cowered back towards the men, flattening itself submissively. It wanted the comfort, the control of the men.

Rain and dark pressed down on them as they struggled back over the black hill to the house. The boy went in front to light their way. Sure-footed himself, he shone the torch back at the ground in front of them – heard their boots squelching – their harsh breathing as the men struggled under the load – a gasp, now and then, as one of them stumbled and the collie whining out its fear, its misery, as it trotted after.

When at last they set the door down outside the kitchen, it crept in again, nosing, nuzzling between them.

"Hey – get this bloody bitch out o' my road," Jack Ashe shouted.

The boy called her, trying to make his voice hard and harsh as a man's, but she wouldn't come. Not to him. Dug in her claws and cowered, as he tried to drag her by the collar. He had to lift her bodily, clutching her to his chest, his face pressed into the thick, wet stink of her, and weeping as he struggled with her over to the stable. When he came back he saw the door lying where they'd left it, in a beam of light from the kitchen.

Strange, it looked. Dreadful. Lying there like that – with the flat drumming on it of the rain.

Fearfully he slipped in at the kitchen door.

They'd laid him on the floor in front of the fire, and were stood looking down. They were big men, the Clarksons. All the bigger, they seemed, above the body on floor. Yet the boy sensed in them, the big Clarkson men, a helplessness he'd never known before. A dreadful nullity.

His dad was kneeling, putting a cushion under his grandad's head.

Shocked, he gazed at the puddles, the raw smears of mud across his mam's kitchen floor – the gap where the larder door was missing. No one seemed to notice him standing there, until Maurice Clarkson turned and saw him, shuddering in his saturated jeans and jumper, his sodden wellies – took in at a glance the hair stuck together in black rat's tails, the pinched face, the lips blue with cold.

He put his big hand round the boy's head and drew him to his side.

"I should get this lad to bed, Ellen, if I were you," he said quietly.

"I were going to make some tea," his mam said, in a queer, dazed voice.

"Aye. Get him off to bed. I'll see to t' tea," said his dad.

She took off his wet clothes in the sitting room, in front of the fire. He stood, shoulders hunched, thin arms pressed together. Now and then little tremors shuddered through his body. All shrivelled, he seemed to her: his childish flanks blue and goosefleshed.

"Dear, dear, you must be perished," she said, and wrapped her arms, cloaked in a heavy towel, around his body.

He still carried, forgotten, the scrap of paper he'd taken from the collie's collar.

She prised it, screwed up, from his fingers.

"What's this?" she asked.

"It were under Meg's collar," he replied mechanically, shuddering again, his eyes fixed in the fire.

She flattened the scrap, saw the pencil scrawl: GONE DIZZY.

A shudder of horror ran through her as she thought of

him. Bitter. Unyielding. Now dying at last. And like an animal. Alone, out in the open, with the rain drumming down.

She recoiled from the horror of it. All her revulsion, her bitterness at that old man and his ugly, lonely farm rose in her, and she flung it from her – flung it into the fire.

"Is he dead?" the boy asked suddenly.

A dread came over her. She began to rub at his head again with the warm towel.

Suddenly, she saw the death dawning in him, spreading, darkening. In horror she hugged him to her.

"Oh, Tommy," she cried. "Tommy. ."

He was in bed when the doctor got to the dale. It was still raining. Wind swaying the trees behind the house. The yard lamp wincing on its wire. The lamp swept over the ground a downward beam that shed no light on the upper windows, so the boy knew that the light leaping suddenly in his room, shrinking across his wall, was the headlight of a car.

He scrambled down the bed to the window. Yes. Lights were coming up the dale. All the gates must be open, for they came on together, not stopping, the headlights swinging weirdly over the banks and black plantation. Then the dogs started. Lights blazed in at his window as a car turned into the yard. He watched Dr Gresham hurrying over the wet stones, through rain blowing in gusts against the swinging beam of light. Fear stirred his heart at the solemn strangeness of the scene: the yard blocked with cars, Clarkson's Landrover, the wet gleam of Dr Gresham's car, ghastly in the pallid glare of the lamp.

It was bitter in his bedroom. Shivering, he crawled back into bed and drew his legs up to his belly, cuddling the hot water bottle his mam had put in for him.

The wind was getting up. The heavy boughs behind the house were rousing, protesting.

Winter gales frightened the boy: a stormy battling about

the house that woke him in the middle of the night and he'd lie there filled with dread at the sound of the trees lashing, battering at one another, threatening to come crashing in through slates and ceiling. It frightened his mam too. She hated it. *Ah, it's grand though*, the old man said slyly. *Just listen to that.* As the gale screamed in the trees, and the stream came crashing down the clough. Whatever was going on out there, out in the night, that old man seemed at home in it.

He was a queer old man. He could talk to owls. He could. Once, coming down together at dusk through Slip Wood, the old man lifted his face to the softly stirring twilight that was leaves, branches, and hooted softly through his cupped hands. *Hoo-hoo-hooo... hoo-oo-oo-oo-ooo. .*

If ever you come across one, leave it be, the old man whispered. *It'll go for a full grown man, will a tawny owl. I knew a feller once lost an eye. Fiercest bird there is, a tawny owl. .*

There was a sudden noise below. Men's voices, low and solemn. On the narrow stair someone stumbled.

"Mind the corner there," a low voice muttered.

It was his dad. Then he heard Dr. Gresham's softer accent. He guessed they were carrying his grandad up the stairs. Then the heavy boots clumped down again. The door of his grandad's room closed quietly.

He would like to have slept then, to have slipped away, but he was still vulnerable to whatever visitant came in out of the night and into his imagination. He couldn't drag his mind from what had entered the house. Something he'd seen only as bleached bones, bundles of feathers, carcasses of sheep, had of its own accord come in from the moor, and he feared that if he slipped away it might slip after him.

Owd or young, when your time's up he'll come for you, his grandad used to say.

His mind floated over the cairn beyond Guttery Clough, that heap of stones near the waterfall, where the men had died in the dale. He used to think the men were buried there. When he was little. Solemnly his mind held to the stones, the running water, and the solemn strangeness that marked such places: the jagged flake, pointing like a finger out of the stones; or the great cairn over on Derwent where a shepherd lad froze to death in a blizzard long ago. *Lost lad*, he scratched on a rock. Up on Howden there was a wooden cross where an old shepherd died, an old man his grandad knew, and Tip, his dog, that stayed by his side for weeks. *While owt were left o'Will, he'd mind it*, the old man chuckled softly. A figure on a rock turned a leather face.

He woke with a start. The dogs were barking. He heard quick steps in the yard. And scrambled out to look. The yard lamp was off but the moon was shining. He saw a woman pass between the dark, looming barns, pass through the moonlight. Her head was covered with a scarf. It was Mrs. Clarkson.

He scrambled back to bed. Was asleep again in seconds. He never heard the steps on the stair, nor the soft opening of his grandad's door. And when the women had finished and the Clarksons drove away at last, neither they nor the clamour of the dogs could wake him.

The Clarksons had gone at last. Their plates and glasses still littered the table. Ellen Ashe wanted to clear them away, but he wouldn't hear of it.

"Oh, they'll wait till morning," he said. "You get off to bed."

Yes, they'll wait for me, she thought. But she was too worn out to argue. She went on up.

It was hot and steamy in the kitchen. He'd banked up a good big fire to dry out the wet clothes. He still had the barns to see to. But he sat on by the fire's sunken glow. Now, as much as anything, he felt relief at being, at last, alone. Or maybe it was sheer weariness left him that drained, played-out, as if he couldn't feel for anything any more. Whatever it was, he didn't fight against it. He sat dully in the red fire glow, his mind drifting vaguely to the dead man upstairs.

He raised himself with an effort and went out into the yard. It was a dark night. The wind, that had threatened earlier, had dropped again. A still air hung about the yard. Cold, wet, heavy. The dogs growled uneasily, yet even in sleep they knew him.

"Give over," he growled back.

He made his round of the barns. Then, as he paused a moment to fasten the yard gate, the moon rose suddenly. A bank of cloud moved on and, icy, remote, the moon, rising behind the house, picked out in a ribbon of snaky light the river down in the dale bottom. Only then it struck him. He hadn't thought of it before, but now it stood out rock-like. Dalehead had come to him. Through seven generations Ashes had farmed here. Now the farm had come to him. He gazed at the moon-blanched land by the river where his sucklers lay, and his mind went back through the old man's memories of *his* father and grandfather, *their* tales of the Irish labourers who used to mow those meadows a hundred years before, and the great-aunts and uncles, each with a little fork or rake, spreading the new mown grass, turning it, raking it into winnows, a great grass rampart, like a wall across the dale. They loaded forkfuls on to the slowly moving cart, then rode home at last on top of it, sunk in the snug, soft, warm, sweet-smelling grass, with the Kerry men singing, under the summer moon.

Then Jack Ashe knew a moment of pure loneliness. Icy, intense, it flooded through him as he stood alone under the black rim of the moor.

He turned, and went heavily to his bed.

For three days the dead man lay in the house. She wanted him moved to the undertakers but Jack Ashe wouldn't hear of it.

"He'll go from here," he said. "It's what he would have wanted."

Jack's sisters came, looked him up and down for the last time, and left. They came to coffin him that same afternoon. Jack Ashe went upstairs with them. After a while the undertaker's foreman came down to her, a big, affable man, fair and ruddy in his black clothes.

"Do you want to look at him?" he asked her gently.

She shook her head. She'd helped wash him. Lay him out. She wouldn't look at him again.

Then, for three days, he lay upstairs in the house. And she had to suffer it. Inwardly she raged, but she put up with it.

"It'll pass," she muttered to herself.

She stuck it out. But she kept her children close about her.

So the old man was buried from the farm. She stopped in the kitchen as they carried him downstairs, glad the children were at Alice Clarkson's. She heard the men struggling on the narrow stair. They took him out through the front door into the yard.

She sat stiffly beside Jack as the car crept on behind the hearse, heaving up and down along the rutted track. She heard the thin, shivering sound the wind made in the thorns. Flakes of snow were travelling on the wind. All down the dale the in-lamb ewes looked up to watch them pass.

The sisters rode behind in another stiff, black limousine.

"Well – he were t' last on 'em," said Jack.

She didn't answer. She had a sudden vision of Lizzie, the old man's favourite: Lizzie, whose picture, so faded it might have been the photo of a ghost, still stood on the chest of drawers in his bedroom, the ghost of a thin-faced little girl in a white frock, her long, fair hair caught up in a white ribbon. She couldn't have been more than eight or nine, yet she did the darning for the whole family. The lads might have worked on the farm but they did nothing in the house. Nothing. He never had. *They* were sent to school. Not the girls, though. *My mother couldn't spare 'em,* he used to say.

I don't suppose she could either, thought Ellen Ashe. What with sewing, scrubbing, mangling clothes, churning butter, whitening floors . .

At the end of the track young Maurice Clarkson was waiting to open the gate for the cortege. He took off his cap awkwardly as they passed.

At least the children were safely out of it with Alice Clarkson. Then she remembered the boy's face, rigid at Alice's kitchen window. He thought the world of his grandad. It might have set her weeping then, but for the thought that followed: Oh yes, he took to the lad but not to her. He never cared for her.

Dry-eyed, bitter, she sat silent all the way to Hope.

Afterwards, she felt nothing. Only relief that he was gone.

But for days after the funeral Jack went about quiet and withdrawn. He looked more gaunt than ever. The skin clung tighter to his bones. He seemed to be holding himself together. As if some cover had gone from over him. Left him exposed.

"At least it was quick," she said, concerned for him. "He didn't suffer." Conscious she was only repeating what everyone else had said at the funeral. "You wouldn't have wanted him dragging on like Jacky Longden."

He stared into the fire.

"He liked a good fire," he said, at length stirring himself.

She waited, ready to respond. But he lapsed back again. He seemed no longer to have any connection with her. As if, after all these years, he'd lapsed back to being just a son again.

At night she sensed him lying beside her in the darkness. Silent. Wide awake.

"Jack," she whispered.

"What is it?"

She lay watchful, uneasy, striving to pierce his silence, to see if he had read her secret exultation. Nights were tense.

But in the daytime, when he was out about the farm, or on

the moor, she threw off the darkness he brought into the house. Buoyant, enlarged, she swung about the kitchen, baking, washing, singing as she worked. The infants crawled or toddled after with solemn faces. They'd never known her sing.

She was going to paint the kitchen.

"Just emulsion. It'll not take but a couple of days," she pleaded.

"What d'you want to do that for," he grumbled. "In November?"

But he brought her the paint. He brought it back from Bakewell. She surveyed the dingy, yellow walls. The paint dark with age. Yet *he* would never have it done. *That paint's sound enough*, he'd say. *Last another year or two, will that.* He wouldn't spend money on paint. *But it's so gloomy*, she protested. He hadn't cared. He hadn't noticed.

She felt a wave of revulsion. Now she would expunge him totally. She would sweep him out of her kitchen.

First, she took down the old 'Good Shepherd' plaque. It had been there since his mother's day. Each spring, when she took it down to wash the wall, it had to go back in its place. It must have been up there for eighty years. It used to infuriate her, that religion of his. She used to hear him sometimes, singing snatches of old hymns. It hadn't done him much good, she thought. Or us, for that matter. She tossed the plaque into the rubbish pit behind the house. Triumphantly, she tossed it away.

It was a bright, cold morning. The boy was playing by the stream. He was trailing a twig for the kitten. Solemn, intense, it watched the trailing twig.

She felt a flush of tenderness; was glad, again, they'd let him have the kitten.

"What do you want to bring cats into the house for," Jack had grumbled.

"It'll take his mind off things," she'd argued. And for once even he'd seen the sense of it.

"Don't you get into that water," she called fondly.

She stood a moment longer, breathing in the sharp, moist air, her eyes travelling up to the dark rim of the moor across the dale, and the vast space of sky beyond. Then she went back indoors and began to carve great swathes of lather through the muck on the walls. The radio blared its music. She sang as she worked, and chattered to the children, squabbling on the kitchen floor.

Then the boy came in. With one hand he held the kitten pressed against his chest. His other hand held out the plaque.

"You're not chucking this away, are you? It were grandad's."

She turned on her stepladder, saw the loyalty written all over his face. Fierce. Absolute.

"I'll have it then," he said.

He went off with it across the kitchen. She heard him climbing the stair to his room.

All the joy went from her, all her lightness. She saw him locked away in the same dark, clogging life that had buried alive that dead old man. That was burying them all.

She longed to break free, to get away, to get them out of this.

*

It was some time before Hardman could bring himself to visit the Ashes. Usually, when colleagues went they simply slipped out of sight. Mostly, you forgot about them. Moving on, retiring, dying – it was the same. You subscribed to the presentation, or sat for twenty minutes at the crem – and then forgot.

Maybe, he thought, I should go over to Dalehead. But even as it sprang up, so it died in him, that impulse. It was a habit now. The second-thought. That split-second in which one put a gap between oneself and the world. Fictional grief he could have coped with. He could handle that. He even liked it. Would note with satisfaction the rapt faces of his students as he picked bare this or that tragedy. He had a way with fiction. But people suffered, and he had no adequate response.

Instead, he took his condolences down to the *Bridge* to sit with other friends and neighbours paying their respects over pints of bitter.

"Last o' the old school, was Tom," said the red-faced man.

"Jack'll miss him."

A silence descended on the company. The men, drawing on their cigarettes, were tasting the emptiness the old man left.

"Aye, well, he'll have to manage wi'out him now." That was the landlord's brother, who worked for the forestry, and whose name was Eric Smith.

"I suppose the tenancy will pass to Jack," tried Hardman cautiously.

They stared at him

"*Tenancy?* Tom Ashe weren't the tenant."

Now it was Hardman's turn to stare.

"He told me he was."

"He was pulling your leg," chuckled the landlord. "Dalehead's been in the Ashe family for generations."

"But I saw the agent.."

"More likely some feller from the bank," said Monty. "What d'you call 'em – small business something or other – keeping an eye on the loan."

At last, after what seemed to him a decent interval (when, as he supposed, the last traces had been cleared away, life flourishing again) Hardman walked down to Dalehead.

He found a restless vigour ranging in the dale. Up on the moor a moist wind was streaming that threatened rain later in the day. In the yard dead leaves were stirring. The great trees bustling above the house.

As he passed through the yard he spotted the boy hanging back in the gloom of one of the barns, swinging idly over a half-door. Off school again. Perhaps he hates it too, he thought, with a flash of sympathy.

"Hallo!" he called out brightly.

But the boy hung back in the gloom. He didn't answer.

"Come in!" a voice cried, when Hardman knocked.

She was painting the ceiling, clinging with one bare arm to the ladder, stretching with the other, in imminent danger, it seemed, of toppling over.

Sheets of newspaper covered the stone flags. Only the great dresser was still in its place against one wall. The rest of the furniture, pushed to the centre, formed a playground for the kids. Engrossed, they crawled or clambered here and there.

"I just want to get across this ceiling," she called down to him. "You feel you've made a start then, don't you?"

Already the warm, creamy paint had transformed one wall. Wide open, the low windows. The room seemed steeped in clean, cold air.

"I must look a sight," she laughed, as she came down from the ladder.

Hardman, though, was staggered at the change in her. The long hair, now bound up in a scarf, left exposed a face flushed, animated. Splodges of creamy paint had settled on her skin, clung in gouts to the fine hairs of her arms.

"I don't know where you get the energy," he began, "for all you do."

"Case of having to," she laughed.

Awkwardly he offered his condolences. Briefly she acknowledged them, offered him tea.

" Why don't I make it, " he offered.

"Then you'll not mind me getting on," she said.

They chatted as she worked, she in little, breathless spurts, craning her neck and bending back as far as her arm could reach. Hardman watched her, took in the broad hips, the thickening thighs and buttocks. For all the sparkle, the animation of that face, there was something heavy, earthbound, about her. It came, he supposed, from all that childbearing. That labour. And yet it drew him. The vigour, too, in the arched back, the bow-bend of the arm laying its swathes of creamy paint across the ceiling.

He asked after the boy.

"It must have been a dreadful shock," he said. "Finding him like that."

"Yes," she said. "It was a shock for all of us, really. He had a lot of time for Tommy. That's what he'll miss, I think."

"It's his birthday, too, next week," she went on.

"Not the twelfth," said Hardman, with sudden, sinking certainty.

"Yes, that's right," she said, surprised.

"It was my son's birthday." He experienced the shock of a word he never used. "Well, it would have been. He was premature. Stillborn."

"Oh, I am sorry," she said. "I'm so sorry."

He could see in her face the measure of the impact on a woman, and suffered again the pang of an old disloyalty.

"My wife remembered the day he was born. I didn't." He'd no idea why he was blurting this out, but went on anyway. "She took the day off work to stay at home and remember."

She'd been angry for a week. Angry with everyone and everything; him, the weather, the junk mail coming through the door.

"She didn't see any of the others, but she did hold him. Just for a moment.."

Ellen Ashe's face was full of sympathy.

"Since losing him," he went on, " she won't have anything to do with babies."

The threatened rain had arrived, great gusts of it, blown across Blackden. Ragged clouds, like smoke from a conflagration, were driving over the Kinder plateau. The wind moaned in the chimney, a thin, listless sound.

It was, he thought, a disastrous mistake. Getting her to hold him. She knew he was dead inside her. Even so, she'd cherished a forlorn hope of hearing him cry when he was born.

He sat listening to the wind's lamentation, playing over snatches from the horror movie of their life together. The trauma of yet another pregnancy. Her panic, rocking as he tried to hold her. *What's going to happen now? What's going to happen? Please tell me, what's going to happen. I'm so scared..* The bitter, self-flagellating lashes. *I don't feel as if I'm having a baby. I feel as if I'm having a miscarriage..* The nights lying beside her, sensing them clinging to her, the dead babies..

Waves of the old helplessness swept over him. He had sought to cancel the past. To blot it out as if it were irredeemable. Yet what had brought him here but his own past?

Elizabeth rang that night.

" Roger says he hasn't heard from you yet. He wonders if you're OK."

"I'm touched," he said dryly. "Do reassure him."

"You might at least answer his letter. You owe him that, at least. He really does need to know what you intend to do."

"I've already done it," he said wearily. "I've resigned."

A sudden spasm of dislike for his professor swept over him. That summer he'd second-marked a batch of exam papers that had passed through Seton's hands: scripts covered in a hieroglyphic scrawl which erupted, now and then, in bursts of peevish irritation: *Yuk! Oh Gawd! Gush! Illiterate nonsense! Dear oh dear. Words fail me!* Here and there you could see where words had actually failed: where the black ink trailed away, seemed to stagger incoherently. *I've just endured three hours' exposure to the Mind of Roger Seton*, he'd complained to Elizabeth. *That man is arrogant, intolerant, dogmatic..* She, though, had simply thrown his words back at him. *So are you, Anthony. Most academics are. You must try to live with it.*

But she was still banging on about Seton's letter. Had he read it yet?

"I don`t suppose you have. You probably stuck it behind the clock, where it wouldn't be visible. I know you, Anthony."

He looked away, out of the window, aware of her words tumbling into the space between them. He had a sudden sense of it, that space, a wasteland of unmown grass, leaves lying where they fell.

"You know, what I hear you saying in all this, Anthony.."

Sooner or later it came trotting out. Her therapist's jargon. Whatever was immediate, warmly personal, she rejected as untrustworthy. It had to be deconstructed, interpreted. It was her way of *not* connecting, a kind of psychic contraction back and away from the painful human world.

But she had rung off. It was, he thought, like all their communications these days, unfruitful, inconclusive. But that was their marriage

Sighing, he opened Seton's letter. 'A magnanimous offer', Elizabeth called it.

> *Dear Tony,*
>
> *Do you really want to resign? We'd be sorry to lose you. Won't you reconsider?*
>
> *Think about it, anyway. In the meantime I've fixed it for you to have some time off. You've never had a leave of absence. I'm sure you could make use of one. It'll give you a chance to get started on that book of yours, and think out what you want to do – and, hopefully, come back to us in January. .*
>
> *Yours ever...*

And really, he reflected, it *was* a very decent letter. Conciliatory, agreeable, it conveyed the felicitous insincerities of a civilized professional.

He thought of the gang of old men who'd ruled the roost

when he'd first joined the department. The imperial guard of English Letters, Seton called them. Scholars, most of them, of such entrenched opinion they rarely convinced one another of anything. In fact they hardly ever changed their minds at all. Half a dozen old turtles, scratching over the dustheaps, each encased in its own particular shell. It grew thicker as one got older. That shell. More massive. Thus encumbered with the accretions of decades, wheezing, grumbling, they creaked and trundled about the campus. Well, Seton soon put the skids under them.

Then was it borne in upon him that the university had become the place where he had learnt to hate himself. He hated his own sourness, his cynicism. Above all he hated his cleverness. He looked at his students, his colleagues – his wife, even – and he thought of something *clever*.

He knew then that he must wait patiently; wait for as long as it took; wait until that part of him languished and finally died for lack of any stimulus or nourishment.

*

Across from the dale, a little way above the Ashop river, rose a grassy knoll. A cottage stood there long years ago. The old man's grandmother lived in the cottage.

One-and-sixpence a week she paid for that cottage. The familiar voice no less audible for being underground. *Aye, all them farms and acres, yet he took his one-and-sixpence a week off that old woman.*

The boy was discovering that things both can and cannot be.

When she died they pulled down her cottage and took the stone for wallin'. My mother never forgave him for that. Not as long as she lived she never forgave him.

Did he come himself, he wondered. The Duke? To get his money? He used to think so when he was little. He'd lie on the knoll and see in his mind's eye that carriage stopping down below on the Snake: a dark green carriage with great spoked wheels, with shields and suchlike painted on the doors (there was a postcard of it on the wall at school) and the Duke, all in his noble robes, coming to collect his money.

"She were me great-great-grandma, weren't she?"

Aye, she were that.

" Had she got a cat?"

Aye – and a broomstick.

"Were she a witch, then?"

Oh aye. A good 'un, too.

The boy stared. But the old man's face was solemn. Sharp-eyed, over the glasses. It gave nothing away. And he wasn't sure. Wasn't sure.

She were a queer owd woman, though. She used to talk to my grandad. He'd been dead thirty year but she'd talk to him just as if he were sat there large as life. "Can't you see him?" she'd say.

He fixed the boy then with a *look*. Transfixed, the boy stared back at him.

I can still see her, plain as day. Wi' that white apron, and her starched cap. Very partic'lar she was about her caps.

At Dalehead opinion was divided as to the old man's tales.

"He made up stories," said his son defensively. "That's all it was."

"He told lies," said Ellen Ashe.

But the boy sensed it acutely; that backward glance. A portion of his own life, it might have been, running back below a surface. Never before had he sensed so sharply the proximity of life and death. He was anxious to get things right. He needed to know exactly how things stood. He still suffered from a primeval dread of misunderstanding the situation.

He sometimes wondered about those strange old women: his great-grandma, his great-great grandma. They'd been buried in Derwent churchyard. And then dug up again. All the bodies dug up and buried again in Bamford, when they flooded Derwent. *Crossed over*, his grandad used to say. Of dead people.

I'll be there, I'll be there, the old man used to sing sometimes. *In the glory over yonder I'll be there..* He used to sing it forking hay in the barn, or lifting potatoes. Doing the rough jobs he liked best. Sometimes he put in words of his own: *In the glory.. in the glory.. In the glory over yonder I'll be there.* Whether he sang to let forth a sudden blaze of fervour, or to hold a torch to the advancing darkness (he was an old man, well over eighty, well past his time) the boy, of course, couldn't say. But did wonder whether the *glory* lay, in some mysterious way, behind the strange transparency he sometimes sensed within the shapes and forms of things, and living creatures. Light, streaming through green leaves. Or the great beam of light that cut through mountainous clouds above the moor, *Jacob's ladder*, his granddad called it, plunging down from heaven.

Sometimes, as he stood engrossed, he seemed to feel it. The pressure of another world.

Trees moved softly overhead. The river roared below. And something hung in the air. Mysterious. Compelling. It slipped into his wars. This place. That cottage. Its whitewashed walls, levelled long ago. Scene of an old disaster, where the King's men struck without warning. Killing, destroying.

As Hardman came from his house he saw the boy down by the bridge, stamping about, slashing the air with a stick.

He waved. And was seen. For the boy stopped his pacing. Stared back. But gave no answering wave.

They would have been, it struck him, much the same age. He stood for a moment, watching the small figure now escaping down the bank, shaken by the recognition. Not for years had he been stricken so by the pain of the old loss.

You're in at the start of it, he thought, and then nothing. Men don't have babies. Yet the loss was real enough.

He wandered on along the track uncertainly, without purpose or direction, shaken at this welling up of the old unmanageable confrontation. Perhaps that had been his mistake: seeking to sever a part of himself that couldn't be denied or disavowed. He had seen its heart beating on the screen; had watched his son, as it seemed, waving to him from the womb.

So they went on together, part of a larger story from which, somehow, he had wandered away.

Across the river the dale changed character. For the whole valley side was scarred by a monstrous landslip, a mile of sandstone cliff that had parted company with the unstable shales, spilling down to the Dale river in a jumble of mounds and hummocks. Hard, now, for the eye to pick out among those grassy hillocks, those lumpy terraces of oak and head-high bracken, the outline of that eight-thousand-year-old crash. High on the hillside, though, in a deep bowl backed by disintegrating cliffs, was hidden a giant stack of splintering sandstone: a huge segment sheared away from the plateau, still upright, amid a gargantuan heap of rubble.

It was to this atmospheric place of crag and tumbled rock that they came, the man and the unborn child, an unseen presence from whom came feelings, emanations which lit up that lonely place. Things shone in that light. Weirdly tilted rock, walls of yellow sandstone, glowed like a boy's adventure, waiting to be taken down, the pages turned.

Far below, its buildings huddled round the Puritan barn, Dalehead lay defenceless under the sky. To the man gazing down, hearing an intermittent trickle of shattered stone, it seemed as if the reverberations of past centuries were still present here, unexorcised. They'd have kept a guard, surely. Posted sentries. Someone with sharp eyes. Keen ears. A lad, maybe, like Jack Ashe's lad. Hardman saw that pale, pinched face lifted to some grave minister. *So you're to be our little David, keeping watch over God's flock..*

As suddenly as if he'd stepped into another skin he felt the shock that must have gone with that responsibility, the appalling lurch of a world turned upside down. He thought of the boy wedged here among the rocks, peering into the mist. Then a key turned in a lock. A door opened to distant voices raised in a hymn.. then a clatter of hooves, the clink of steel..

On a day like this, maybe. A cold, raw day. That saturated air that clung to everything. And the troopers sour, ill-tempered, at everything damp, having to be dried and polished again. Looking to give short shrift to those psalm-singing bastards. And their officer. Young. Hardnosed. *I'm not here to debate with you. I'm here to carry out the King's law..*

The imaginative moment filled him with excitement; with the desire to know what happened, to *do* something.

Then it faded. He was alone again on the wet hillside, alone with the shattered rocks.

In the days that followed, Seton's letter, in its insidious way, began to work on him. Not its offer of time off, but the assumption (a pretence, of course, but still it served to point to a norm) that he'd come here to *do* something. To do some work.

Mere loafing, it seemed, this drifting through each day. A kind of mindless bashing about the hills. Of course there'd been compensations. His legs were stronger, arms and back the better for having swung an axe. From a physiological point of view he was undoubtedly a healthier, hardier specimen. Yet all around him other men were at their labours.

He'd heard the whine and rattle of their engines in plantations. He looked from his window over towards Blackden where the Clarksons were taking their ewes up on to the moor. In the dale bottom Jack Ashe was seeing to his sucklers. He'd come into this solitude to find out who he was. He saw now that it was merely a resting place, a stage in a transition. It couldn't be an end in itself.

One morning, eating his breakfast beside the ashes of his fire, he began to think seriously of starting work.

So he began to spend his days in libraries again. The narrow road took Hardman down the wooded valley of the Derwent. He drove beneath bare winter canopies, through stone villages, with flashes of river between the trees, and the long march of the gritstone edges for company as he travelled south.

His mind, though, was travelling in the seventeenth century, dredging up all he could recall of those apocalyptic years after the king's execution. Yeomen, labourers, apprentices, craftsmen of all kinds, taking the road. *They sprout out by huddles and clusters*, he remembered, *like locusts out of the bottomless pit*. The born-again men. Driven by the Word, the 'in-dwelling Spirit'. Seekers, Ranters, Quakers, Anabaptists, Fifth Monarchy men. Men whose dreams were filled with fearful visions, whose heads rang with malignant texts, haunted by accusing voices, pinched, buffeted, pulled this way and that.

In Matlock, that pleasant town, under the eccentric pleasure dome of Smedley's Hydro (it now housed the County Archives) where rheumaticky Victorian dames once dipped, discretely draped, in tepid springs, and sat down after to *bouchées aux huîtres*, haunch of venison, *meringues à la Chantilly*, Hardman pored over old instances of man's inhumanity to man. The Act of Uniformity, the Act against Conventicles, the Five Mile Act, the Test Act..

In a lofty room, under a mock Gothic window, he slipped back comfortably into the reading, the research, taking, in spite of himself, a grammarian's pleasure in the elegance of those instruments of oppression; intricate, comprehensive, each a model of clarity.

Every person above sixteen years of age, present at any meeting, under pretence of any exercise of religion, in other manner than is the practice of the church of England, where there are five persons more than the household, shall for the

first offence, by a justice of the peace be recorded, and sent to
gaol three months, till he pay 5L and for the second offence, six
months, till he pay 10L and the third time being convicted by a
jury, shall be banished to some of the American plantations..

On it went, the sonorous prose. Stately, measured. Seventeenth century, yet wholly familiar in its catalogue of tyranny.

At the ejection on Black Bartholomew Day, three excellent
clergymen in Derby, and forty-three in different parts of the
county, were cast out of their livings and exposed to cruel
persecution..

Government, it seemed, so far forgot itself as to lend its weight to one sect in persecuting another. For ten years or more the ejected ministers could not be suffered to live in peace. Men and women could not meet to pray in private, but it was deemed a seditious conventicle. The upright man was known by the zeal with which he informed upon his neighbour. Meetings disturbed by bands of soldiers, *to the death of some, and terror of many..* men hunted down, their houses rifled, property confiscated, themselves seized, convicted without benefit of jury, thrown into close and noisome prisons: all this for the heavy crime of preaching and praying: for refusing to subscribe to the Book of Common Prayer.

In a *Memoir of John Hackett* (a lengthy encomium in praise of that prelate's kindness, his care even for his dissenting clergy) Hardman found part of a letter. From one, Billingsley.

I knowe not how to mollify oaths by forced interpretations, or
stretch my conscience to submit to human will in cases
wherein, if I should be in the wrong as I sharply suspect I shall
be in this, I knowe human power cannot defend me..

It was obvious what Bishop Hackett had been up to. Compromise. Sweet reasonableness. The serpent voice that finds a way round, or under, or over.

Yet Hardman read of him with pleasure. Old Bishop

Hackett. Who'd excommunicated Thos Wood, Dean of Lichfield, in his own cathedral, to the great delight of the chapter. He had, they said of him, *the old apostolic spirit of discerning.* Wood had paid the king £100 to get the deanery. Three years later, when Hackett died, he bought the bishopric. Oh, what a consternation of canons, he thought delightedly. I bet they jumped about then.

But it was the Derbyshire men he was after. Anything that might throw some light on the temper, the essential spirit, of those clandestine meetings in that isolated barn. He had a sudden image of the boy, huddled under the lee of a rock, his coat pulled up about his face, peering into the mist, straining to hear the chink of steel, the clatter of hoofs..

As he drove back north to the Snake, it struck him that maybe the past is never really there at the far end of the historical microscope; that history always springs out of a relation between a present and its past.

He felt, then, like a man who had thrown away a part of himself. Elizabeth had never let go. He could see her, waiting in the car outside the university *crèche* as he came back from the bookshop. *He'd be three now. I'd be taking him to nursery..* He had tried to write off that part of his life. He knew now that a past was never over and done with, that it was always present, waiting to be lived and relived, until it was purged out of him.

*

Since the day of the funeral the boy had haunted the edges of a precipice. He might have been floating in a void, dislocated by the incomprehensible fact of death. Voices floated around it, but it remained, that void. Things he knew were unfamiliar. Books at rest on their shelves that wouldn't move for him now. That might never move again. Even his mam and dad were different. Only the twins and Jacky stayed the same. He took to playing with them, a thing he'd rarely done, letting the twins crawl and roll all over him, surrendering himself to the press of warm, urinous little bodies. Yet he felt infinitely older, wiser, than the children. Something, a part of his life, had gone for ever.

In the weeks that followed his mind was drawn, again and again, to the last sight he'd had of the old man. His hand reaching out uncertainly, as if in a dream, the door swinging ajar, the room pitch-black, except for where the moon shone in at the window, the blanched light falling faintly over the draped figure, the weirdly jutting chin.

It haunted him. The thought of his grandad under the gleaming lid of that long, narrow box. Even by day he couldn't shake it loose. What it was exactly, the thing he feared, he couldn't have said. Yet the sense of being attended by something fearful was very strong. It waited for him as he climbed the stair at night. It followed him over the gaunt marsh, with grey rain-smoke drifting over the dark plantation. It sat, a draped figure, on a grey edge of rock against the sky. *You don't want to go out on them there moors at night, lad*, the old man whispered. *They crawl.*

Then he woke, pressed down in darkness. The yard lamp was off and his own light switch was distant, across a dark divide. A scuffle there, though, was the kitten.

"Treacle," he whispered, in the darkness.

Only the kitten made him forget. He carried her with him as he went about the house. Solemn, wide-eyed at the astonishing world, baffled by bits of itself that always seemed out of reach, it twisted its tiny body in impossible contortions. It leapt, tumbled, skipped like a lamb, pranced like a pony, danced like a March hare: then, in an instant, plunged down gulfs of sleep.

At night it slept on his bed. He felt the warm pressure of the living thing against his thigh. And was reassured. Yet feared to sleep himself.

He told no one of his dreams. He had no words to speak of

dreams. Nor did it occur to him that anyone would care. His mam rattled about the house, singing as she worked, but for all her bustling activity he sensed in her a preoccupation that was wholly private. It shut him out.

One afternoon Mr Clarkson arrived at the kitchen door with a terrier under his arm. The men were going over the dale to look for a fox. His dad said they were vermin, that had to be shot.

As soon as he'd finished his dinner the boy slid down from the table, and set off after them. He could see the two men already crossing the dale bottom, heading for the river.

Two nights running he'd heard the high-pitched bark of a dog fox in the dale. Every man's hand against it, yet it survived, and lived implacably its own wild life. That self-sufficient loneness called up in the boy some unquiet spirit buried in the bone. Alerted, he lay waiting, the tip of his nose freezing in black, icy air, waiting for the vixen's answering scream. But no answer came.

That morning he'd slipped out early, down to the dale bottom, close to the bridge that carries the Snake road. There on the steep bank above the river, where the trees grew thickest, were tunnels cavernous with age. Fresh red earth was spilt down over the sandy bank. He'd crawled in at each dark mouth, sniffing for the stink of fox. Not everyone could smell a fox. His dad couldn't. But he could. He'd combed the rich, soft grass under the trees, scavenging for signs of fox: bitten feathers, crushed and bitten bones, or droppings, purplish in autumn when they'd been eating berries, the tell-tale, whispy twist of fox shit. There was nothing. Yet he'd come back with foxes in his head.

He could see the two men up ahead, slowing as they started the toilsome climb up through the wood towards the stack, Maurice Clarkson with the little terrier huddled under his coat, Jack Ashe carrying the shotgun.

The boy hurried after them. He still inhabited, at least in

part, a universe in which everything was special. Everything had a different face. He had not quite started the drift away from creation. Was not yet stuck down in the certainties of the adult world.

He was made to stay lower down, behind the gun. Out of harm's way, his dad said. Meanwhile, Mr Clarkson was climbing a little way up the slope to put the terrier in among the rocks.

Then, just emerging at the base of the rocks, not thirty feet away, he saw the fox. At the hot stink of man it froze. Lowered its muzzle. The boy was conscious of close-set, glowing eyes. The out-gazing of the wild, face to face with the world of men. It had not been told what was said of it. It was its own wild truth.

All this the boy, in his difference, saw, since the same was true of himself.

What came, though, as the fox turned, was the double *bang* of the shotgun, and what had been running was bowled over, rolled over and over, tumbling down to come to rest among the rocks.

Afterwards he squatted by the body. Stared at the gouts of bright blood, the cruel muzzle that tore out the throats of lambs. Wonderingly, he put out a hand to touch the thick, coarse coat. Still warm with life. But it was dead. At one with all dead things he'd ever seen on the moor. Maggoty crows. Carcasses of sheep. Whatever it was that had challenged him wasn't here. Something had vanished from the empty eyes. A blind had come down there

That night the fox was back. It was there, alive in his head. The spear-blade ears, the coals of its eyes fastened on him as if something was expected. As if it was waiting for a sign. He lay, scarcely daring to breathe, for he knew the slightest noise or movement would set off the blast of the gun.

But the fox went anyway. A wild thing, it wouldn't stay for him. He could not keep it back. Its passing left doors set open in his mind. But dark. Opening on dark passages.

So, caught up in the inextinguishable vigour of creation, the boy struggled to fit himself as best he could to the mystery of his own existence.

*

There followed a succession of tranquil late autumn days. Long, soft shadows dappled the dale. Trees, stone walls, the steep green fields serene under that special light that falls only when the sun is low, subdued, and colours come into their own. To Hardman, sweeping leaves from the cobbled yard, the very sticks and stones were steeped in peace and silence.

One afternoon, as the light was fading from the dale, he brought down the folding photograph from the bedroom, set it in the window space. Elizabeth, at twenty, gazing down at a book. The smooth, young face, half-averted, unmindful of the empty years. She seemed, it struck him now, the opportunity he never took.

And what of the crew-cut youth facing her across the frame, heedless, vain, a coil of rope round his shoulders, posing under the bridge at Ogwen Cottage, with the Afon Ogwen thundering down. Lean, healthy, filled with the strength and exuberance of youth.

He felt a sudden access of compassion for that sporting innocent, among his rocks and mountains. Knowing nothing. By turns frightened, or deliriously happy. *Somewhere*, he thought, distressed, *I let him down*.

So, gradually, he stumbled on his life again. Oh, not as it was. That would have been too much to hope for. Though it took some effort he found he could transport himself back and forth among the debris, shuffling here and there, turning over the bits and pieces, painful to the touch, yet each a fragment of the story that was himself.

He began to see, uncertainly at first, how the parts might be assembled. Not perhaps as they were before. But assembled, none the less. It wasn't easy. He had to empty his mind and wait, in stillness and silence, waiting for whatever might be lurking in the half-light, waiting to venture in.

Gradually, as the outlines of the room receded, another room declared itself. It might have served as a set for a play, a piece of make-believe. The cot in a corner. The chime of bells above the cot. In a chair, a jumble of woolly animals. A teddy bear. A rabbit in a knitted dress. On the wall, pictures for a nursery. A buggy, folded against a wall. The consultant's eyes, though, were fixed upon the scan. *Have you decided on a name?* She shook her head. To have given him a name would have made him real. She wouldn't risk that. Even though four months pregnant she didn't want anyone to know. She couldn't believe she could have a baby. Her womb was not a safe place for babies. *They're much more defined at this stage.* Look, there was the heart.. the stomach.. the bladder. *Quite a little person.* A fuzzy movement turned out to be an arm. *You see, he's waving...*

He was the last. The end of it. The end of their attempt to have a child.

Only some time afterwards she said, quite calmly, *I'm not going to go through that again.* She'd arranged it on her own, without consulting him. She'd punished the body which had killed the babies.

He sat at her bedside after it was done, staring at the wall.

A half-remembered line sprang into mind: *I did not weep, so much of stone had I become. She wept..*

No, he thought. She didn't weep either.

Rain fell heavily in the night. He woke before dawn, to hear the rain drumming against the window. He stared out at a low sky, pressing like a lid upon the land.

He set off for Matlock as usual, peering through the murk and spray of lorries at the lamps of oncoming vehicles, troubled by a sense that he was clinging to a part of his life that was breaking loose. So it was almost a relief to get the old Hardman safely to the library where he was known, greeted. A mousy girl stacking the shelves smiled at him, and he smiled back. As he resumed his usual seat at the table, the archivist swivelled pebbly lenses in his direction. Mouthed a silent *Hello*.

So far his search for the Derbyshire Dissenters had plunged him into turbulent waters. He'd hunted through *Lives*, memorials, histories and antiquities, memoirs, books of characters, recollections, spiritual testaments. A laborious trawling of parish registers had produced a list of names. Though sometimes the record scarcely ran to that. Sometimes it was simply the date of an ejection, and the formula: *non subscribendo juxta statute*.

They must have hawked the Act right round the diocese, he thought, as he flicked through his notes. Taken it into every parish. Put the question formally to each incumbent. Sober, learned men. Men who preferred to be ejected from their comfortable livings rather than renege on their convictions.

*Many fled from their homes and went into hiding, coming
privately by night to their wives and children. Not a few
resolved to preach in the cities: to preach openly, till they should
be sent to prison..*

He studied the list of names he had jotted down: Oldfield.. Scholes.. Bagshaw..

There was a time when he would have interpreted their refusal to conform as just another form of 'false consciousness', masking another, more material interest. Really, though, he knew nothing about them.

He looked again at the note he had written against one of the names.

NB: Text preached at Bingham's funeral. 'I will put my law upon their inward parts. In their hearts will I write it.' [Jeremiah]

Was there, perhaps, some accession of insight, some illumination in which intelligence, skill, learning, all these counted for nothing? Indeed, to the extent that they were resorted to, actually became an obstacle?

He sought for the meaning without grasping the life. And to assume one could truly interpret matters of which one had no first-hand experience, things not felt in the blood, and felt along the heart, it was, he thought, the scholar's hubris.

The new philosophy calls all in doubt..

He had embraced it, the new Enlightenment, because it was the thing. The way forward. Older, more traditional colleagues who refused conversion were simply swept aside. Besides, the young zealots spoke with such exceptional self-assurance, such conviction that what they had to say was obvious, once one had liberated oneself from the shackles of old ideologies. They had freed the present from the past. In exposing the literary heritage industry as nothing more than a sham, a swindle, a long gallery of distorting mirrors in need of a suitable correcting lens, they'd demonstrated a wholly different understanding of the individual, and the individual's relation to society. They'd raised literary theory to the realm of scientific truth.

Liberated from the mystification of centuries, they flashed triumphantly, like so many skaters, over the surface of the pond. Clever people all of them, at last they'd found something to be clever about. And so had he. So had he.

"Have you turned up anything yet?" enquired a wheezy voice. A moon face bent good-naturedly. It was the archivist.

Hardman smiled. Shook his head.

"Not much, I'm afraid. Some names. Very little else." He pushed the list towards her.

She read it, frowning.

"Look," she said. "Leave this with me. Maybe some of these wrote pamphlets, or published sermons or something. There's all sorts of stuff in the old catalogue. Things we scarcely know we've got."

He dragged on a while at the table, pushing his notes around. At length he pushed back his chair, and went out from the library.

A bleak half-light lay on the town, a wintry pallor reflected from the roofs of houses, scarcely glimmering on distant hills, where earth and sky seem shrunk together in melancholy conjunction. It was bitterly cold.

He walked for a while in the little park beside the river, past piles of dead leaves awaiting collection. A heavy, flooding rain had fallen during the night. A fast stream was flowing, full of fallen, broken things: twigs, litter, dead leaves, scurrying past on the swirling, slate-grey, slate-green water.

Matlock was busy. He threaded his way between shoppers well-wrapped against the cold, thronging shops tricked out with fake leaded lights and cotton-woolly snow, to buy back the dream Christmases they never had.

He felt ashamed, then, at this sudden access of the old sourness. However provoked, the goodwill he sensed around him was real enough. Other folk were happy. The non-holly cheered, and cardboard bells rang out, if not for him. The Christmas scene, people buying presents for children, grandchildren, brought home to him the nature of his own deprivation, his and Elizabeth's, outcasts, both of them, from another of life's feasts. The fear that he had somehow mutilated his own life, cut himself off from some rich stream of loving-kindness, filled him with desolation. In this busy street, where not a soul knew him, or cared anything about him.

For a moment he was overwhelmed. Had to step aside, into a doorway, anywhere.

He found himself blinking at books displayed in a window. Bright jackets. A snarling dragon head against a low, red sky. A line of Gothic print: *Hammer of the North*.

It brought to mind a low-ceilinged room, shelves of books, an old man reading to his grandson.

Maybe it was that image carried the childless man into the shop.

"That one. There," he said. "The one about the Vikings."

An elderly assistant reached it out for him. Stood waiting while he flipped past swords, black silhouettes of standing stones, a vast beckoning sky, *forever further than the furthest known..*

"A Christmas present," she asked him pleasantly.

"Well, maybe," said Hardman. As the impulse slackened. He snapped the book shut.

"Yes. I'll take it."

And hurried back to his car hugging the wrapped package almost as if it was the pressure of a human arm he had there, pressed again his side.

The golden light had gone from the dale. Now, as the year waned, the dark moors loured against the sky, shutting out the light from the south. The last shreds of autumn were slipping from the boughs above the gable. The boy's birthday had come and gone.

Hammer of the North remained where laid down on the sideboard at Moor House. The death's head helmet staring from its empty sockets, mute evidence of another stillborn impulse. Another failure to connect. The disengagement, it seemed, of some failed father-figure, no more than an empty husk of what it shrank from so regretfully, a half-life longing for wholeness, even as it backed away from the unmanageable encounter.

Something bitter was taking root in his existence. Bleakly, he set himself to meet it. If he lay down, let it wash over him, there was a chance he might not come up again. Yet, as he sat at the long table, gazing at the dreary day, he felt utterly without resource.

In the end he rang Elizabeth. He heard the answer-phone cut in with its formulaic response: … *please leave a message*.

"Come up this weekend, if you can, Liz," he muttered into the phone. "Please come up."

So grief began again for Hardman. And with its onset he knew he had reached a destination of a sort. Sooner or later an isolated man drops all his poses.

Winter

'Tis a common tale,
An ordinary sorrow of man's life,
A tale of silent suffering, hardly clothed
In bodily form.. '

William Wordsworth   *The Excursion*

FOUR

If Elizabeth Hardman had not suffered more than many women, her sufferings had cost her more. They had opened her eyes to the inherent disappointment of existence. She had been betrayed by life. Worse, she had been betrayed by her own body, a treachery that cast a shadow over all allegiance. But she wouldn't talk about that. She couldn't put that into words. Even so, what was not to be thought of continued to be borne. She carried in her heart the souls of her dead babies. It was something she had to do for them, a recompense for the hard usage they had suffered. Asking nothing, they'd received less than nothing. No coffin, no funeral, no outward sign. They weren't even a reality for anyone else.

She felt she had killed them. Nothing could rid her of that feeling. Just as nothing since had cured her conviction that she was not a normal woman. It had never crossed her mind that it could happen to *her*. A miscarriage. She'd lain on a couch with her belly exposed in a beam of sunlight that turned suddenly to ice. They checked the date of her period. Asked if she was sure. Of course she was sure. They said there was no heartbeat. *What do you mean, there's no heartbeat*? She saw the nurse had tears in her eyes.

She was still young, of course. So she kept hearing. It was a truth which they repeated to one another, lying in each other's arms, together affirming the right to life.

Then, as if in confirmation, she was pregnant again. That time she'd seen for herself there was no heartbeat. A fortnight before she'd seen it quite plainly. The tiny flickering. The consultant, a woman, had fixed on her a look of piercing tenderness. *This pregnancy*, she said, *is not going to continue*.

After a while, they tried again. *I should be all right this time. It's not going to happen to me again, is it?* What if I fail, she wondered. She was haunted by dead children. She grew ugly, and repulsive to herself, shuddering away from the body that had murdered them, shivering as he tried to hold her. *It's rare to have two*, he whispered. *Three's even rarer*. If he told her that again she thought she would scream.

Six weeks, and all was well. No pain, no bleeding. At seven weeks Anthony went to a conference. She went for her scan. *It's not good news. I'll show you on the screen*. She knew it. Her breasts had changed. *If you look to your left..* She'd even packed a bag, expecting to be kept in. *I can't see any heart beat there*. Twenty-four hours later another child had been removed from her womb.

They desired one another less than before, consoling themselves instead with solitary moments of past sorrow. Grief, it seemed, could be more satisfying than passion. And was keenest savoured alone.

She turned more and more to her clients and a life apart, a vantage point from which she could operate at a distance from herself. She and Anthony had less and less to say to one another.

Or, if either spoke, the other was not listening.

They stopped trying for a child. So it came as a complete shock, her final pregnancy. She was devastated. She waited for the worst to happen. But the pregnancy continued. The baby began to kick. At eighteen weeks he was clearly visible, even to her. He was becoming real. And still she couldn't believe. At twenty weeks he gave up trying to convince her. Giving birth to him had been an unspeakable, soul-shattering horror. She made sure it wouldn't happen again.

After that, their sense of each other darkened. All they were left with was an unlived life.

So why, she wondered, was she doing this? For him? For their marriage, an empty space around which they continued to forage for warmth and comfort? If it hadn't died exactly, nothing of it remained alive.

He came down the path to greet her.

He looked thinner, she thought with sudden solicitude, and wondered if he was eating properly.

"How are things?" he said, as he took her bag.

She stood awkwardly in the kitchen while he made her tea, bobbing along on a flood of chatter – yes, he was fine, he was working on something – that will do to furnish a silence. Or fill a gap. What either understood of the other was doubtful as they sat in front of the fire drinking tea. Uncertainty began to make the woman restless. Then she saw that the man was starved of company, that what he wanted was a human presence at which to aim his words, a mark preferable to furniture or wallpaper.

"Look, Anthony," she said with sudden irritation, "what am I doing here? What do you want?"

"I'm sorry," he said stiffly, suddenly on familiar ground again. "You didn't *have* to come."

They were addicted to pain as a confirmation of their identity.

He'd prepared a salad, for which he apologized ironically.

"It's mostly lettuce, I'm afraid. Bamford doesn't cater much for vegetarians."

It was another of her failings, for which she was expected to pay. Even so, she availed herself of the relief of eating, grateful for the silence it permitted.

"What are you working on?" she managed eventually, between mouthfuls.

"I don't suppose it'll come to anything." He wouldn't be drawn.

Snubbed once, she wouldn't try again.

After the meal he made up the fire, piling fresh logs in the grate. She, meanwhile, had noticed *Hammer of the North*, still lying on the sideboard. She picked it up, was flipping though the pages of what was so evidently a child's book. Maybe I should tell her, he thought. *There's a boy*, he might have said, *who lives at the farm up the dale. He was born on the same day.*. Yet before the words were out he could see her recoiling, shivered into that psychic contraction of hers in which she was no longer present to herself.

She, though, had replaced the book on the sideboard without comment. He was conscious of her moving about the room, staring out of the window, picking things up, putting them down, hearing the echo of her heels on the bare boards. Most of all he heard her silence.

She was closed, he saw. He raged inwardly at the pointlessness of her coming here. Of his asking her.

Even our failures, she was thinking wearily, have no depth. They keep us living on the surface of ourselves.

"You know, Anthony, I sometimes think we're really a hopeless case."

" What case is that?" he enquired icily. " I wasn't aware we were a *case*."

The walls shrank intolerably.

"Oh, for God's sake – let's go to the pub."

It was Saturday night at *The Bridge*. The night of the Christmas draw.

Grand Raffle, declared a notice stuck to a bar pillar: *Proceeds to be donated to the Derwent Mountain Rescue Team. Winning tickets will be drawn by Eric Smith.*

The place was packed. Thumping with a merriment that only aggravated Hardman's isolation, pushing him further out. They were all there, he saw morosely. Everyone he knew. He forced a passage through to the bar, nodding at Norman, at Monty, at Malcolm, helping out behind the pumps.

"Come to check up on you, has she?" the burly youth shot sideways as he pulled a pint. With a grin for Elizabeth.

She found herself wedged up against a broad red face, a watery eye, hair slicked back above a shiny brow. On the bar beside her a pair of heavy hands unstapling raffle stubs in a fumbling, thick-fingered way, pushing them through a slit in a cardboard box.

"Ah'm feedin' 'em into t' computer." He winked a rheumy eye.

George was counting a fistful of notes and silver into a pint pot.

"Ne'er mind talkin', Norman," he called out. "Get sellin' them tickets. We're not drawin' till we've taken another fifty pound."

"Got yours, 'ave yer?" asked the red-faced man.

"What do we get if we win," Elizabeth smiled back at him.

"Well, there's a nice turkey.."

"Nice and fresh," put in George. "It were running round here this morning."

"There's a Christmas hamper, and a bottle o' malt whisky.."

"Fourth prize is me for a week," George added loudly. And winked at Elizabeth.

"You've no need to buy a ticket for him," called a sharp voice from the snug. "You can have him for free."

"Aye," a woman called, "but is he worth having?"

"Beryl, Iris wants to know if I`m worth havin'."

"Tell 'er I s'll ask her after."

For the man and woman who were strangers here, who did not belong, this place was offering a refuge of a kind. Here, at last, amid the smoke, the clamour of voices, they could escape one another. Drawn apart into the broad, good-natured flow around her, the stories and the laughter, Elizabeth Hardman had reverted to the bright, impersonal non-Elizabeth she favoured most. So it seemed to her husband. She was standing under a lamp above the bar, head inclined, as she listened gravely to one of Monty's tales. Then, turning, she caught his eye, and smiled.

"I hope you've bought a ticket," said a voice at his shoulder. Hardman looked round to see Eric Smith.

"I didn't know you were in the Mountain Rescue."

"That's right."

"I was a climber once," said Hardman impulsively.

"Oh aye?"

"Then my wife had a miscarriage, so I had to pack it in." Enclosed by the noise, the racket of other voices, he felt a sudden urge to confess, to tell his tale.

"I was climbing on Great End. Central Gully. You know it? I was on my own. I should never have been there. It was a terrible day. Thick, wet, sleety snow. No visibility. I should never have been there. But I'd gone up to the Lakes to climb. You know how it is."

Eric Smith nodded. He knew how it was.

"I was at the top of the gully, right under the cornice, when the whole bloody lot started to avalanche. I ended up in hospital. I was lucky to get away with it."

Hardman gulped at his beer. He might have said more, shed some of the woe which is in marriage to this rescuer who, he half hoped, might offer a top-rope.

But Norman was offering to buy them all a drink.

Smiling, Elizabeth refused.

"Go on, have a short."

"I try not to have too many shorts," Monty put in delicately, "in case the wife requires me when I get home."

The shout of laughter left Hardman feeling got at. Though he grinned, with a great show of teeth.

"Ah 'ave to get as many down my missus as Ah can," said Norman ruefully. "On'y chance Ah've got of gerrin' it. If she's kettled."

Elizabeth was laughing with the rest, when Anthony's voice cut at her ear, clipped, cold.

"Are you ready?"

"But they haven't drawn the raffle yet," she protested. "We might win the turkey."

"Oh, for Christ's sake! What would you do with a turkey?"

Give it away, she might have said. But he was already ploughing his way towards the door. She had to follow.

They woke, and breakfasted together, talking in stiff voices, exchanging words like sticks that might have snapped, given rough usage.

"What are you doing for Christmas?"

She was going away, she let him know, before he could reply.

"You remember? Maura has that cottage in Glen Shiel."

You go on trying and trying, she was thinking. *How many failures can you take? When do you say, 'Enough is enough'?* Yet he was still her other self, who continued to dwell in her loneliness, and made it authentic.

The drone of her engine faded down the Snake.

It was a cold morning. The stars had gone. A pale moon stood over the plantation, with Mars a last light in the west. There was snow on the hills.

Hardman shivered. He put some scraps out for the birds. Then he went inside and closed the door.

Helpless, repetitive, their lives went round in circles. They couldn't live together, and they couldn't live apart.

*

Ellen Ashe was a Glossop girl. Born in a stone-built back-to-back in Hadfield. Her grandfather had been a weaver at the Wren Nest mill. He'd fought in the war, survived, come back and voted Labour. But nothing changed. He still worked at Wren Nest. Dragged on in the same dark, damp, dreary house.

It was a rented house, built at the time of the Franco-Prussian war. No bathroom. No inside lavatory. Under the pre-war

Housing Act it might have been declared unfit for habitation, but it wasn't. By the time Ellen Ashe came along it still showed no sign of collapsing. *That's the trouble wi' gritstone,* her grand-dad used to say. *The bugger won't fall down.* The men he voted for had passed another Housing Act after the war. It offered grants to landlords if they would improve their properties. Not many of them applied. Not in Glossop. An eight per cent increase in the rent didn't make it a commercial proposition. And you couldn't sell the house when you'd improved it. Not unless the tenant died.

For years after the war there were very few private houses built in Glossop. It was never a fashionable place. It was hardly worth a speculator's trouble to build houses. The middle classes wouldn't buy 'em. The working class couldn't afford to. By the time the council were prepared to build, people wouldn't move. After twenty or thirty years in the same dilapidated property most folk preferred to stick it out where they were. At least the rents were low. The Council were asking three times as much for their new houses. Most folk didn't bother to apply for homes they couldn't afford. Less than six hundred sent back the application form the Housing Department had distributed round the town.

So, like most other kids in Glossop, Ellen Ashe grew up in the same decrepit house she had been born in. She'd married twice. The first time to a lad who'd ignored her when he was sober, and knocked her about when he was drunk. It was a relief when he ran off with another lass. She'd married Jack as soon as the divorce came through. *Take the chance while you've got it,* her mam told her. *There's not that many fellers'll take a woman wi' a child.*

All her life, one way or another, she'd done what she was told. What people said she ought to do. *A farmer!* her mam said. *You'll be set up for life.* She'd the same daft idea all towns-folk seemed to have. All farmers were well off! Well, she knew

better now, she thought with savage satisfaction, as she filled
her basket with wet woollens, and went out to peg them on the
line, her fingers, wet from the warm suds, chilling quickly in the
cold air.

It was a bright day. A sharp breeze was filling out the shirts
hanging on the line. Sun, after snow, lit up the hills with a
bleak, wintry sparkle. There was no warmth in it.

Across the dale Jack was bringing in some unsheared sheep
driven down from the moor by the bad weather. She could hear
him shouting to the dogs. She wondered sometimes if she'd
ever really loved him. Then she told herself it must be something every woman wonders at some time or another.

Even so, that first day, after those flat few minutes in the
Registry Office, had revived in the young woman some inextinguishable dream of life abounding. He'd driven her back over
the Snake. Fresh snow had fallen in the dale. The snow curved
from edge to edge of the black, fractured crags, a pure solid white
hemming in the dark forest headlands, flowing as far as her eye
could follow down the dim recesses of the moor. Almost weight-
less, she'd felt then: a lightness, a largeness she'd never known,
as he threw open gate after gate.

"It's as much yours now as it is mine," he'd told her. In
fact, it belonged to neither of them.

A week later they were into lambing. Her days and nights
were filled then with the thin whickering, the scraggy bodies of
little lambs. She moved, the child toddling round her, with
new wonder about the big farm kitchen where lambs lay heaped
in cardboard boxes round the range. He showed her how to
make up the feed and she sensed her life joined now to his,
absorbed in the life she felt pulsing against her fingers as she fed
them the warm glucose drink.

It staggered her, how hard he worked. At lambing time he
put in eighteen hours a day. Always cold. Always wet. She took
him tea to the barn and stayed simply to be with him, watching,

as he crouched, shivering, cupping the mug of steaming tea with shrunken, bloodied fingers, his eyes fixed on an orphaned lamb he'd sewn up in the skin of one who'd died: bent-kneed, tail wriggling, it bumped at the ewe's belly. He gave no thought then to cold or wet. His eyes were quiet, content. His peace seemed to flow through her.

Then there was the child. Seeing him grow had seemed a vindication. Proof that she'd been right. On hot summer afternoons, when the river was low, she used to take him for an hour or so, watching over him as he strutted, splashing up and down. Or she'd go out to feed the hens, or stoop to pull a cabbage from her garden, when a piping whistle across the dale would fetch her head up to light on a tiny figure, stood with Jack on the steep bankside as the dogs worked the far-off hollows. These things had filled her with content.

I have married a good man, she told herself.

If all that sometimes took on a bitter flavour now, it was because she had become a different woman. She had only to look at herself to see how she had worn. The red, swollen knuckles. The rough skin that soaked up like blotting paper the cream she would sometimes lavish on the backs of her hands. She would look round at the pots waiting in the sink, the piles of ironing, at the old man asleep in the chair, slack-jawed, mouth gaping, and recognize, with a sinking heart, that this was her life now.

Of course, *they'd* wanted their own kids. She'd been expected to bring more Ashes into the world. That went without saying. She'd wanted to put it off as long as possible for her own child's sake. She'd had a sense of him sometimes swept aside in the crush of new demands upon her, two men, a house, farm animals to care for. She'd wanted to give some time to the child.

But then Jacky was born. Then the twins. So now there were two Ashe lads growing up in the dale, as well as a little sister to wait on 'em. And she'd been dragged back into that sucking, grasping world, the clutch of little bodies.

Days came to an end, but never the work. That was endless: kids to mind, clothes to wash and mend, meals to cook, an old stone house to tend to. She slept, her eyes opened, and it began again.

Always she was short of money. There was never money enough for the farm, never mind the house or the kids. Yet the men complained if so much as a cake was lacking. *A tenpenny bun costs me seventy pence*, she told 'em sharply. *I've seven mouths to feed.* Jack said nothing. But she knew what he was thinking. *My mam baked her own.* *Your mother*, she would have flashed back, *had three girls to help her in the house.* But it was useless to complain. *We get by*, the old man used to say, as if nothing mattered. Nothing bothered him. *Yes, because I scrimp and save, we get by*, she cried, seething.

She pegged out the last of the woollens, thinking of all the dead girls who must have scrubbed and mangled at Dalehead. It fell on her with the weight of centuries, that succession of Ashe women, shut up in this narrow dale. Her own life was shrinking, narrowing to follow theirs. Whenever she saw Tommy now, racing on the banks, it gave her no joy. She thought of the twins and Jacky growing up wild, ragged, with the moor closing round them. And Tommy. Sometimes he seemed lost to her already.

As long as they stayed at Dalehead things could never get better. She knew that now. On the few hundred sheep Dalehead was able to support they could do no more than scrape a living. If it wasn't for the money Jack brought in, walling. And the subsidy. Sometimes she thought their only hope was to get out. Get away.

It could have been a providential guidance the woman looked up so eagerly to see coming round the corner of the house. At that moment she would have welcomed any means of escape.

But saw, with disappointment, it was only Mr Hardman from Moor House.

"We've not seen you for a while," she managed. If a little bleakly.

She stooped to pick up the empty basket.

"If this is a bad time?" he tried, brightly.

"No, no. Come in." And led the way, leaving him to trail after her into the kitchen.

He might have known she'd be up to her eyes. Pots bubbling. That swarm of infant life under her feet.

"I'm off tomorrow. I thought I'd better let you know."

"Going home for Christmas?"

"Well.. sort of."

It struck him suddenly, he'd really no idea if he'd be back.

"Oh," he added, as if as an afterthought, "and this is for the lad. I know he had a birthday."

Now it was her turn to be confused. She wiped her fingers and took the glossy object, turning it over in reddened hands.

At that moment the boy himself slipped through an inner door. He seemed smaller, thinner than Hardman remembered.

"Look," she said. "Look what Mr Hardman's brought you."

The boy looked. But made no move to touch, to take.

"Here y'are." She held it out encouragingly. "Take it, then."

"It's about the Vikings," said Hardman, smiling. "I know he's interested in the Vikings."

He had the feeling they were snaring a wild creature.

"You'll have to teach him to read it, then." Jack Ashe stood, darkening the porch with his presence as he pulled off his coat.

The boy's first instinct had been to drop the book, and run. When his dad said that. But Jack Ashe was blocking his path. So he just stood. And since the book was in his hands, he clung to the book.

"Well, he can look at the pictures," said Mrs. Ashe defensively. She reached out to draw her son to her side, but the boy shrugged her off.

"Oh, there's lots of pictures," smiled Hardman, with a sinking heart. Christ, what was he *doing* here, distributing books.

Jack Ashe clumped heavily across the kitchen. Began lathering his hands at the sink.

"Well?"

She gave the boy's arm a little tug as he stood mute, impassive, clutching the book with both hands.

"What d'you say?"

Hardman cursed himself for coming here. For inflicting this.

"Perhaps," he suggested gently, "you could take me up the dale one day. I'd like that."

The boy said nothing. His eyes met those of the man a moment, then flickered back to the snarling dragon prow. Briefly, awkwardly, he nodded.

*

Inside the gates of Hardman's university stood a relic of the industrial revolution, a formidable contraption of wheels and cylinders, of gleaming pistons and connecting rods. Retrieved from one of the cotton mills of northern England, it represented the bequest of a former vice-chancellor, a professor of engineering, who had left a sum of money for the erection of some appropriate monument that might embody the character of the university.

It was a beam engine. It had been, in its time, an instrument for the enslavement of thousands.

Moloch, Arkwright had dubbed it, wittily. A *grisly deity of the Philistines*. It should, of course, have been the Ammonites, as Arkwright, a Milton scholar, knew very well. But *Philistines* suited better for the engineers.

Hardman had come on foot. Walking easy. He was stronger

physically. His body told him that. Yet, though set free by leagues of sky and moor, and nourished by soft air, his spirit was dejected.

Hostilities with Liz had resumed within a day or two of his getting back.

"The trouble with you," he told her cuttingly, "is that you don't really want people to act like people. You want them to function properly. Like machinery."

"Well, maybe that's what they are," she snapped back. "And sometimes they break down."

She stalked away, tight-lipped. Exasperated.

But his attack had hurt. Afterwards, he felt bad about it. Was conscious of her moving stiffly about the house. It was a relief when at last she left for Scotland.

At the same time, roaming about the empty house, he felt implicated by the silence that surrounded him.

Though term had ended some days earlier the campus was busy with comings and goings. The university hardly ever paused from its labours. Beds vacated by the undergraduates scarcely grew cold before they hotted up again for conferences and short courses. The cramped spaces between the various blocks of buildings were packed with cars, slotted into lots whose rightful occupants might be identified from inscriptions screwed to the walls, or painted on the tarmac: *Vice-Chancellor.. Pro Vice-Chancellor.. Senior Academic Registrar.. Dean of Humanities.. Head...* (of this, or that). It was an offence here, punishable by fine, or even confiscation of one's permit, to park above one's station. Seton, though, would lend you his. *Oh, look,* he'd say. *Here. Use my space.*

Six months had passed since Hardman passed this way, and the heart within him stirred uneasily as he passed the fountain in a wide quadrangle, picking his way between the parked cars. For what might be revealed. One disclosure he'd suffered already. The three months' salary paid into his account. At

first he'd thrashed about in an orgy of self-righteous indignation. He'd got on to Elizabeth straight away. It was monstrous.
Iniquitous. Seton had absolutely no right..

"Oh, for God's sake," she cried, at last. "Send it back. If
you're really serious, send it back. But you're not, are you? All
this is just a tiresome, childish game."

He came at length to a dull, flat-roofed building, like a
collection of shoe boxes set at angles to one another, with doors
of grimy glass, the paint peeling from the metal frames. A
concrete plaque built into the wall above the doors: *School of
Humanities, Social & Sports Sciences*. As he entered the dingy
foyer he saw, coming out of the *Gents*, the short, ruddy-faced
figure of Arkwright. Who, the moment he recognized his other
half, ducked, as if warding off a blow.

"Relax," said Hardman dryly, dropping into character. "I'm
quite cured now."

"Well," he added, gazing round. "What's new?"

"Well, as you see," said Arkwright, indicating a cabinet
displaying the jackets of latest publications, "Seton has shrivelled another famous head."

The wrapper bore a picture of the author poring over a
book. Head in hands, brows bent, face well-nigh invisible, he
seemed locked in relentless inner struggle. The effect was of
some unremitting mill of the mind.

"Fogg has stepped up his campaign on behalf of fallen
women. *More Sinned against than Sinning.* You know the kind of
thing. Break three fictions into a pan – say, *Madame Bovary*,
Anna Karenina, and *Effie Briest* – beat vigorously together, then
scramble over a low heat with a thick wooden spoon."

"I like the thick wooden spoon," murmured Hardman,
who'd worked in the kitchen where such things were cooked.

But the old knockabout with his sparring partner failed to
lift. He felt himself hardening into a brittle glaze that might, at
any moment, shiver into fragments.

Outside the door of the Senior Common Room a thought-ful-looking, bearded man was listening to a colleague.

"I'm much more interested in what women's writing shows us about female struggles," declared a sweetly fluting voice, "than I am in whether or not it's good *literature*." The speaker was a tall, slender woman with a high brow, and smooth, untroubled face. "Besides, there's a great deal of work now to show that ideas about 'good' writing simply help prop up the values of white, middle-class, heterosexual men."

"I'm inclined to question whether literature, in our time, isn't essentially an impossible enterprise," replied the bearded man reflectively. "Indeed, whether we can speak of 'literature' at all."

The woman's eye fell on Hardman, sliding past.

"Anthony! How nice to see you back." An expression of glad welcome slid on to the smooth screen of her face. "We've been *so* concerned about you," she went on, with patent false-hood.

He saw then how he was to be received.

" Hilary," he said huskily, "I never doubted it." Taking her arm he bent forward and, before she could recoil, kissed her lightly on the cheek.

"People are so unbelievably *kind*," he said earnestly, turn-ing to his companion.

"Still the best o' th' cut-throats," purred Arkwright, as they passed through the door.

The SCR bore all the signs of a room at the fag-end of a week's festivities. A stale air hung over the sagging decorations, as of gaiety exhausted; the paper streamers torn, the balloons deflating, the Christmas tree askew as if barged into. The bar, though, was heaving with beefy figures in tracksuits. Evidently a coaching course was in full swing. Every breast, it seemed, sporting a Union Jack. Every back emblazoned 'ENGLAND'. A scrum of bodies forking up the food from cardboard plates.

Air a-fug with curry and fried onions. A hub-bub of voices raking over the usual grouses. "An hour's more teaching is an hour's less research," complained a voice Hardman recognized as Fogg's. No, he thought, with a resurgence of bile, teaching never got anyone anywhere. And Fogg was thirsting for a Chair.

Oh, God! What was he doing here?

There was, he reminded himself, the matter of his salary. He meant to have it out with Seton.

He looked round, scanning the room. There, unmistakably, was his professor, that frowning watchtower of a head, with its crop of iron-grey hair.

No, he reflected. Seton was really a kind of Black Hole that sucked up everything, moons, stars, rushing in. Well, he had no intention of disappearing up that arse.

He had been spotted, though. An arm went up. A beckoning hand.

"Tony!" cried the familiar voice. " Tony! Over here."

Whereupon began a shuffling round of chairs as the Department made room for its black sheep.

Hardman's colleagues were enjoying an amusing Christmas game.

Young Culler was deconstructing *The Wind in the Willows*. It was, it seemed, a pretty nasty book.

"You only have to look at the cultural coding," he was saying. "Who invades Toad Hall? The stoats and weasels. Who, we're told, spend half the day lying in bed, guzzling, drinking and singing vulgar songs. The kind of uncouth creatures who'd piss in the sinks and keep coal in the bath. Where do they live? In the Wild Wood. A place where decent river-bankers go only when they have to, and then only in pairs. A grim, teeming place where evil little faces peer at them from ugly black holes."

"So you're saying it's a veiled attack on the social housing movement..."

Seton, though, had turned to Hardman.

"Lizzie tells me you're working again," he murmured. "How's it going?"

Hardman heard the rumbling of iron doors. For a moment he felt a wild desire to throw the grinding wheels into reverse, write out a cheque for three months' salary, hand it to Seton and walk away. Clean. Final. The big finish.

Yet even as he mumbled some reply he knew he was confirming what everyone else had known all along. His leave of absence was a fact. Offered, and tacitly accepted, months ago.

Heart thumping, he left the common room, crossed the yard, and climbed the stair to his old room. As he unlocked the door he'd felt the old distress coming on.

The room was just as he'd left it. The slogans still on the walls.

To see things as they are.

Long ago, he'd chalked it up for his students. A fiction, of course, but a useful one. The classic formulation ironically requisitioned for the new Enlightenment. An apt maxim for a casting off of old, dead ideologies. The passing years had seen the breeze blocks covered with inscriptions from dead masters: fragments he had shored against his ruins. Urgent at first (*Leave for Cape Wrath tonight..*), they had grown increasingly despairing as the years dragged on.

Eyeless, in Gaza, at the mill with slaves..

Rotten, and rotting others..

It was as if he'd never been away. No, worse. He had come here looking for some reinforcement of himself, and he had found it. The old lag back in the institution. Prison life settling round him like a well-worn coat.

Could what happened here *really* define his human essence? Who he was? What he lived for? This place, these people? However little they had to offer, they were a part of his life. He had been here for over twenty years. Twenty years gnawing away at the fabric of English Literature. Reducing it to dust. He had spent his life in that which least concerned life. And the dust heaps grew ever greater, leaving him stranded further and further from any human centre.

How did it go, the Larkin poem? *How we live measures our own nature..* Was it true? Should having no more to show, at his age, really make him pretty sure he warranted no better?

Abruptly he left the room, clattered down the stairs, and strode off across the campus. As he passed the place where Moloch rested on its massive pillars, Hardman directed an anguished glance at the huge wheel, the great black belly of the furnace. There *had* to be something more than this.

Hardman spent Christmas on his own, one of that multitude of souls for whom the feast is an ordeal somehow to be endured. Never had the austere harmonies of his home seemed so desolate, so void of comfort. Seeing no one, speaking to no one, he felt himself succumbing to the estrangement, the desertedness of being truly alone. He wandered from room to room, unable to settle. He went up to his study. There was his desk, his laptop. Untouched since his defection. He had no children, nothing but a shelf of books. He looked at them. His books. His contribution to knowledge: destined, he knew, to sink into oblivion, of no interest to future generations. Already, they had a cellar smell about them. He thought of them mouldering among the 'lit-crit' shelves of some second-hand bookshop. Shelves no one ever visited. Books never taken down.

His eye ran over the volumes, arranged systematically according to content or chronology. The primary texts, as he used to call them, the focus of theoretical arguments which reached conclusions quite contrary to repeated aspects of his own experience. The prevailing ideology did not encourage the expression of any personal encounters one might have had with the stuff of literature.

On the shelves given over to the literature of the seventeenth century he came across *The Pilgrim's Progress*. Warmed by a memory of those Derbyshire dissenters – *I knowe not how to mollify conscience by forced interpretations..* – he took it down from the shelf, read again the famous opening:

As I walked through the wilderness of this world, I lighted on a certain place, where was a den; and I laid me down in that place to sleep: and as I slept I dreamed a dream..

There was a time when he and his students would have set about dismantling it with spanners and monkey-wrenches to see what it was made of, to determine its material context, its ideological base. Maybe that is why, he thought, in the accounts we gave of them, works of profound imagination were made to seem so much less than one felt they truly were.

Sighing, he closed the book, replaced it on the shelf. Yet the cry of Bunyan's wretched man resonated in his mind: *What shall I do?*

You profess, he told himself, to be a thinking man – well then, bloody well *think*.

He went downstairs. His heels clicking against the stripped boards gave out a melancholy echo in the silent house. The bare, white walls had nothing to say to him. There seemed to be nothing there where he was, nothing for him to cling on to.

He sat on the black sofa in Elizabeth's dining room, beside a vase of dried grasses, and stared at the sleek glass table, memories of colleagues wined and dined mingling with a sour aftertaste of table-talk. They'd all joined battle here at one time or other, the shock troops of the Cultural Revolution: disciples of Derrida, of Lacan, Straussians, neo-Marxists, cultural materialists, proponents of Saussurean or Jacobsonian linguistics, Laputans, post-Laputans, scholars for whom discussion in any depth was possible only with those with whom they were fundamentally in agreement. Though in practice the advantage usually lay with those who could best deploy the strategies of disbelief: Hilary Vane-Tempest's falling jaw, her gasps of incredulity, Wiseman's pained silences, Seton's grim head shaking and furrowed brow.

Language belongs to all of us, he thought, or it is nothing. Yet words had opened up a gap between him and the world.

Suddenly he felt an overwhelming longing for simple, elemental things. Things you could trust. Things you could be sure of. A form of life in which nothing was spoken. The candour of bodies. The touch of a loving hand. Eyes that told the truth.

He remained a long time sitting there, keeping vigil. He did not read. He did not switch on the television. All man's trouble, he remembered, arose because he did not know how to stay quietly in his room. Well, he was doing that now. He had been left to ponder and reflect on what he was. On what he should do. He had thought long and hard. And the truth was he did not know what would become of him without Elizabeth.

It was growing dark, but he left the lamp unlit, sitting in that half-light in which, it was gradually borne in upon him, the great mass of human kind must somehow make its way.

*

Hardman drove back. He had to go. To have stayed, tinkering with some piffling research, would have meant sinking back into the old stultifying habit, drifting on the eddies of campus life, the backwash of petty feuds and jealousies, showing up at the lectures, the films, the student shows, one of those sad, middle-aged academics who clung leech-like to the young.

He saw the darkening perspective offered by increasing age, without some kind of inner light. The boy, had he lived, might have become a focus for that further life. A child brings hope, and thoughts for the future.

I have to find out whom I am, he told himself. Dr Anthony Hardman, Senior Lecturer in English; author of various unremarkable volumes of literary history.. ? No, that least of all.

He knew now a phase of his life was over. He saw it receding from him, slipping past with the trees and hedges, as if he were no longer to be allowed to cling to it, part of a past that was itself being rejected.

To be free of all that, to escape them totally, he must become unrecognizable, a person none of them would understand, a man no one knew. He felt a moment of bleak joy at the thought of some inner space where the archetypal man might live at peace with himself, a being closer in truth to the dry-stone walls, the in-lamb ewes on the hill, the wind scouring the moor.

Impulsive, Elizabeth called it. *A regressive spasm*. And what if it was something far deeper, far more fundamental? No, what had started as headlong flight had, somewhere along the line, become a journey.

It was dark when he arrived. On the car radio the weather man was warning of north-easterly air streams, snow on northern hills. Arctic enough already. The rutted track like iron. The dark wood shrinking into the hill. The iron gate biting at his fingers.

Hardman, ferrying boxes of provisions, boxes of books, shivered at the thought of frozen pipes. Icy, echoing rooms. But there was mail for him in the box. A square manila envelope. His name printed in clumsy, toppling capitals. No address. Puzzled, he pulled it open. Inside was a crude, crayoned drawing of hounds and huntsmen. *The Meet*, it said, under the drawing.

Ellen Ashe had had misgivings. *I'm sure I don't know what Mr Hardman'll think.* All the same, she'd supervised the spelling. Made him practise it on the back of a bill.

Hardman studied the spindly nags, misshapen men, huge,

angular hounds, all cut-throat teeth and slavering jaws. He looked for the fox, but couldn't find it. Then spotted a brushy tail tucked away among the hard hats and hunting pink. Hidden with the bloat faces and bristling moustachios was a tawny orange muzzle. For the fox, too, was mounted. It rode with its pursuers.

That had caused a great to-do at school. Particularly as everyone else had got their foxes racing away properly, with hounds and horses streaming after. As they should. *What on earth have you done that for?* asked Mr. Clarke incredulously. *Cause he's daft, sir. Daft,* they chorused. *Daft.* But the boy had put his enigmatic beast where he wanted it to be. And there it stayed. The black sardonic eye half-closed, not a whit less savage than the hunting faces. But more cunning.

What Mr Hardman thought, or rather felt, as he studied it, with something of a shock of recognition, was the mordant wit of the internal émigré. The loner. That winking, sardonic eye. *Cunning*, it signalled. *Silence.*

He carried the card through to the sitting room. Seton's letter was still on the mantelpiece.

Hardman screwed it up and tossed it into the grate. In with the dead ashes. He put the card up carefully, so he could keep before his eye the lit imagination. And the message, in its crude cartouche of bells and holly: *To Mr. Hardman. A Mery Xmas. From Tommy Ashe.*

Next morning he looked out to see a thick white frost had stiffened everything.

He wrenched open the front door to find the lawn a tufty carpet. Above his head the honeysuckle hung, studded with ice. He went out into the garden, his breath steaming in the bitter air. Beyond the gate, the dale was shrouded in a freezing fog.

He walked round to the yard to find his washing line a

shaggy rope. In the window of the outhouse the spider's web, hoary with frost, hung down in shreds. Leaves he'd piled in a corner crackled as he stirred them with his foot.

Huddled on a branch a solitary blackbird, feathers fluffed, looked mournfully about a bitter world.

As he stood there, on the edge of the copse, a sudden, soft, swelling hiss showered his face with ice.

At first most of his time was taken up with keeping out the cold. Lagging pipes with sacks. Keeping alight the small stock of spirit lamps he'd found in the outhouse together with some sacking and old blankets. He stuck them under the plumbing.

It became total. This battle against the cold. He wedged blankets under doors. He tracked down draughty cracks round windows, tacked strips of sacking to the wood. Split mountains of timber. He pulled out all the blankets from the dower chest on the landing, and piled them on his bed.

One morning, dragging fallen boughs from the copse, he was struck by a certain flatness of the light. Air seemed warmer. He stared at the sky, at whisps of cirrus hauling over Featherbed Moss.

Next morning he woke to a white glare.

Pulling back the curtain, he saw that the track was a track no longer, nor the path down to the gate, nor the lawn on either side. The snow had claimed them.

FIVE

Hardman's real winter started with the snow. The road blocked. Landscape, a monochrome. The muffled trees lifting imploring arms. Day, a few hours that scarcely struggled into light. The house silent, but for a trickle of water in the pipes. On the Snake nothing moved but the drifting snow.

The world's whole sap is sunke. So it seemed to Hardman, watching from his window. And so cold. Air numb, so that sounds seemed to arrive fractionally late.

He fetched in armfuls of logs. Stacked them either side of the hearth. Then, huddled at last over his fire, he brooded on Elizabeth. He couldn't ring her. The thought of her voice, cold, deadened against him, filled him with pain. He couldn't face the possibility of that.

To see things as they are, he'd written, in the days of his pride. Now he realised that her tragedy was another thing he'd seen only from a distance.

He sat in the gloom of a dying winter day lit only, now and then, by a few, fitful gasps from the damp logs, and looked again at this unknown woman who, long ago, had tried to have his children. Only it was not to be. It was not to be. And the thing had nullified her. She was *re-begot* – the line bit into him with jagged truth –

Of absence, darkness, death; things which are not.

Love's grief, he saw, was a state in which one suffered things as they were *not*, just as he suffered now the not-ness of non-Elizabeth. Elizabeth, frozen.. iced over..

What, he wondered, was needful for the transformation of a heart which was profoundly lonely? He didn't know. Then it dawned on him that maybe he would remain forever distant from this woman. That human beings in their essential loneliness were not recoverable.

And still it went on snowing. One morning after a fresh fall he dug a path to the gate, only to stop there, sweating, breathing hard, staring at the skeletal thorns, iron black against the snow. He trudged round to the back yard to see a smooth expanse of snow that swept unbroken up to the forest. Hardman went back inside.

For several days he had no contact with humanity. The Rover, obsolete marvel of an earlier age, sank gradually, its outline blurring under successive layers of snow. The world he knew had dropped away. In the morning, coming down to see his tracks wiped clean, he felt a shiver of mortality.

He watched the flurries of snow howling over Blackden. He watched the birds, flitting disconsolately from branch to branch, or making swooping passes over the snow.

> ... and now they range,
> Busily seeking with a continual change..

Troubled, he watched, as other, ominous lines followed after:

> All is turned ...
> into a strange fashion of forsaking;
> And I have leave to go of her goodnesse
> And she also to use new-fangleness.

A good few must starve, he thought.

He fed them. At first light, hunched against the cold, they gathered in the trees. He cut bread in large lumps so it wouldn't sink, and placed it carefully on the snow. But the birds stayed put. One or two made darting passes over the snow. Mostly they waited. The bread lay where it fell. The next fall buried it.

And he thought maybe if he were to spread it where he'd trodden. And did so, trampling out a path in the fresh snow. But the birds stayed where they were. He began to see in them a dreadful resignation. The apathy of the condemned.

Next day, at first light, he cleared a wide patch in the yard and scattered bread over the cobbles.

They came down in dozens.

Each day after that he cleared the patch in the yard. Famished birds crammed the tiny island in the snow, feeding as if they were feeding for the winter. As if they might never feed again. Hardman baked potatoes, cut up cheese, fruit, put out bacon rind, some leftovers of lamb. And put the bone out too.

A pure joy possessed him, to feed so many. Birds he knew, tits, finches, thrushes, starlings, blackbirds, the doves, robins, others he'd never seen before, milling about his yard.

His own stores were running low. Soon he would have to make tracks for the village. But he felt no desire to go. He was content to tramp about the snowy yard and garden, and the copse beyond. One afternoon he kicked his way up to the drifted ridge behind the house. Below, around, all the land lay locked in silence. Pallid hills. The sun a dying furnace somewhere beyond a frozen vista of moor. The profound stillness that had settled on all things, he felt it settling on him.

He wrote to Elizabeth. A strange, long letter filled with emanations of his winter solitude, its frozen sounds, the arctic twilight, the brittle, iron trees. He told her about the birds: starlings, that got on with the business of surviving, hunting out the tiniest scraps. They took his mind back to a cat he'd had as a boy – a ginger cat with a fat belly and a pink, freckled lip – its passionate pursuit of food.

He tramped down to the village to post it.

"Any mail for me?" he asked the woman. Not that he was expecting anything.

She leafed through what she had. Shook her head.

He tramped back, disappointed.

That afternoon, poking through his box of books, he pulled out one at random, flipped it open, saw the opening line – *There was a man called Mord..* – and was carried back to a land he hadn't visited in years.

He lit the lamp, piled logs on the fire and gave himself to the saga world again. Wind and snow raved on outside as Hardman rode with Gunnar back from exile, back to Hlidarend. *Lovely, the hill. Never lovelier than now the white cornfield, the new-mown hay. I shall not leave. I shall go home..* Though death lay waiting.

Wind and snow raved on forgotten. Hardman engrossed, his legs stretched out before the blaze. He wasn't conscious of being alone. Only when he thought of Elizabeth his loneliness returned.

Then, for the first time in a week, the sky was clear. A low wind blowing off the moors. He felt an urge to be up there again. He needed to get moving.

Stick in hand, he set off down the Snake. No one was about. The road empty, but for a few tracks of local vehicles. The cold air nipped his nose. Nipped the tips of his ears. Spiced the blood flooding his body. Flushed, alert, he tramped as far as the track below Hagg Farm. His way lay up there.

Northwards a dark wood rose out of the hill. Trees springing up steeply. Branches bare and black against the sky. It was dark under the trees. Silent. Only the sound of his breathing as he plodded upwards. Snow squeaking under his boots. He made his way uncertainly, stepping over fallen trunks, ducking under branches, the only living soul in a snow where nothing else had been. Now and then he paused, to enter into the stillness, the silence. Once, he was made aware of movement. Up in a tree. A small, mouse-like bird with a thin, curved bill. Silent, secretive, it crept up the rough bark, peering, probing. Hardman smiled. The scholar bird. With a short, dismissive *peep*, the bird dropped slanting to the foot of another tree. Began again its minute, laborious examination. Watching it, Hardman found he was happy simply to be here.

He wandered on, gladness flooding through him like a tide. The canopy of branches, thinning as he climbed higher through the wood, was showing patches of pale sky. Here and there, in the lee of boulders, where snow had failed to penetrate, little green sea horses of fresh bracken. Now and then a soft sussuration, shed from a branch. A scent of pine mingling with the moist smell of fresh snow. The sun's disc, pure silver, coming at him through the trees. So solid, presented with such weight, he had a sense of something given.

So he got slowly towards the inexpressible. That which reveals itself. For it was all around him. Rich. Dense. Like a sea. A life beyond language. Now that he'd learned silence, other things had begun to speak.

Minutes later, he came out from the trees onto the high, open ridge, and turned to look back.

Far-off in the south, where a translucent haze lay over the land, the sun burnt like ice. It glowed with an icy flush on distant ridges. Below him were silent forests enclosing ribbons of water. Hills, blue with cold. He felt a tremor of strangeness. As if he'd crossed a frontier. As if he'd entered a wood in Derbyshire, and somehow come out in Iceland, or Arctic Norway.

Turning, he began the steep pull up the ridge. His boots crunched into the frozen snow crust. He breathed deep. Sucked in the sharp-edged wind. Higher and higher he rose, striding on over Rowlee. Now and then a grouse went up, whirring away with a harsh *go.. go.. go.. go-back.. go-back*. Stretching away north, west, further than his eye could follow, fainter and fainter, were the Bleaklow moors.

So, at last, he came to the brink of the shattered cliff above the dale. Far below, Dalehead looked like a child's toy. Grey walls and roofs clustered under snowy tiers of trees. An arc of light hung over the farm. The light picked out the side of a barn, a coil of smoke above the roof, and slanted up the spur of Ferny Side.

Locked in a loving glance it seemed to Hardman. As it might

lie in a man's mind who'd brought his little world through iron winters; who'd shifted stones, dug drains, felled trees.

A faint bleating reached him. Thin. Wintry. At the back of a barn sheep were gathering. A tiny figure throwing out armfuls. Jack Ashe was seeing to his ewes.

*

Five miles the Dale river ran, from its source in the swampy heart of the moor, cutting its way through the accumulation of many thousand years of peat, through dark shales and livid sandstones, to the Snake bridge, and the River Ashop.

One January morning they went up the dale, the man and the boy together, under a sullen sky full of snow. A hard frost had followed several days of thaw. It was still freezing. The boy loped along, silent, sure-footed, flitting up and down the bank a dozen yards ahead. Hardman called after him. Tried to slow him. And the boy turned, his face expressionless, then hurried on, as rapid as before.

The man dawdled. Asked about things. Tracks spotted in a patch of snow. Two light dots in front, plunging holes behind. Lopsided exclamation marks, they looked like. The boy studied them.

"That's a hare," he said. And added gruffly, "That's where she starts to run."

A little way above the farm the dale drew in abruptly. Snow lay longest there, where the winter sun could never get for more than minutes. Soon the swollen stream was forcing them up on to the steep clough side. They were following a deep V-trench, a hundred feet below the skyline of the moor, a funnel for win-ter blasts that sometimes reached Arctic intensity. The boy, alert as any wild creature. The man too, roused, it might have been, by some long-buried, disinherited self walking the bare bones of this river bed, among the strangely-coloured grits and shales, veiled pink, sudden black, glowing sulphur-yellow. His senses, pressing down hard, collected images of razor-edged distinctness. High up in a bank, where a huge split block leaned drunkenly, a mouth flashed, agape with rage. For a split second. At the edge of vision. Stony again, as he passed on.

To see the land like this, it struck him, must be to see it like the primitive men who once lived here. Or like a child.

Beyond the Crookstones the dale opened out a little. Here and there a stunted birch or solitary mountain ash clung on beside the stream. They made their way again along the rocky bed, creeping under fallen boughs, straddling branches thick with ice. At every turn the man's eye was alerted to the mystery and summons of creation, earth, stones, water and vegetation singing the radiance of sheer presence. Now and then he almost fancied he saw it stirring. That presence. Here and there. Under ice not wholly frozen. Scuttling over stone. Small things took on a terrific intensity. Slender grasses the frost had thickened. Beads of water threaded on a stalk and frozen there. In black hollows under banks gleamed fangs inches thick. Icicles like tusks. Once a whole fern frond encased in solid ice. A fresh green marvel.

"Look," shouted Hardman..

The boy had often seen them. Ferns frozen up like that. He'd broken one off once to take home to show his mam. All the way back he felt it slipping away between his fingers. Draining away. What came out was unrecognisable. Black. Shapeless.

He looked, and went on.

They were now a good way up the dale, with the roar of water constantly around them, pouring in torrents off the moor, roaring louder as they drew near each narrow feeder clough, dying away as they passed. On they went. Glittering Clough. Hesleden Clough, where the stream came leaping down huge, blocky stairs, as through a splintering defensive wall. At every step hung curtains of ice, freezing from the outside inwards, so that the water raced through a narrow channel at the centre, penned, hemmed in, yet crashing down, energizing thunder.

They had to shout to be heard. Even face to face, they had to shout.

"Hey! Look!"

"What?"

"Look at that!" Hardman raised an arm.

The boy raised his face to the fall. Though the worn look of the mother was already shaping there, it was still a child's face, lifted dreamily, on which the faint spray settled.

They came at last to a small bay below a fall, where the youthful river raced through a slot in beds of harder rock, spilling out in bubbling pools. Hardman saw a heap of stones beside the water, a cairn topped by a jagged flake. A scratched inscription:

R.I.P.

MCMLXIV

"This is where they were," the boy said suddenly. "Where they found 'em."

Ellen Ashe had provided biscuits, sandwiches. Hardman had brought a flask. They ate there beside the stream. The boy munching, avid, his eye fixed on the man. Who related what he could remember of an old tragedy.

They would have started from Holmfirth, those young men, down past the site of the old Isle of Skye Inn at Wessenden Head, then the long slog south over Black Hill, down to Crowden in Longdendale, then up on to Bleaklow, heading for the Snake. *How old were they?* Strong lads. Twenty. Twenty-one. They would have travelled light. In those days it was more or less a race. Driving rain. A wind that stripped the flesh from the bones. They should have quit at Crowden. Last chance they got. At that age, though, you don't quit. You don't know enough to quit.

Difficult, on such a day, to imagine Bleaklow Head. A black quagmire at any time. You wouldn't see it until you were on it. And then there must have seemed no limit to it, for they stretch away endlessly, the hags and groughs, the waves of black peat bogs. In that storm-driven sleet and snow it must have been appalling. So cold you ceased to feel it, you wouldn't feel yourself walking. Sinking at every step, the peat sucking, gripping, an icy wind cutting through sodden clothing, chilling blood drawn up from its deep core of heat to go back colder to the heart. Long before they even knew it they were fighting for their lives.

"My grandad said he could ha' told 'em where they'd be, but he weren't asked."

"No" said Hardman. "I don't suppose he was."

The boy was fishing about at the edge of the stream. A skin of ice had gathered there, out of the eddy. Hexagonal crystals. Wafer-thin. Each filmy segment slotted into place.

"Would it have hurt, dying like that?" the boy asked, oddly. And raised his head.

"No," he said carefully, conscious of the watchful eyes. "No, I don't think so. I don't think they'd have known much about it."

And would have left it there, but for the prompting of those eyes that urged him to go on, to complete the truth, not soften it.

"They must have felt very frightened and alone," he said, thinking how swiftly a winter blizzard here could reduce a strong young man to a poor, bare, forked animal, no different from any other creature of the moor. "Floundering about up there. In and out of the groughs."

"That's a Viking word, you know," he added, glad of a chance to change the subject. "Gryfa. It means a ditch, a hollow."

"Did the Vikings come here, then?"

"Well, quite a few of the names hereabouts are Norse words.

'Grough', 'grain', 'hagg'. So there was probably a Viking settlement round here somewhere."

"What, in the dale?"

"Could be. More likely in Longdendale, I should think. That was part of a great forest then. Full of wolves, wild boars, things like that."

The boy's hand was still busy in the stream. Dabbling among the ice crystals. Suddenly, he held one up, wafery, translucent, between finger and thumb.

"Open your mouth," he said shyly.

Hardman smiled. He bent forward, offering his open mouth, received on his tongue the slip of ice. Tasted an elusive presence chilling his tongue, his teeth. He pressed it into the roof of his mouth. Numbing. Then it was gone.

They went on, with the dale, shallower now, gradually bottoming out before them, and came at length to a watersmeet in a wild bowl of the hills, a place of stony frozen pools, and drifted snow, soft, slushy, under a crusty top. They floundered about, laughing. Hardman, clumsy, plunging through, felt a rush of cold wet, snatched back his boot.

"You've to watch out for that," the boy said, solemn-faced. "There's no bottom t' th' bogs on Blakelow, mi grandad says."

Hardman scanned the ground ahead, around. Nothing. Only snow and tussock, broken here and there by sparse clumps of sedge. Gingerly he stretched – thrust his stick down at an angle through the snow. It went in right up to his hand. He had to wrench it back. It came with a distant sucking, gurgling, the liquid gurgling of bowels. Left behind it a kind of arsehole, bubbling in the snow. And a stench. Fetid. Corrupt.

He drew back gingerly. Skirted round in a wide, cautious arc.

They went on in silence, with the mist on Bleaklow Head drawing in behind them. Slopes of snow and cotton-grass rolled away westwards towards Hern Clough. There, too, mist was gathering.

They walked in an eerie light. In gloom themselves, yet two or three miles across Derwent, a snow flank, lit by a sun they couldn't see, gleamed a faint blood-red.

Then, quite suddenly, the sun appeared. It was as if some-one had switched on an extraordinary lamp. No heat. But this immense glowing lamp low down in the south-west. And every-thing was changed: peat hags, to monstrous mounds of choco-late pudding, garnished with brilliant bilberry green; stones bloomed lime green; even the bleached grass glowed copper. It lasted no more than minutes. And so dazzled Hardman he would have stopped if he could, simply to stare about him, to be part of the illumination. But the boy, all unconscious, was trudging on with the light blazing in his face.

So the man followed. And then the lamp went out. It was again a winter afternoon. He was sinking into thick brown dough, sliding into groughs, kicking his way up sticky banks.

They came back, plodding side by side, along the top edge of the forest. As they passed above the dark trees, it was as if a door had closed behind them. The river hushed, distant. Below them ranks of larches, like an army of young giants, stiff, silent, arms extended, fingers stretched.

Down in the dale lights were twinkling. High up on the steep side of Blackden a glimmer of lying snow. Almost dark. A glow, though, in the sky beyond Kinder, as if all the lights were on in Edale. A world of light beyond the dark edge of the moor.

The man became conscious of the boy. Poised on the spur below him. Waiting. Looking back.

"Go on, then," he called. "I'll race you down."

In a flash the boy was off.

"Don't fall in t' river," he shouted back. And vanished in the gloom.

Hardman jolted down behind him.

The boy was in the kitchen making tea when he got down.

"Me mam says you're to go through," he told Hardman.

She was in the sitting room. Ellen Ashe was getting the twins ready for bed. They were on the rug in front of the fire, the boy in pyjamas, the girl, all pink cheeks and golden curls, in a pink nightie with little lacy collar and cuffs. Each was sucking at a bottle.

"Yes," she said dryly, "they look like little angels now. They'll be little sods, the pair of 'em, before long. Hold *still*." As she began to brush a silky head.

Hardman ran his eye along the shelf of books.

"I don't suppose he gets much reading now," he said. "The lad."

"No. It's a pity, really. But we haven't the time. You can see for yourself."

She flashed him a wry smile. Her face, eyes, bright from the fire. There was, he thought, almost a zest about her.

"I'll read to him," he said.

She stared, her hands stilled.

"It'd make a change from students," he added wryly.

*

The days passed, and still there was no letter from Elizabeth. Sometimes, coming down Blackden Brook, or returning over the hill from Heathy Lea, he would see the post van going up the track to the farm, and wonder if it had stopped at Moor House. Then he would quicken his stride, eager to get back and see. But there was never anything for him.

There could be half-a-dozen reasons why she hadn't written. She might be up to her eyes in work. Or she might be away from home. It was even possible she might not have got his letter. There was no telling with the post these days. Then, again, she might not want to write.

The thought of his own letter, its sentimental guff about cats and birds, struck him as inept and foolish.

One afternoon, he looked from a window to see the van returning along the track. He heard it draw up as usual, the engine running, for the driver to open the gate.

He was halfway down the stairs when he saw a slim envelope dropping through the letter box.

As nervous as a boy, he recognised her writing. A single sheet. No heading.

How strange to get a letter from you. Hardly anyone writes letters these days. Not personal letters, anyway. I'm not sure I remember how to go about it. Though there must be certain advantages to letter-writing. So much kinder than meeting face to face, where everything is so instant, so up front. Not having to suffer an accusing look. Or hear a bitter voice. Then there is the time it gives you. Time to unsay things you wish you'd never said, without anyone knowing you ever said them.

I had a cat, once. Though it wasn't mine, exactly. She belonged to herself. A wary little thing. Far wiser in her way than ever I was. Like the fox in a story you once told me. Or was it the hedgehog? I knew many things but she knew one big thing. As if, in her own wild way, she'd learnt what I never learnt till she hung, a limp, loose weight, in my arms. She was killed, you see. I was scarcely more than a child then, finding out for the first time how the worst can happen. That to love is to be hurt.

Perhaps people should write to one another more often.

Elizabeth

He was exhilarated by her letter. Exhilarated, and moved by her disclosures. Tenderness, at the thought of her as a child, drew him closer to her. A sense of a deeper life beyond the life he knew, a realm beyond the closed, unchanging worlds in which they had imprisoned one another, excited him beyond measure.

He still hesitated to ring her. Nor did she ring him. It was as if some unspoken accord existed between them not to do so. As if they were content to wait in separate apartments, parties to a negotiation who couldn't trust themselves to meet in the same room, but needed a go-between to take soundings, make overtures. Or else they had made strangers of themselves, that they might be re-acquainted.

So it went on, this ferrying back and forth, delving after memories when everything was unknown and mysterious, before each knew what life was like, when they were open to whatever it might offer.

He told her of his winter walk with the boy.

At that age, I imagine, yours is the first and only world. I can't help wondering what unique perceptions must he have of it: what things unknown to you and me. What if there is much more to life than we imagine..

She saw him reaching after something in himself he could never quite come at, the divine child, the magical child, who redeems the suffering of life, and releases joy.

Sometimes in dreams, she wrote, *we may see the energies of the psyche striving to heal itself.*

For absence, she had discovered, could take on a presence of a kind. That may be cuddled, and put to the breast. Or, if older, taken to a park, and pushed on a swing.

All those things that never quite happened during their life together had the potency of nostalgia now that it was in the past. In the intervals of waiting each began to listen to what might lie concealed in the silences they'd shared. To what was unsayable between them. She wondered if he was conscious of the wounds he had inflicted on her.

As they began to venture over the dangerous ground they had never traversed together, each was gentle with the other, as if only gentleness could protect against the briars they'd bound about themselves.

Then Elizabeth Hardman felt a welling up of love and pity,

but whether for herself, or for her husband, she could not have said for sure.

*

A week of gales had driven the hardiest ewes, those left to lamb on the moor, down to the dale. They were dotted all over the bottom land, on grazing meagre enough without their extra mouths. And couldn't be let stay a day longer than was necessary.

"We're tekkin' the flock back up tomorrow," the boy said to Hardman. "I'll ask me dad if you can come."

Next morning at first light Hardman, an unlikely shepherd in mountain boots and breeches, found himself with Jack Ashe, and the boy, and the two dogs, working their way towards the open moor, the flock, a fluid amorphous mass pouring like a white tide among the humps and hollows, flowing anywhere except where it was intended it should go, separating, reforming, dark liquid eyes in the mottled faces looking back reproachfully before the surge carried them on.

"They're a bit like shepherds," shouted Jack Ashe. "Not very domesticated. They don't take kindly to being interfered with."

Sheep were pouring through gaps in walls, flooding into hollows, checking, overflowing, the dogs racing round to head off a break away, the boy darting ahead, dashing back and forth, staff in hand, to turn back deserters, his child's shouts mingling with bleating and baa-ing, so caught up in the life surging round him he seemed present everywhere.

Hardman, watching, himself felt lifted, dispersed.

"What sort of sheep are they?"

"Swaledales, mostly. Some Derbyshire gritstones. A lot of 'em nowadays seem to favour Swaledales and Dalesbred. On these moors you need a ewe as can fend for itself. These were born and bred 'ere."

The dour voice had taken on a warmth that startled

Hardman, for months on the receiving end of grunts, nods, or the sudden sardonic flash that broke off contact altogether.

"We get a lot of rain up 'ere. I dare say you've noticed. So you need a ewe with a nice tight fleece. One that don't collect the snow."

The shepherd's eye, no less vigilant than the scurrying dogs, was running with the flock. He was looking for one ewe in particular.

"They all look the same to me," yelled Hardman.

"Aye. They would, to you. Oh, there's ways of tellin'. The way she walks, turns. The way she sets at a dog. I can generally tell who she is half a mile away."

They jolted, stride for stride, down into a dip. It was the geld ewe Jack Ashe was looking for. Docile, inert, she lay in the crook of his arm as he felt at her belly. She was barren. Though he'd kept her for three years. And now a man he knew had offered to take her. *If I can find 'er*, he'd told him, *you can have 'er.* But reluctantly. He never liked parting with an animal.

He dropped her off next day on his way to Longdendale. Hardman went with him.

"Put me down anywhere along Torside," he said. "I'll walk back over Bleaklow. I'd enjoy that."

His intention was to scramble up Wildboar Clough, a steeply-angled watercourse cutting deeply into the northern flank of Bleaklow, and then negotiate a route across the moor to link up with the dale. As he passed between the dripping walls of the clough he found himself wondering how Jack Ashe would cope now single-handed. All the way over from Dalehead, the shepherd's talk had been filled with memories of his father. A tangle of sayings, doings, the younger man was forever picking at. All his life the old man had been there. Now gone, he seemed to have left behind a mystery for the son to ponder over. *He lived in a time of 'is own, if you know what I mean. He didn't hold with the farming industry. He preferred the old ways. Workin' with Nature. The real work, as 'e called it.* Hardman thought of huge, cracked hands that might have borne the burden of the world from the beginning. *He could do any job on a farm. Never said much. Raining cats and dogs, it never bothered 'im. He just got on wi' it. Just got it done.* He sensed at the back of these terse disclosures the bleakness of a man alone in the world, a man looking back to a time of all-but-vanished grandeur. *Ah, well. We s'll 'ave to manage wi'out him now..*

The air was dank, heavy, in Wildboar Clough, where the bedding planes tilted sharply westward, forming a channel down which, after heavy rain, the torrent crashed in a series of cascades, roaring over thin, flaky sheets of millstone grit. For once the simple pleasures of movement upon rock, reaching, balancing, stepping up, failed to lift his spirits. He climbed in the angle of the retaining walls, avoiding the stream, moving up the short, ledgy risers with none of the enjoyment he had looked to find. His mind was filled with gloomy thoughts, as if some harm hung in the melancholy gulfs of the ravine, some thickening of the clogging air, and was relieved, on gaining the shallows of the upper clough, to see a widening arc of sky above his head.

He came out at last, the tumult of water dying away behind him, into an oppressive silence.

Ahead, wastes of peat and cotton grass stretched away, cheerless, forbidding. He took a bearing for the western end of the mile-long summit ridge, the watershed of the moor. In failing light he thought it best to follow the Pennine Way south, rather than cut across the swamps towards the head of the dale. Not much more than an hour's daylight left. He pressed on for Bleaklow Head with the Ashes darkly present in his mind, the feral boy, his pupil, Ellen Ashe with her trail of her infants.. *Like it! She bloody loathes it..* He could see nothing but trouble. Nothing but pain for all.

Then, at the Wain Stones, he came upon a figure squatting

there among the rocks. A man of indeterminate age. Dressed as he was dressed. Breeches, Icelandic sweater. Who lifted a lean, leathery face. But gave no greeting. At his side a tall, tapering sac. He was stuffing something into the sac, some voluminous orange material that might have been a shelter tent. Or a body bag.

Hardman nodded, swung past without a word. Further down the track, he turned to glance back. There was something compelling about that lone figure, silhouetted now against the sky. Motionless, by the strange stones.

When he looked back again, Hardman saw him shouldering his sac, and moving off, heading into the darkening heart of the moor.

*

In the days when names were given to hills and rocks, men named what they could see from their own tracks and valleys, the edges of their visible world. Along the Ashop, gazing up at the jagged outline high above Blackden, they named Seal Edge and the Seal Stones. From Derwent side they looked across to the Wheel Stones and Dovestone Tor. Of human travail, too, they left a record, memorialized in the landscape. Lost Lad, Cut-throat Bridge, Madwoman's Stones, preserve echoes of old sorrows resonating through twenty generations of folk history.

Yet the worn uplands offer evidence of countless lives. Remote hilltops hold the charred bones of innumerable cremations, interred no one knows how long ago. On the bleak sheep runs of Abney, Shatton, Moscar, still stand, after three thousand years, stone circles where men's fires, at the winter solstice, reddened the skies to propitiate such powers as governed their precarious world.

Their descendants are to this day dour, mystical men, profoundly conscious of irascible gods that bury ewes alive, and send the killing frosts at lambing, or the cold rains dragging on and on, pushing back the time for shearing into the time for making hay, the good, tall grass withal, the winter keep, beaten down and rotting in the fields.

"It's half the battle, the weather," Jack Ashe shouted, as they battled down through flurries of sharp-edged hail.

"Must be a chancey life, then," yelled his companion.

"It's like anything else. There's good years and there's bad years. In the bad 'uns y'ave to live off your back. Like a hill ewe in hard weather. That's what they say round here."

The shepherd's face, set against the hail, took on a look of stoic endurance.

Strange, thought Hardman, reflecting on it later, how it was the momentary glimpse that touched the heart. A face clouded over, or lit up as the shadow passed. And in that moment one was grasped .

He was in the kitchen, preparing breakfast, when he heard the news that some sort of pestilence had broken out on a farm in Essex. Another case had been confirmed by Ministry vets. The public were advised not to make any visits which might bring them into contact with livestock until the outbreak was over.

He had little idea what it might mean. It was not a thing he'd ever given much thought to, except as a remote malevolence, a bane of lives distant from his own. Weren't infected animals slaughtered? Only then did it sink in that he had himself been in contact with livestock.

The following morning, as he was about to set out for Bamford, he heard the sound of the quad bike on the track.

Jack Ashe was fixing a box to the farm gate. He looked up at the sound of steps.

"I suppose you've heard?"

Hardman nodded. He didn't know quite what to say.

The red-haired man took a screw from his mouth.

"It's all we need," he said. "We're working for next to nothing as it is."

Hardman helped manhandle the big straw bale from the trailer.

Together they laid a thick layer across the entrance. Jack Ashe doused it liberally with disinfectant. Then he closed the gate, securing it with a chain and padlock.

"This is for you," he said, handing Hardman a key. "Don't lose it."

He bent to pick up the can, then straightened, staring for a moment at a crow which had just alighted on the road.

"Not my favourite birds, crows."

Then, reflectively, after a pause..

"You can't help wondering where the buggers have been."

Like everyone else in the country the authorities had been taken unawares. Their reactions were entirely understandable. No one at the Ministry remembered the last outbreak. And though they might have agreed that history has a way of repeating itself, they found it difficult to imagine it suddenly crashing down on them one Tuesday morning, so to speak, out of a clear blue sky. True, there had been one or two cases in the southeast. But they would be dealt with. It was only a matter of doing what was needful. Then the outbreak would come to an end, because it was unthinkable that it should continue unabated.

Though furnished with records of the earlier epidemic, officials with no experience found the figures difficult to envisage. A few thousand cases added up to perhaps a couple of largish fields full of cows. Rounded up, transported to Whitehall, and slaughtered in heaps around the Cenotaph, they might have furnished the authorities with a clearer picture of what they were facing.

Whatever hopes the authorities might have had of containing the outbreak were short-lived. Within a very few days the disease had made startling strides. From Essex to Anglesey, from Northumberland to Devon, the funeral pyres were burning, flames from the tonnes of coal and railway sleepers whirling sparks across the darkness, thick, black smoke from the oil fires hanging low over the land.

To the man crossing the yard to feed his sucklers, the world seemed as it always was. A faint mist hanging over the in-by. Dawn reddening the sky above Slip Wood. The first *chirrups* of stirring birds. A quietness and peace. All things abiding in their proper place. It seemed unthinkable that things should not continue as they were, run on as they had always run. The memory of the old man was still a refuge. *No, we never get it. In Edale, aye. In the valley farms. Not up here.* As he crossed the paddock the tups came up to him, nuzzling for food. Nothing had changed.

He stood in the close, dark peace of the byre, his sucklers, eyelids lowered, at their munching, and thought of the TV pictures. A cow with hanging jaw, saliva drooling, standing in field, trembling with pain. You could see the pain in its eyes.

He leafed through old farming magazines, looking for information; pictures of blistered tongues, blisters that came off in the hand, leaving raw ulcerated patches.

He rang round his neighbours, those old enough to remember the last outbreak.

" We 'ad some fat on us then," said Dicky Swain gloomily. "It'll be different this time."

No one seemed to know how it was spread. Dicky reckoned it were the dairy lorries carried the disease from farm to farm.

He went about his daily foddering dreading what he might find. The ewes were watching for him on the high ground above the dale, and would descend in a rush, milling around the quad bike with its ration of hay. Always present was the fear that a man might have it on his farm, and never know. According to what he'd read it could be difficult to detect in sheep. Sometimes only a small proportion of an infected flock showed any signs.

His heart sank when he came across a limping shearling in Slithery Clough. He tipped her up on her backside, and examined each foot in turn, brushing back the hair where the horn joined the skin. He pulled back her head, prizing open her jaws to look inside her mouth, as gently as the job allowed. She seemed to be clear, as far as he could tell. Just a bad foot, after all.

All the same, she gave him a baleful stare when he left her.

That night, over supper, Hardman considered his position.
I can't go back, he'd written to Elizabeth. *That much, at least, is clear..*

There was a wisdom that knew when to stay, and when to go. What was bondage and what was liberation. His work at the university seemed marginal to any kind of real life. Its discourse, the rattling of withered twigs.

I don't know what I shall do. Perhaps I shall stay on here. For the time being, at least. I might be of some use..

Jack Ashe had given him instructions about disinfecting his boots, and making sure all the wheels of the car went over the straw.

"I can't stop you going over farm land," the red-haired man added. "But I'm asking you not to."

Hardman nodded. It was, in any case, only a question of time before the footpaths were closed. Besides, what else should a man caught up in a siege do but throw in his lot with the defenders. The only barrier was his readiness.

The next day, walking up to the farm to give the boy his lesson, he came across the red-haired man gritting the track. And gave a hand. Jack Ashe didn't ask him. Hardman didn't offer. He saw a shovel sticking up at the back of the trailer, so

154

he took it, and began shovelling cinders into the icy ruts.

They didn't talk much. Though once or twice Hardman caught the blue eyes under the pale lashes studying him perplexedly.

They were studying one another.

If ever there was an opening for casual labour at Dalehead it was the time between back end and lambing, a time for cutting and clearing drains, checking walls, mending fences. Now, with Hardman sitting in the farm kitchen after his session with the boy, if Jack mentioned some job or other that had to be done, it seemed accepted, in an offhand sort of way, that Hardman might go along and lend a hand.

One of the heaviest, most awkward tasks was rescuing the water gate that had lost its moorings after heavy rains off the moor and drifted downstream. After much slipping, splashing, pulling, swearing, the two men lugged it back to its place.

"What's a clever man like you want to be doing this for?"

"It's not enough to be clever," gasped Hardman, heaving on the rope. "You have to have.. something.. to be clever about."

Together they walked the walls of the in-by, and then the walls above the dale. Once, going up to Rowlee Pasture, they put up a mountain hare that lit off like a flash of white lightning, with the dogs streaking after.

The shepherd gazed after them, bony face impassive as ever.

"It'll leave 'em, y'know," he said abruptly. "Then it'll sit. But it puts down such a scent they'll get up to it again. Then off the bugger'll go."

He resumed the trudge up the steep bank.

"That's why the hounds kill 'em," he went on. "It's not that they're faster. But they never lose the scent, d'ye see. They just keep going."

His voice held a note of respect for things that just kept going.

"Aye, but it's a lovely creature, a hare. A marvellous thing to see."

Then, after days of mild, wet weather, winter began again. Hard frosts at night. Snow on the moor. The Snake road blocked. "Wouldn't you know it," folk were saying. "Just before lambing."

Already, up on the moor, the first premature deaths were taking place. Lambs would die, frozen within minutes of being born, that might have lived had their ewes been brought down to the dale.

Now Jack Ashe was working fifteen hours a day. Sometimes Hardman went with him, muffled, shivering, watching the dogs streaking away with that extraordinary instinct they had for their business. They needed no directing. The shepherd, following them in his binoculars, would pick up in a distant flurry of snow what they had sensed minutes earlier.

Now and then they cornered a ewe that wouldn't budge. "Either she's just plain daft, or she's got a lamb."

They trudged across to see. They found her in a hole she'd scraped to give birth, with her lamb huddled up to her chest and the bloodstained snow piled up at her back. Hardman stared about him at the desolate scene: black rocks, wind-ribbed dunes of snow where sparse grasses clung, life itself seemingly at the end of its tether. There was nothing else. Not a tree, or brake, or a clump of heather to be seen.

"Strewth," he said, "it's a bleak place to be born."

"A winter lamb expects nowt else," said the shepherd dourly. He took it up, tucking it under his coat.

They set off back, with the ewe running back and forth, calling anxiously, following after.

In the farm kitchen they warmed numbed hands around steaming mugs of tea, and watched the news. It came with a Devon accent. *What I want to know is when will I be able to move my in-lamb ewes out of that field? It would've been for hay to feed next winter's stock.* The camera, panning across a trampled quagmire, lingered on sheep up to their hocks in mud. *They've been there for three weeks now. They're cold. They're wet..*

The voice stopped abruptly, its owner shaking his head, turning away.

"Where will it end?" Ellen Ashe looked uncertainly at her husband.

"It'll get worse before it gets better."

The outbreak was increasing by leaps and bounds, ten, twenty, thirty cases a day, as the foci of infection steadily extended: Wiltshire, Northamptonshire, Cumbria, mid-Wales, the south-west.. It was now beyond dispute that a pestilence was loose, and galloping about the land. There was, too, a capricious quality about its will-o'-the-wisp appearances, almost as if it was teasing its pursuers, now here, now somewhere else, a hundred miles away, with a virtuosity that left the authorities unable to predict where it might crop up next.

The speed and unpredictability of its progress provoked much discussion as to its means of propagation. Some argued that it must require a human agency to enable it to travel so fast. Others said it was spread by birds or wild animals; others, on infected particles borne by the wind from the fires burning up and down the land.

It must be like living in the blitz, wrote Hardman to his wife. *You know the bombs are going to fall, but you don't know where, or when. We have the papers and the post left in a box fixed to the gate, and ferry our rubbish down to the road. The dustbin men pick it up the other side of the gate. Jack is paranoid about passing lorries maybe carrying the virus. The other day I helped him transfer animal feed from the wagon into the trailer. No one's allowed in..*

This sudden, rapid escalation marked, one might say, the end of the first period, and the beginning of another, in which the complacency of earlier days gradually gave place to desperate measures. Once the policy of wholesale slaughter had been decided on, naturally it was impossible to take individual cases into account, or make exceptions for such things as healthy animals.

Look at 'em, said a farmer, blinking back tears as the camera switched to a group of sheep bounding across a field. *I don't think there's much the matter with that lot!*

Inevitably, perhaps, the effect of these brutal visitations was to compel those responsible for the culling of livestock to act as if they had no feelings as individuals.

Yet what might have appeared instances of callous indifference were, more often than not, the result of stupidity or casual incompetence, as in the case of the farmer who had to milk what was left of his dairy herd because the killers hadn't brought enough equipment to cull the whole lot quickly enough, or that of an old Lakeland shepherd who went up the fell to feed his Herdwicks, only to find no more than a handful of them left alive. He hadn't been told they were to be slaughtered. He wasn't on the phone.

For families cut off from one another, the phone had become a lifeline. Neighbour talked constantly to neighbour, clinging together like survivors of a shipwreck, knowing full well that if one of them went under, the rest went with them.

The spread of misinformation did nothing to ease anxieties. Emotions ran high at rumours of sheepdogs killed. And was it rats, folk wondered, rats in their thousands feasting on the corpses heaped up in farmyards, that were now spreading the disease? Each day seemed to generate fresh fear. It spread with the westerly wind that ran over the bent, brown moorland grasses. It bred in farm kitchens, and blossomed in the faces of the men and women.

"You don't know what to believe," said Ellen Ashe.

In the farm kitchen she had the radio on continuously, picking up voices from all over the country. Even in areas so far free of the epidemic, anxieties were mounting. *It's a nightmare*, said a man from the Lincoln wolds. *I've got lambs as were born last spring ready to go, but can't. And the worst of it is, not knowing how long it'll last.* Desperate men were inundating the help-lines, only to break down in tears. Many women were worried about their menfolk. Dreaded coming home to find a son or a husband dead.

One day she heard that the Minister was considering a plan to cull half a million sheep trapped away from home on winter grazing. She knew Jack was anxious for his yearlings, still trapped over at Longshaw. The constant worry was causing him sleepless nights.

How, she wondered, did folk manage to keep going.

Yet all around her the year was unfolding as it always had, the cycles going on from everlasting to everlasting. The swallows were back, darting in and out of the big barn. Day by day Jack was bringing down more ewes to their lambing quarters in the bottom land. Ellen Ashe would see them, a grey smudge drifting down through the dwindling daylight.

Two-thirds of the flock were gathered now on the in-by land, with only the hardiest left to lamb on the moor. In the field, where the growth of grass had been sparse after the winter, Hardman, armed with a pitchfork, was breaking up bales of hay for the shearlings, raking the hay over a wider area. Or else he was humping straw bales into the barn, ready for setting up the pens.

Ellen Ashe was preparing another batch of meals ready for lambing. There would be no time then for cooking. In farm kitchens all over the country women were doing the same, and wondering just like her. They were talking about it going on till August, she'd heard Jack saying. Even if they escaped it, would they ever be able to sell their lambs? How long could they last with no income? The stores couldn't be sold on, and there'd be no wallin' jobs for Jack while it lasted. As she went out to the dairy to put another big shepherd's pie in the freezer, she found herself wondering how much longer she would be here doing this. Looking out at this. That was a track she daren't allow herself to follow. All the same she felt a fierce surge, like a flare of light inside her, a split-second, momentous blaze.

There was always a good fire burning, those days Hardman read with the boy. Pot of tea on the silver tray. Biscuits. Cake, if she'd been baking.

Together they read from *Hammer of the North*. Sometimes the boy sniffed at the pages. They had a strange smell. Queer. Spicy. Like the smell of polish. He was curious about all things that could be fingered, smelt, savoured, watched, wondered about. But not words. Hardman's eye followed him as he dragged through his lines with the hobbled gait of a backward child. Patiently, Hardman picked him up when he stumbled. Lifted him over the longer words.

But the book told him things the old man couldn't have known. Wisely, Hardman let him puzzle out the discoveries himself

"Didn't they wear them horns, then?"

"Doesn't look like it. Not according to this. They seem to have worn them just for ceremonial occasions."

Together they found the sentence and re-read it carefully.

"Besides, they would have been very awkward, I should think," said Hardman. "Those helmets. In battle, I mean."

Now and then they crossed swords once more with an old foe of many battles, Harald Finehair. They found a story about Ulf the berserker, another of the king's enemies.

"What were they?"

"Berserkers? They were the wild men of the Viking world.

`Hard men whom no iron could bite' it says in the old sagas. Frightened of nothing. They were often said to be shape-changers. Men who could turn themselves into wild animals. Bears, or wild boars."

"Was he a shape-changer?"

"Well," said Hardman gravely, "people must have thought he was. They called him Kveld-Ulf. It means 'evening wolf'."

He could see the face, the eyes, working on that.

But the boy was thinking of his grandad. He really changed at night. When it grew dark. Queer. Not speaking. He'd take his stick and go out into the dark. Then the dogs 'ud start up, and he'd lie in bed waiting for the *bang-bang* of the stick and the sudden, snarling shout.

The boy thought of him, silent under the dark trees, hearing the cries of night creatures, sniffing the darkness, and the soft wind over the dale. He was not yet lost to the strangeness of things, still open to a world in which all things were possible: hares that danced (*They do, you know*, the old man murmured in his ear, *oh aye.. round and round..*), a drowned village that rose up out of the waters, a ghostly legion marching over the old Roman road.

Outwardly, he seemed a good deal tamer. Would sit happily wolfing his teacher's biscuits.

"You have 'em," Hardman said, noting the avid eyes. "Cup of tea'll be enough for me."

After that it was established that the boy ate Hardman's tea. It was a secret they kept from Ellen Ashe.

Spring

'You may remember, now some ten years gone,
Two blighting seasons, when the fields were left
With half a harvest. It pleased heaven to add
A worse affliction in the plague of war:
A happy land was stricken to the heart!
'Twas a sad time of sorrow and distress:
A wanderer among the cottages,
I with my pack of winter raiment saw
The hardships of that season: many rich
Sunk down as in a dream among the poor,
And of the poor did many cease to be,
And their place knew them not.'

William Wordsworth *The Ruined Cottage*

SIX

Shepherds, dour men at the best of times, are more than usually taciturn during lambing.

There were men in that part of north Derbyshire who said *Good morning* to their wives and children, and that was *all* they said, except to speak to their dogs. But for Jack Ashe it was the best time of the year. Not that he said much either. Yet each year at this time, for almost as long as he could remember, he'd assisted at a marvel. Kneeling in darkness, often in snow, pulling a bloodied, smoking, yellow egg-yolked scrap from the womb, blowing into the bleary, crumpled face, rubbing its rump against the ewe's nose. Then he'd sink back on his heels to watch as she began to lick her lamb. For it was still a marvel. At length he'd pick up his lantern. Set off again to the next.

Most lambs were born at night. At dawn some were still arriving. At six, the shepherd was out and about in the dale with his lantern and satchel, stuffed with vaccines, hypodermic, iodine, antiseptic pessaries, a thermos of warm milk. Hardman carried another filled with extra feed. He was up before five each morning. Crunching across frozen fields in the bleak hour before dawn. It was what he wanted. Life, he knew now, dependent though it was upon reason and intellect, had its wellspring and source of power elsewhere, and he yearned to be part of it, as one might yearn for a country and a home. It was like setting out again in the Alps. Stepping over the Mer de Glace, dazed with the cold, fearful, yet full of wonder. Here and there lambs were just wobbling to their feet, bleating a baby cry at mothers who seemed to stare in amazement at what had popped out at their nether end, reaching forward to sniff nervously, licking at last the splay legged, spindly object bumping at their muzzle.

For others, birth was a hard, bloody business. Hardman held on queasily to the head of a prone, panting ewe as the shepherd delved with an arm.

"They generally come head first," he grunted, "but there's always some awkward little bugger that won't.. bloody.. *shift!*"

He drew it out at last by the back legs in a loop of bloodied cord.

Every ewe that lambed in the field was brought into the barn and given hay to eat, and a water bucket. Hardman had the job of topping up the hay and water several times a day, and adding clean straw to the pens. Then, when each couple was turned out into the paddock, he had to sprinkle the dirty bedding in each vacated pen with disinfectant powder, and set down more clean straw.

There were the inevitable deaths. Part of the barn was turned into an orphanage for lambs. They lay in cardboard boxes under the lamps. Feeding lambs, the new hand soon discovered, was a battle of wills: a novice's impatience clashing with the intransigence of infants who had not yet worked out that the warm milk was for them to swallow. It dribbled out of their mouths, ran down his over-trousers, collected in puddles on the floor.

The newcomer had a lot to learn. Sent with a bag of concentrates to fill the troughs in the paddock, with ewes milling round him, he was lifted off his feet and carried about, hanging on desperately to the bag, until the boy, howling with laughter, pulled him upright, and set him back on the ground.

Jack Ashe, watching him floundering after lambs in the barn, remembered how the old man would pluck them up by the armful, three or four at a time.

"I don't doubt he's a very clever feller," he said dryly to his wife, "but he's no dab hand wi' sheep."

Then, one morning, just as the two men were coming in for breakfast, Jack got a call from his cousin Arthur at Grainfoot. He'd heard a rumour of a suspected case somewhere on the other side of Kinder. He didn't know where.

All that morning the lives of men and animals appeared both helpless and haphazard events before the terrible contingency of foot and mouth. The shepherd's stocky frame moved about barn or paddock ministering to ewes and lambs, but it possessed his mind to the exclusion of himself.

By dinner time it was definite. Ellen Ashe went over to the barn to tell them. The local radio had picked it up.

Hardman was topping up the hay and water in the pens.

"Can't you ring someone?"

Jack Ashe shook his head.

"They won't give out the names. Only if you name a farm will they tell you *yes*, or *no*. No, you have to find out from friends or neighbours."

"Maurice knows the NFU rep," said Ellen Ashe. "Why don't you ring him?"

It was nine o'clock the next morning before Maurice Clarkson knew the location of the suspect farm. He came over straight away with a map. They spread it out on the kitchen table.

"I reckon you're right on the boundary, Jack. But I'd definitely be inside the Infected Area."

"What's worrying me," he went on, "is this. That farm's open to the moor. There's a lot of sheep grazing up there, mine among 'em, and they'd all be suspicious contacts."

The work went on, sorting out the new arrivals, checking the lambs to make sure they'd suckled, savouring the old excitement of finding out which ewe had had what kind of lamb – *Ah knew it*, the old man used to say delightedly, *Ah knew she'd be a good 'un* – but all these tasks and memories were circumscribed by what was going on just the other side of Kinder. And there was nowhere you could hide from it.

Hardman, gripping the throat of a ewe that had been scouring for the shepherd to clip the shit-caked wool from the tail, asked the only question that mattered.

"What happens now?"

"They'll slaughter everything, then test afterwards. If they find anything, they'll very likely move over here."

"When will you know?"

"It could take anything up to a week."

Jack Ashe was staring at the paddock where his new lambs were jumping over one another, and running races. They had just discovered life was fun. The shepherd, though, was standing at the far end of the village, where the lane became a track, dwindling up into the hills, standing where other men in overalls were waiting around vehicles parked at a farm entrance. He'd never been there, but he knew it. He knew the women clustered in the yard, all with the frozen faces of disaster, and the young lad setting off for school. He knew the shepherd on a quad bike driving the last of the flock down towards the farm, and the pens set in place. He knew the men in white walking where the sheep had been gathered in the field beside the pens. The noise of their lamentation was ceaseless.

The arms of villagers were closing windows, drawing curtains, but couldn't keep out the bellowing of cattle as their lives were taken from them.

In the field, some of the sheep were making frantic efforts to escape, jumping repeatedly at the fence. In a distant corner of the field a ewe was giving birth to a tiny lamb. It was scooped up, and carried down to the pens with the ewe, bleating loudly, following after.

Then the revving of engines, a heaving and sighing of brakes, as the wagons reversed into the yard. Then the chunter and clatter of a yellow JCB, grinding down from the byre and manoeuvring over the wagon to tip its load, the great, heaving weight of a fully pregnant cow, eyes rolling, tongue hanging, falling with a thud. Back and forth, again and again, until the wagon was full.

Then the men were pulling black plastic sheeting over the legs, the heads and hooves.

The lad, coming home from the school bus, stopped dead at the sight of four calves, hanging, chained together, from the bucket of the JCB. Stood rooted, as another bucket-load swung over the wagon. It was the tups, the lovely tups he used to reach at through the gate, stretching out his hand to the strong, curling horns. Tangled, bloody, they tumbled into the wagon with the rest.

The first thing that the pestilence inflicted on the country as a whole was a feeling of division.

To start with, people had been shocked by the pictures in their newspapers and on their televisions screens. These were, after all, horrors everyone could shudder at. Even so, they found it difficult to grasp what was happening in the countryside. Besides, they were preoccupied with their own affairs. For them everything was still possible. They went on studying maps and gazetteers, making plans for fishing trips, camping holidays, walking tours in the hills. How could they ever have imagined that these ugly events should be used as a pretext to close footpaths, suspend rights of way. Thus cut off from their various pastimes and entertainments, their reaction was to blame the authorities.

For those imprisoned on their farms the consequences were divisive in a different way. Babies were born that couldn't be shared with the rest of the family. Folk died, yet could not be laid to rest in their own burial ground. Children, sent away to relatives to study for their exams, were not allowed to visit their families in case they spread infection. The anguish of this separation, inflicted on folk wholly unprepared for it, was immeasurably increased by a feeling of exile and isolation from the rest of their fellow countrymen, a sense of abandonment which left a void around their lives.

Meanwhile, in those areas of the country as yet untouched by the disease, there were many cases of individuals now suffering the traumas imagination will inflict on those not usually

considered susceptible to such attacks. Men and women through-
out hills and dales waited with haunted faces, fearing the worst.
It dogged their days. It filtered through their sleep to trouble
dreams. No longer were there individual lives and fortunes. Only
a single, collective fate. The pestilence had swallowed everyone.

After two weeks of lambing the cold snap lifted as suddenly
as it had come. Winter still clung on here and there under rocks,
on leeward banks, clutching with long skeletal fingers behind
dry-stone walls. Each morning, out in the yard, Jack Ashe
checked the wind. He did so instinctively. The ministry vets
had found no evidence of infection among the sheep and cattle
culled the other side of Kinder. Yet now and then during the
day, Hardman would see the shepherd's glances directed anxiously westward.

Then the weather turned wet. Wet and windy. Jack put a
tyre in front of the barn door, and tied up the door, leaving just
a gap for the hens to shelter from the weather.

"They like scrattin' about in the straw," he said to Hardman. "And they're company for the ewes."

A fresh moist breeze was blowing in the dale. Everywhere,
the noise of running water. Even the reluctant grass had a fresh
wet gleam to it.

The boy, ever keener than the men, picked up this change
in the air, a sense of the cramped land stretching, swelling. At
first light he was out scanning the bottom land to see what fresh
white dots had blossomed overnight.

For lambs were still being born. Though every day now
there were other pressing tasks for the shepherd to see to, marking, inoculating, notching ears. Every day ewes and lambs, a
batch at a time, had to be driven into the holding pens, and the
lambs, kicking, struggling, carried into the barn.

"You can't keep 'em apart too long," Jack Ashe yelled above
the din.

Hardman, clinging flinchingly to his kicking armful, nodded grimly.

But the boy drank in every minute. He loved the sounds sheep made. The little purring noise a mother made with her newborn lamb. The din the ewes kicked up in the barn, bellowing for their breakfast. He loved the smell, the infant squalling of lambs, the urgent *blaaa* of anxious mothers as they milled about below his boots, perched on the half-door between the barn and the pens, anticipating the moment when he would jump down from the door, swing it open, and be swept aside by the inrush of ewes frantic for their lambs. Yet all was sorted magically in seconds. *Mothering-up,* his grandad called it.

But it was all a mystery to Hardman. A confusion of woolly bodies.

"Whose is this?" he would cry in bewilderment, holding aloft a lamb he'd come across, wailing forlornly in the barn. Was it hers? The lone ewe in the pen? Or was *her* lamb that bloody carcase Jack was skinning.

The shepherd was stripping the pelt from a dead lamb. He started at the neck, pulling hard to get the front legs out of the skin, but the rest was easy – along the back – down over the back legs.

"You've to keep the tail on, whatever you do," said the shepherd. "She sniffs at the tail."

He fitted the skin to one of the orphans, and stitched it with twine along the back. Then he took up the shrunken little carcase, slit the belly and pulled out its insides, searching for the bladder, which he smeared over the rump and tail.

"She smells there when it's feeding. Mek's sure it's hers," he added, with a sideways grin. It was a rare thing to see him grin.

They set the lamb in a pen with a single ewe. Stiff, unused, it looked, in its bulky, bloody overcoat. Bleating thinly. The bereaved ewe, still distracted at its loss, backed off nervously. The lamb followed, whickering its need.

Jack Ashe was watching keenly.

"Will she take to it?" asked Hardman.

"Mebbe. Mebbe not."

"He loved this, you know," he went on dreamily. "I remember one year he'd been that bad with bronchitis, yet he *would* come down. He came out here all muffled up, coughing and spitting, just to see for himself. It did him that much good. What he'd 'a made o' this business.. "

The slow voice tailed off into silence. He'd be holding a lamb to a ewe's teat, or dabbing a bloody cord with iodine, and it would strike him like a knife in the chest.

Yet even the foot and mouth couldn't obliterate the wonder of it, this miraculous renewal of his flock. It was still a marvel.

"Hey up," he said, softly nudging Hardman, nodding to where the foster-ewe was suckling its lamb. "Just look there."

But as the days passed the shepherd seemed more withdrawn.

"He's not sleeping," Ellen Ashe told her sister-in-law over the phone. "He's worried about the expense. I know he is."

Where there was a job to be done he got on with it methodically, without explanation. Hardman, following as best he could each terse instruction, felt like a man assisting at some inexplicable ritual. He *asked*. But what he was told conveyed nothing.

Wherever one looked there was something wanted doing. The shepherd went dourly about the mountain of work. After his sessions with the boy, Hardman went back to a bath, a meal and a bed. For Jack Ashe there could be no respite. He needed to keep a close watch now the sucklers were close to calving.

A red heifer had been walking about for hours with her tail stuck out. She was having a bad time. Now Ellen Ashe stood holding back the tail while Jack slipped an arm into the hot, slippery tunnel, right back to the port hole of the pelvis. He could feel a tail, but no hoof.

After twenty minutes agonizing, still he couldn't make up his mind what to do. In the end it was Ellen Ashe who rang the vet.

"We can't afford the vet," he told her.

"And can we afford to lose a cow?"

"What's she worth now," he flared up at her. "She's worth nowt."

"That's silly talk," she flashed back at him.

It was the old vet that came out to them, old Mr Savage.

"Another young bugger with its hind feet round its ears," he grunted, as he delved with an arm.

Jack, meanwhile, was applying traction with the puller. Absorbed in what he was doing, he had escaped his fear, his anger, into the task of delivering this calf. Only it wouldn't come.

"No use," grunted the vet. "It'll have to be a Caesar."

The woman watched her husband, who was murmuring soothing noises to the heifer as he scrubbed her flank with antiseptic. He looked up at her, and managed a smile.

He is a good man, she thought. *A decent man.*

Yet the truth was the work was almost more than he could cope with. Not that he said anything. Each day he was up before dawn. He'd be back for his dinner and tea, and out again the minute he'd eaten. And when, late at night, he came into the kitchen, the skin seemed stretched tighter than ever over the gaunt, bony face. Drawn with fatigue.

"It's too much for one man," Ellen Ashe told her sister-in-law. "Only he won't admit it. And of course he's worried sick."

She was so tired. She came into the kitchen one morning after helping with a calf, and sat with a mug of coffee listening to the farming programme. A woman like herself. Six children. Suckler cows and sheep. Shepherd for a husband.

She sipped the hot coffee, listening to this woman describing the culling of her ewes, and realised she was weeping.

Weeping, and hadn't noticed. She'd not done that since her mam died.

This won't do, she told herself. She got up to mix the pet-lamb feed.

One of the unfortunate consequences of the measures taken to halt the epidemic was to present the authorities as if they were devoid of normal human feeling. Yet they were, undoubtedly, men and women of good sense and integrity, government ministers, politicians, leading figures from the agribusiness world, experts from the universities, professors of this and that, highly qualified professionals of wide experience. There was no questioning their good intentions. But when it came to combatting an epidemic of this scale and virulence their competence was more or less zero.

To many country people, though, it seemed as if the government was hell bent on uniting forces with the plague to hurl themselves upon the farming community, and bring it to its knees.

At the end of each day families would gather in farm kitchens up and down the land to hear news of some fresh atrocity. At Dalehead the two men were sipping the hot tea Ellen Ashe had poured for them as they listened to some young fellow up in the Scottish Borders. His voice was flat, without expression, as he told how the slaughtermen and two Ministry vets had herded his beasts into a small shave of land, and shut the gates to prevent their escape. The men then shot at them with rifles. The vets stood and watched. *They shot the bull three times. I don't know if he was dead then.* Jack Ashe was staring at the screen, his face a blank. *Didn't they use a captive bolt?* a voice was asking. *They're supposed to use a captive bolt, aren't they?* Somewhere in the kitchen a chair scraped against the flags. *No. There was no captive bolt used here..*

Sometimes the boy would be present, staring at a truckload of lambs, separated from their mothers, taken away for slaughter, while a big Cumbrian farmer wept openly in front of the camera.

"And the cruelty of it," whispered Ellen Ashe, "is you can't even go and put your arms round folk whose hearts must be breaking."

Then the boy would go with Hardman for his lesson. As he stumbled through his reading, the man was put in mind of some crippled wild thing, the struggling of some broken-winged bird. Yet the boy seemed indifferent. Or else he accepted it with that passive, fatalistic wisdom of the wretched of the earth who *know* things will never get better. Who struggle on because they have to. Sometimes he would stop at a word, look up expectantly – "Yes?" the man would say encouragingly – then stab at it forlornly, without hope, and look up anxiously. And the man saw they were travelling a dark, much-travelled track, going round and round together on a cruel treadmill.

He began to set aside a part of their time together simply for talking. For drawing closer.

They sat together across the fire while the boy ate Hardman's tea, and chattered about the dale, the moor, his family, his grandad. Tales, related in his blunt laconic way, that gave to moor and crag, a heap of stones on a bleak ridge beyond Back Tor, an aura of things unseen.

He told of the great white Alsatian that came over the moor one winter, that killed a hundred of his Uncle Arthur's sheep over on Derwent side.

"A gret white wolf of a thing, me grandad says it were. They all got together to shoot it. All the men round 'ere. They shot at it, but it kept coming at 'em."

It was a tale he loved to hear. *It were dead. Oh aye. Stone bloody dead. But it came at us all o' twenty yards before the bugger dropped.*

The man was amazed how deep the roots of the boy's life

ran back into his native ground. He was full of tales. A dog that stayed for fifteen weeks beside the body of a shepherd who'd died on the moors one winter. 'Lost Lad' – to the man no more than a curious name on a map.

"He were called Abraham.." As matter-of-fact as if they'd been school mates. Though the lad had died maybe two hundred years before. "He went up on Howden one day to fetch down the sheep, and got lost in a snowstorm. So he crawled under this rock for shelter, and he scratched LOST LAD on t' rock. They found him after a time. And they built that cairn. And every time a shep went by 'e put a stone on t' cairn."

"But all your stories," the man teased him gently, "are about death. About things dying."

But the boy only looked away. When he raised his head again Hardman saw that his eyes were filled with tears.

"Why did they separate the lambs from their mothers?"

"I don't know," he said. "I can't tell you." He knew only that there was a horror going on, and he, like most people in the country, couldn't understand it.

He took up the book to read to the boy. He'd discovered that the old man used to read aloud bits he liked himself, without relating them to any context. And the boy liked best the old things read again. The best bits of Dickens. Oliver asking for more. Pip and the fearful man on the marsh. Hardman would do them all with gusto, beefing it up for all he was worth, with a bravura he'd never have dared in front of students. His Magwitch a fearful man whose snarling throaty menace had the boy flinching, as he warned of that young man that had a secret way, *pecooliar* to himself, of getting at a boy, and at his heart, and at his liver. Of how it was in *wain* for a boy to attempt to hide himself from that young man. That a boy might lock his door, might tuck himself up, might draw the clothes over his head, might think himself comfortable and safe, but that young man would softly creep and creep his way to him and tear him open.

"I am a-keeping," whispered Hardman, "that young man from harming of you at the present moment, with great difficulty. I find it *wery* hard to hold that young man off of your inside. Now, what do you say?"

There was a pause, a silence: the question seemed to hang, alive and menacing, in the leaping flames, in the dark, crooked corners of the old room.

"Did 'e get 'im the things?"

"Would you?"

"Yes," the boy said swiftly. "I'der bin frightened, but I'der felt sorry for 'im too."

"So did Pip"

"I know a place," the boy burst out before Hardman could go on, "where 'e coulder hid. On Dovestone Tor. Where nobody coulder found 'im."

Even close to, it is almost undetectable. Just a small, black recess in the rock. Just a pocket, you might think. One of many in the pockmarked rock of the Tor. Yet wriggle inside, you find yourself in a domed, circular chamber, like the inside of an egg, or a stone igloo. Just big enough for a small man to lie full-length. The floor flat, peaty. The archetypal outlaw's cave. A refuge for any fugitive on the run.

"I know it!" cried Hardman joyfully. "The bivouac cave on Dovestone Tor."

For a moment the boy looked at him guardedly. But there was no mistaking the eager truth in the man's eyes.

So they had something else to share.

As the government's flurry of orders and restrictions fastened about the farming community, the shutdown of the countryside was causing serious hardship. At Dalehead, Jack and Ellen Ashe continued the desperate endeavour to keep their animals alive and free of the disease. Yet even if they escaped the epidemic would they ever be able to sell their lambs? And the store cattle that ought to be going soon. That lost their value after thirty months.

"There'll be compensation, surely?" said Hardman.

"Aye, if your animals are slaughtered there'll be compensation. Not otherwise. Now they're telling us it could go on till August.

It was a mystery to the other man how, in such circumstances, they were able to carry on with their daily lives. Something of his anxiety spilled over into his letters to Elizabeth.

When I first arrived here I wasn't much interested in my neighbours. Now, with this business going on, I feel this is where I belong, at least for the time being. If I can't avert it, at least I can suffer it with them..

He was growing so passionately defensive of the place, the boy especially, she feared another of his obsessions

I fear for him, Elizabeth. He lost his grandfather in particular distressing circumstances. And now this abomination, which is crushing the life out of them. The wife, stripped of all capacity for joy, the man swallowed up in a vast despondency. Above all, the father's darkness. And the boy picks it up from the man..

She began to wonder if unexpiated grief might not project itself, in some strange inversion, on a resurrected child. Anthony, though, seemed terribly persuaded.

I tell you, slowly, surely, the light is going out..

Yet the boy's mind was far from dark. The old man's death had ceased to be the painful thing it was. Only the old collie bitch seemed still to suffer the old man's passing. She lay all day in her stall. Sometimes, on a fine day, the boy might come across her, limping out to curl up under the stone wall of the rubbish pit. She'd lie there, curled round, her nose tucked under her tail.

"Come by, Meg," he cried, "Meg.." Whistling her after him.

If a rheumy eye slid in his direction, the grey muzzle never moved. She knew he had no use for her. And the boy knew, in his heart, that she was finished. That she belonged to an older, earlier life that was done with now, and that his part was to live on.

Always there was the living present, that was indefatigable, not to be denied. The turn and return of the populous world, that reflected the workings of his own vivid spirit. Up on the moor cock grouse in glowing plumage were strutting their borders. Go.. go.. go.. go-back.. *go-back*, they shouted, heads down, eyeball to eyeball. On wild, windy days he would look up to see small parties of golden plover coming low over the land, dipping under the gusty wind, so close and low he could look deep into the jet black of their breasts.

He had to work now. With the old man gone he was needed. As he turned the soil, clearing the ground for potatoes, he kept a sharp eye for things that had to be killed. Wire-worms, earwigs, leather-jackets, bright yellowy centipedes, he scrutinised them all, and meted life or death accordingly. Fast runners he left alone. Shiny black things that coiled up like a spring, he killed those. Yet nothing he saw, not even the fat creamy chafer slugs, struck him as ugly or repulsive. It was all too curious for that. Sometimes Nature, in the shape of a robin, took a hand in his executions, hopping just out of range, darting in as he turned a clod. Or he might flick a grub in its direction with a prong of the fork.

It fascinated him. That shrewd assessing eye. Bright. Unblinking. It seemed to have no fear of him at all. Yet the young cat it spotted directly, flitted up to the top wall, uttered a sharp, urgent *tic.. tic..*

Only his dad, stalking about the house, was darkening. Yet he had only to run out into the dale for that weight to vanish, to feel the lightness, the airiness of birds as he ran dipping, swerving. Wagtails, bobbing about in the wet meadow. Peewits, crazily zig-zagging as they hurtled through the sky, rolling, diving and plunging, greeted him with joy. Everything his child's eye fell upon was joyous.

*

For once, Elizabeth Hardman was at a loss to know how to respond to her husband's letter.

She read it over and over again. She did not know what to make of it. Oh, the case was common enough. A man in middle age, whether impelled by a neurosis, or something lacking in his life, quitting the safe, the familiar, looking for something new to focus on. He might think to have found it reflected in another human being, or even in a remote farm buried on a moor. Yet, according to the literature, it was often best discovered in some neglected side of the personality.

Then she had to check herself. She was thinking of him again as a patient.

Even so, as she put pen to paper, she couldn't help wondering if, in living at last the role he had suppressed for so long in himself, Anthony was not reaching for the sky through prison bars.

It would be good to see you, Hardman had tried tentatively.

Yes, we could meet.. She left it at that.

As if a sense of failure shared might metamorphose into something other than a source of bitterness. That they might yet turn a corner. Slough off a skin.

It was Hardman who suggested Leicestershire. As a kind of halfway house. She wouldn't have so far to travel. He would find somewhere they could have lunch.

She would come up, she wrote, by train. She didn't say why. Only that there was a station at Market Harborough. Could he pick her up there?

So they set out, journeying to a destination neither of them knew, who had, in the past, coincided only at points of mutual negativity.

He, though, was traversing a dream-time of memories as the Rover wound through empty lanes, her hand resting on his thigh, passing across the small of his back as they went together into some strange place.

New beginnings, he was reminded,

..surely will find him late or soon
Who turns a corner into new territory..

The man's spirit began to shrink a little amid the patch-work hunting fields of Leicestershire. Not a country for concealment. Maybe the best hope, he thought, as the car bowled through a wide vista of fields and hedges, lay over the horizon, somewhere in the depths of one another.

The woman, gazing from the window as the train sped her towards this reunion, was contemplating the destruction stemming from an unlived life. Years of exile had forced on her a detachment which, try as she might, she couldn't talk herself out of. She sat, her mind reaching for the place words pointed to, but couldn't come at. They seemed to stand there impotently. At the frontier. Lacking the necessary papers. *You must go*, they seemed to say, *these last miles by yourself.* She sighed, over her coffee. Maybe it wasn't words that ailed her, but some atrophy of the heart.

He was on the platform, pacing about, glancing at the clock a full twenty minutes before the London train drew in.

Then the carriage doors, sliding back on figures poised to make an entrance, found them face to face, waiting like actors for a cue, she a slight figure all but swallowed up in the swamping folds of a heavy coat in rich sienna, her face framed by the high, ribbed collar. She wore high boots, a slim skirt of chocolate suede.

She had dressed, he saw, as if for a case conference with other professionals. To subdue, he wondered, or for protection?

"Hello," she said, uncertainly.

"You've grown your hair."

There was a deal of ash now among the faded yellow.

"I felt like a change."

"You look like Joan of Arc," he said, and smiled.

She bent forward. They kissed, as friends do, but not lovers.

She sat very quiet in the car. He made what little talk there was.

"I've no idea what this place is like." He'd plucked it from an old guide he kept in the car.

She stared at the bright flat land unfolding round her. He was conscious of the distance in her. It made him uneasy, yet quickened his excitement. She had become strange again. Not known.

The Rockingham Arms, as it was called, turned out to be a Victorian country house hotel, set in its own parkland. A gravelled drive swept them past fields of grazing cows to a portico, and an area full of expensive cars.

"This is rather grand," she said, in her ironic voice. "Are you sure you can afford it?"

"Yes," he said. "I'm not sure I can afford it."

Inside the porch was a stag's head, mounted above the door, its throat adorned with a faded tie in Old Etonian colours. They entered a dark interior of what must once have been a hall, though now a bar busy with guests and diners, its wooden panelling hung with sporting prints.

To one side a lofty stairwell communicated with the upper floors. At the first quarter-turn, broad shafts of sunlight streamed through stained-glass windows on to the wide shallow stair, accentuating the gloomy depths below.

Elizabeth refused his offer of a drink. Nervous, she seemed intent on getting to wherever they were heading. They went together into the restaurant. He thought how slim she looked. He was as nervous as a boy.

The waiter found them a table for two in a window looking out where deer were grazing under the trees. Her coat, shrugged on to the chair back, uncovered a soft cotton top of dark olive, with loose, wide cuffs embroidered with motifs in coloured wools.

She scarcely glanced at the menu.

"Oh.. the sole, I think," she said, looking up at the waiter.

"I'm afraid I'm not very hungry," she added apologetically.

Beside her on the table lay a queer old leather bag. A sort of wallet. Not much bigger than a purse. Stamped into the leather, a triangle, with a trowel inside it. Some letters. A number, once picked out in gold. A few flakes of gold still stuck to the leather.

"That's a strange bag." It was something to say.

She shrugged, and smiled.

"I bought it in North Street. In that second-hand shop. Near the steps." She ran her long, thin fingers nervously over the leather. "It belonged to some old mason. I expect he kept his apron in it."

Somehow they kept up a desultory trickle of small talk until the food arrived. At one point she raised a hand to smooth her hair. The embroidered cuff fell back on a bracelet of garnets set in silver. He recognized it as one he'd bought for her in Florence long ago. Though he was too unsure of himself to say so now.

He ate the sole too, in deference to her. It was rather good. Though he left most of the spinach. For which he was chided.

"But it's so good for you," she said, with a wife's licence. "Full of iron, and trace elements."

She drank Perrier water, sipping it sparingly.

"I can't go back," he said suddenly. "You know that, don't you."

She nodded.

"No one expects you to go back."

She'd been talking to Seton. He was almost surprised to find how little that mattered.

"Roger thinks he might negotiate an early retirement deal. On health grounds."

"The VC would never wear that." He stared at her. "Would he?"

"Oh, Roger believes he will." Elizabeth looked grave. "A man who bashes an External Examiner? Then there's the sexual harassment of Hilary."

"I kissed her on the cheek. It was an act of charity."

They stared at one another. Then both burst out laughing.

"No, seriously," she went on, "it seems the VC is looking to replace some of the older staff with younger people.`

"*Cheaper* people."

"Naturally."

They sat for a while over their coffee. Talking, it seemed, was easier now. Something had been released.

"You won't get a full pension. What will you do?"

"Well, I don`t think I'd make it as a shepherd."

She smiled.

"I might write a book. There must be lots of men like me trying to relocate their lives."

She smiled, nodded, as he began to sketch out thoughts for a book. How strange they were, and yet how common. These mid-life crises. Whatever it was that happened to men when they reached middle age, it ran deeper than cardigans, slippers. Waking suddenly to a feeling of emptiness. A lack of meaning. *Who am I? What am I doing here?* Then, quite suddenly, the accented voice so clear it might have been uttered in her ear, she heard the words of her own mentor, Leo Goldman. *If you've lost something of value, where might you best look for it? Why – in the most neglected, overgrown part of the garden..*

But it was time for her to catch her train. She went upstairs to the ladies. Meanwhile, he waited for her under the stairwell.

She took an age, as always. He paced about, or stared into the cabinets displaying sporting clothes and Barbour jackets. Then he caught a glimpse of a sienna coat descending the upper stair case, before it was swallowed up in noisy crowd of young people flooding down behind. Then, as the young people scuttled past, Hardman saw his wife. She was standing right under the window, and the sun, streaming through the glass, lit up her hair to a rich corn colour. She was gazing round for him, her face turned aside. Suddenly, with a pang, he saw her as she was at twenty, her head wound round with its coil of yellow hair, oblivious of the tragedies to come. His heart was wrung by an anguish of regret. Just then, Elizabeth spotted him, and smiled, and started down towards him.

It was, he saw, an epiphany of a sort. You had the illumination. And with it, if only for a moment, a sense of what might have been.

Summer

Grey is all theory, green is life's glowing tree

Goethe *Faust*

SEVEN

Out in the fields the lambs looked well enough. Their docked tails were finally dropping off, and for them life was fun. They played, leaped, fought with one another, bounding and rebounding like drops of water from the earth's hot griddle, then having a feed and a sleep, then starting all over again. Watching them, Jack Ashe wondered would they ever be turned out on the moor? Have lambs themselves?

God knows, he muttered, *whether we'll ever get 'em to market..*

The sheep were hungry all the time now, and it was not a good sign. The ewes were short of milk, and it was making for problems. Every time the quad bike entered a field they would lift their heads expectantly, whatever the time of day, in the hope of being fed. They were so ravenous they rushed up, leaving their lambs, every time the troughs were filled.

"An inch o' grass 'ud mek all the difference," the shepherd muttered to himself.

He was out every evening checking for hungry or abandoned lambs. He couldn't rest until he'd made sure each couple was united for the night.

Yet, the work was almost more than he could cope with. Not that he said anything. Each day he was up before dawn, dosing, dipping, bringing down couples that had lambed on the moor for marking and counting, cleaning out the livestock barns, spreading fertilizer on his silage fields. He'd be back for his dinner and tea, and out again the minute he'd eaten. And when, late at night, he came into the kitchen, the skin seemed stretched thinner than ever over the tight, bony face.

"It's too much for one man," Ellen Ashe complained to Alice Clarkson. "Only he won't admit it."

Once, in the early hours, she missed him beside her in the bed. He'll have dropped off in the chair, she thought, and came down to find him still in his heavy boots, bent over the dying fire, his head in his hands.

It stayed with her all the next day. That sight of him alone in the kitchen. She'd always known her love for him had never risen above the average. She went about in a fever of remorse for having failed to love him more.

All that spring and into summer the countryside lay help-less, at the mercy of the epidemic. The authorities, eager for any opportunity to boost morale, now seized on the fact that the number of new cases was no longer rising. It was, said the Min-ister, an encouraging sign. The graph, he said, had now *plateaued out.* Thereafter, he expected to see a fall in the incidence of new cases.

Nothing, though, could obscure the bitter truth. The slaughtermen went about their grisly business. The stench of death continued to sidle through ancient cracks, under doors, down chimneys. The army of hauliers still trundled lorry-loads of carcasses to the mass graves.

For the men and women of the lonely farms, never know-ing where the sickness might strike next, falling further and further into debt with each passing day, there was nothing for it but to hang on through weeks and months that seemed intermi-nable.

Not a few like Ellen Ashe thought wistfully of more fortunate relatives with comfortable lives in nearby towns and villages, with money coming in; thought that they, too, ought to be permitted to enjoy a happier existence.

Next year, she told herself: this time next year. The thought sent shivers through her.

It *had* to be. With four kids to bring up there were no two ways about it. Time and again she'd go through the arguments in her mind. Laid them down one by one. Planks in a rock solid future. They were going to sell up. They were going to live in a dry, properly heated, modern house. There'd be more money, a decent place to live, and a better life for the children. She'd no idea how she was going to bring this about. Sometimes, too, her resolution quailed at the sight of Jack. She felt herself sucked down into his helplessness.

At the same time, she was driven, obscurely, into pushing him towards some sort of crisis that might prove a turning point.

"What are we going to do, Jack, if we can't sell the stores?"

"I don't bloody know," he cried out. "I don't bloody *know* what we're going to do."

By first light he was out with his dogs, gathering as many sheep as he could shear in a day, pushing them down into the dale, herding them into the pens for sorting, the lambs from the ewes. Then he began the mammoth task, hauling each ewe out of the holding pen, stooping over it. He scorned to sit astride a bench. He sheared standing, as his father had done before him.

"You'll be getting in contractors." She took it as a matter of course.

Jack, though, would have none of it.

"I'm getting no one," he told her abruptly.

If he was fiercely present to her, the shepherd's mind was back in the old days, in the old grandeur. Dalehead then would have been full of uncles, aunts and cousins; Swains, Greaves, Wilcocksons, aye, and the Clarksons too, with the trestle tables out in the yard, and plates of ham and eggs after the gathering. There'd be up to a dozen men wielding the shears, others doing the penning and catching, or wrapping fleeces, and the women coming with food and big jugs of tea and orange squash all the hot June day. And at the day's end, with the first stars peeping out, the whole flock would be done and dusted, mothered up, and turned out on the moor. Then the laughter of the men drinking in the yard, the laughter over supper in the big farm kitchen. The plates of ham salad for supper. It were a red-letter day, shearing.

Meanwhile, the sun shone benignly on his labours. Jack Ashe was glad of that. Something, at least, was on his side. His wife, coming out with food and drink, watched him, his singlet covered with grease, mopping his arms and neck with an old towel.

"You're just making a martyr of yourself," she shouted, furiously indignant, above the whine of the shears.

But he affected not to hear, catching hold of another ewe, his hand buried in the fleece of its belly, its neck in the crook of his arm.

She stared bitterly at the bent back, intent on bearing whatever weight the fates heaped on it.

"He'll kill himself," she cried passionately to Hardman, "the way he's going."

She prayed for it to rain. He couldn't shear if it rained.

Next day the sun beat down, remorseless as ever.

If it was hard on the man, it was equally gruelling for the sheep. Brought down at dawn, cut off from their lambs, then packed together, penned all day without food, tormented by the heat, the noise, the terror of rough handling. The dale was filled with the panic of lambs casting about for their despairing, distraught mothers, their little cries flung this way and that. For them, though, after their single day's distress, weeks of peace. Jack Ashe thought of that as he turned them out at dusk, watching the shorn, scraggy bodies trotting nervously away.

Weeks of peace, alone with their lambs, and the larks and curlews.

One evening, after his session with the boy, Hardman lingered in the yard. Took stock of the situation: the fleeces tumbled over the walls, the milling, beldering sheep, the angry mosquito-whine of the shears, the lone man dragging himself to his labour's end. He would do it, since it had to be done. He would stick it out to the end.

Troubled, he set off back along the track.

The next day he rose early. By seven he was at Dalehead. He went straight to the pens. There was the shepherd in his soiled singlet, bent over a ewe, just as he'd been the night before. He might never have shifted.

"Can I help?" shouted Hardman. And stood his ground, though the man looked up, so fierce, so hostile.

"Aye," he said, at length. "I suppose you'll do as well as anybody."

Though that was scarcely true, for the work was backbreaking. And the man ill-suited to it, laying hold of sheep in the pen, lifting, lugging them to the shearer, then rolling the fleeces, cramming as much as he could get into the sacks. As the day wore on each beast grew heavier. The man's arms were racked from the hauling they'd received, his finger-ends sore, bleeding. He sucked at nails, knuckles. His wrist began to ache from forcing the wools into the sacks. By the afternoon, it was painful and swollen. Another hour or two, and he had to pack it in. He could only do so much.

Jack Ashe worked on alone. At the day's end he was bone-weary. Exhausted, as he'd never been before. He had barely strength enough to eat the food she set before him. Tight-lipped, she took off his boots. Got him up the stairs to bed. She wouldn't let him sleep in the chair.

He was up again before dawn, dragging himself into another day. She heard the boisterous greeting of the dogs in the yard. They never grew weary.

The shepherd, though, had given up trying to cope with his fatigue. The woman's heart stirred uneasily at the change coming over him, that took the form of a strange indifference to everything. Only some blind mechanical persistence, something that might have been of a piece with the whine of the motor, kept the hand locked to the shears travelling to and fro along the belly of a ewe, kept him going.

Hardman had a sense of him held together by sheer momentum, as if some rhythm in the cycles he'd served all his life were carrying Jack Ashe onward. His heart went out to the stooping figure. But there was nothing he could say.

Ellen Ashe, though, said plenty. She couldn't talk to him, but she complained bitterly to Alice Clarkson.

"He's doing it on purpose," she protested. "He'll drive himself into the ground just to spite the rest of us."

That night Maurice Clarkson came up the track. He went straight to the pens. He didn't come to the house. Minutes later Ellen Ashe saw him striding back along the track.

What passed between the two men she never knew. But next day two of the big Clarkson lads turned up at the pens. She saw them moving among the ewes.

Thank God he'd seen sense at last.

*

There were many like the Ashes, dragging on in a kind of twilight. Spring had come and gone, May given place to June, and still no sign appeared of any slackening of the epidemic. The long, inviting days of summer found no takers. Crags were devoid of climbers, fairs and shows were cancelled, the ramblers and the race-goers stayed at home. In the tourist districts, where hotels and shops had seen no trade for months, many businesses seemed likely to go to the wall. It had become a land of empty hills, deserted villages.

Much of the south and east of the country had so far gone unscathed. Here, especially, the authorities were berated for depriving people of their sports and pastimes. They now declared themselves determined to get things moving again. In those areas declared free from infection, the Minister now sanctioned the removal of many of the restrictions governing access to the countryside.

With the lifting of the footpath ban, Hardman was able to

revive his old walk, via Win Hill, to the *Bridge*. Late one after-noon he crossed the footbridge over the Ashop, and set off up the track mounting the hill in front, rejoicing in the open space around him, the infinite reach of sky. Soon he could see the craggy edge of the knoll coming in on the right. He continued on his way, a gradual climb mounting the low ridge that runs on to Win Hill. His intention was to go up over Bamford moor to Stanage, then south along the edge to the Burbage valley. First, though, he would call in at the pub.

Half-a-dozen tables with gaily coloured parasols had been set, bistro-fashion, outside the Bridge, ready for the returning visitors. Hardman, though, was the first that evening. He found the landlord's brother behind the bar.

"You'll soon be busy again," said Hardman.

"The mountain rescue? Aye, I expect so. Over a hundred call-outs last year, not counting animals."

"Walkers, mostly?"

"Oh, we get all sorts. Walkers, climbers, boulderers, moun-tain bikers, paragliders. You name it, we fetch 'em off. Last July we had to use a boat for a woman who'd fallen into the reservoir at Fairholme. This year, though, it's been a struggle finding places to train."

Hardman enjoyed chatting to Eric Smith. He was drawn to the other man because he was a mountaineer. The talk turned, as it invariably did on these occasions, to tales of crags and climb-ers, and the controversies of thirty years before, the use of bolts, the pre-placing of runners, and prior-inspections on a top-rope. Most sacrilegious of all, the chipping of holds on gritstone. Eric Smith recalled the heatwave of '75. And the great climbs put up in what had been a golden summer.

So it went on, for the older man a vicarious reconnection which revived, if only fleetingly, the old illusion of a life apart, the real thing, in comparison with which normal life seemed somehow inauthentic.

"It was my last summer, '75." He sipped his beer reflectively.

"Didn't you miss it?"

Hardman smiled.

"The first fine days of spring? Whenever the forecast talked of snow on northern hills? Yes, I missed it. I missed the Alps especially."

He didn't add what now seemed to him a gratuitous abuse: that while she was striving to keep another child alive in her womb, he should be putting his own life on the line.

"It was the Alpine climbing frightened her. We had a friend killed in the Alps. We were in Wales at the time. We heard about it on the news. Two British climbers killed on Mont Blanc. *I hope Jacko's OK*, she said. But of course he wasn't. That really shook her up. Then, six months later, I fell down Central Gully."

The mountain man was thinking you didn't get to any kind of age, and not have friends killed.

He pulled a pint for a newcomer, before shooting a speculative, sideways look at Tony Hardman.

"D' you fancy getting out..?"

"Out where?"

"I were thinking o' Stanage."

Hardman shook his head.

"After all this time? I wouldn't know how."

Somewhat shamefacedly, he owned up to his miserable showing on Bamford Edge.

"I wouldn't worry about that. You just need to ease yourself back into it." He took Hardman's empty glass. "You never know," he added, with a grin as he put it the sink. "You might surprise yourself."

Evening was advancing as Hardman set off over Bamford Moor, the westering sun lingering on the fresh green bracken, leaving soft coves of shadow in the folds of the hills. He was troubled again by the burden of memory, the *strangeness* of events that might have been acted out in another life, the experiences of a self without substance, a self who no longer existed. Or else they were playing back through the memory circuits of a different person, who understood them differently. He was no longer able to separate those days from the shadow that had fallen over them: the troubled years after he'd given up climbing, the ambivalence of a heart struggling to free itself from old allurements, all the while cherishing what it sought to cast away; his longing, amid the blows that befell them both, for that area of tension and release which had been accessible to him. But not to her.

He knew now that he wasn't free. That he'd never been free. That he was answerable to something other than himself. And he knew this now because of the different person he'd become.

He crossed a charred patch of burnt heather, the dead wood like bleached bone fragments, the shards crackling under his boots. The moor rolled away through dreary flushes of sedge and sphagnum, a line of butts dropping towards Jervis Clough, then rose, steeper and steeper, past beds of heather and bracken, jumbles of boulders, to a long rock wall, like a battlement on the horizon, sweeping away south-east, rising, falling, as far as the eye could follow. *I were thinking o' Stanage..* Eric's offer, though, had been made to some other man, a man with an appetite, an enthusiasm that knew nothing of anguish, heartbreak. A man without a shadow. *Go climbing, Eric? I'd love to..* Yet how absurd. No, he'd lived too long among the flat-earthers. Besides, what was it Herzog said? *There are other Annapurnas in the lives of men.*

He came at last to the final rocks of Stanage, and began the tramp down over the moor to the road to Ringinglow. The heat of the day had thrown an amber haze over the western horizon. The setting sun, its brightness fading, was dipping into the haze, leaving the furthest hills in folds ranging from rich mahogany to dark chocolate. Below him, beyond the bridge over the brook, lay the Burbage valley, a wide shallow bowl in the heather moorland, with the clean-cut gritstone edge of small walls and buttresses standing up amid patches of stunted oak, catching the last of the light. Below the edge the pale line of the path curved away to the Fox House, and the Sheffield road.

The last of the climbers were packing gear into their cars, as Hardman set off along the path. He was hoping to eat at the Fox House, before catching the last train at Grindleford, and walking back from Hope. Outlined against the sky, a lone man was climbing an arête. A man perhaps of his own age. Reaching up, a garment of some kind knotted about his shoulders, he moved with a slow, easy grace, as if savouring each move. Hardman didn't know what route it was. How hard, how easy. Only that the man was climbing joyfully, though the light had dwindled to a dying glow, climbing with a child's simplicity – yes, the persistence of a child unable to tear himself away from a perfect day.

The lone man hauled out at the top, and vanished into his happiness.

Suddenly, the man below was filled with a hunger of desire, an eagerness to feel the strong pull of muscles, the body rising as power surged through arms and shoulders. Doing it because you can.

Was it true? Had he lived too long among the flat-earthers? What was it Eric said? *You might surprise yourself.*

As he continued along the path he began to dream of climbing in Wales again. Not, as he'd thought, to start all over again, but to complete the experience, free of the burden of youth, the egotism, the urge to cut a figure. Long easy climbs in the sun, free of false pride, free to pull on a runner, or ask for a tight rope, free to accept one's limitations without regret, or hopeless longing, with joy in the here and now as the route unreels, the upward thrust of rock, the sharp edge of a flake, the stipple of lichen on granite, the glitter of quartz, a clump of heather as one pulled up past a ledge, the flask of tea, that *post-facto* savouring, move for move, stretched on a slab of warm rock. Benevolence in all things.

It struck him then that maybe the core experience could only infuse a soul swept clean of human junk. A child, maybe, might experience its life like that. That simple catching at happiness. Kissing the joy as it flies.

For a while he contemplated what it might mean to live that life, and the reality. The preoccupation with one's own performance, the urge to prove oneself, the self-recrimination, the taint of fear, the shame of backing off, the endless cycle of self-testing. A life recreating itself from day to day, as the climbs get harder and harder. The list of ticks in a guidebook. The unticked routes in one's head. *Spectre.. Sickle.. Ivy Sepulchre.. Cenotaph Corner.. Cemetery Gates..*

Perhaps only in old age might one rid oneself of the tangles of a man. Get down to the bare essentials.

That thought brought to mind an image seen years before on a visit to Chatsworth. A Rembrandt self-portrait. He'd passed through room after room, past walls thronged with allegorical kings, warriors, saints on ceilings, wood carved to look like feathers, or dead flesh. He'd stared at pictures of unsmiling dukes and marquises, almost all of them clutching something, fingering a coin, a roll of parchment, or dressed up in some uniform, each one, it struck him, gazing at *himself* in one guise or another.

Then, in a gallery jam-packed with gods and heroes, the male nude gleaming as no flesh ever gleamed, chiselled, buffed to an icy finish, he'd come across a portrait of the thing itself. Flesh sagging. Swollen, arthritic hands crooked together. Not easy to see properly. Badly hung, so that the glass picked up reflections from other things in the room. And yet the anti-image of those things. It contradicted every *thing* in the grand *palazzo.* A jewel gleamed in the turban. A jewelled clasp fastened the furred gown. But the eyes pretended nothing. They were too old, too weary to be taken in by anything there. Red rimmed, watery, they seemed to challenge whoever looked to see, to contemplate the truth of a man..

Wearying of his own introspection, in chastened mood, he quickened his pace to where the lights of the Fox House beckoned. *There are things that are important beyond all this fiddle..* A truth transcending the self-adventuring of climbing. Yet climbing, too, had a place for the poet's truth: *..the raw material in all its rawness.*

Even so, she was right. Old Marianne Moore was right. For Hardman, too, there was something now that mattered more.

She had begun to figure in his dreams, appearing quite unexpectedly, yet with stunning conviction. Was it Elizabeth of the photograph? Elizabeth as she was now? He didn't know. He never saw her. All the same, he knew it was her. They were travelling somewhere. He was driving, her hand resting on his thigh. Or else they were going together into some strange place. She must have been cold, for she shuddered suddenly, and pressed against him. He accepted her presence as further evidence of the debatable territory they were negotiating together, drifting towards whatever lay in store.

It would be three months before he saw her again. That thought had driven him back home, fussing round as she prepared for her trip to the States. She was flying to Seattle. She was so excited. She talked of nothing else. The wonderful campus overlooking Puget Sound. The rich mix of staff and students. Who she would see, what she would do. What a progressive place it was. How much English universities might learn from Northwestern Pacific. Its stress on personal engagement, on linking theory with practice, understanding abstract ideas by applying them to real-life situations, the very things Elizabeth avoided, in order to protect herself from living. Hardman had heard it all before. Above all, how good it would be to see Leo again..

Hardman remembered Leo Goldman. The domed skull with its sandy tufts, the rimless glasses, the speculative gaze. What was it with shrinks, he wondered, that made you feel so bloody uncomfortable in their presence.

He had driven her to the airport. Pushed her luggage down interminable tunnels.

She wouldn't have him wait until her flight was called.

"Off you go," she said.

She bent forward, held him a moment, kissed his cheek.

"Don't forget. You're to see Roger on the 23rd..."

He felt vaguely comforted by the companionable solicitude a marriage brought.

"Do be nice to him. Just one more effort, then it's over."

At the exit he turned to wave, but she was already burrowing into her schedule.

It was evening when he crossed over into Derbyshire. With Elizabeth gone there was nothing to keep him at home. At Slackhall he turned aside from the Sheffield road, and took the yellow lane to Sparrowpit, threading criss-crossing dry-stone walls, dazzling white and throwing lengthening shadows in the long, low sun. The fine weather had brought the tourists out in force. He passed a party of walkers toiling up the Winnats. The trippers were back again on the narrow streets of Castleton, and the cycling clubs, bowling down the road to Hope. Outside the *Bridge* drinkers lounged over their beer in the evening sun.

He stopped the car in front of the track, and got out to unlock the gate, stepping over the soiled straw mattress, now crushed flat. The tin tray, he noticed, was dry. Had not been filled for some time.

It was cool inside the house. Little of the sun's warmth

ever penetrated the thick stone walls.

Too tired to cook a proper meal, he scrambled some eggs, and ate them in the kitchen. Then he took his bottle of wine, and went outside to sit in the soft, warm summer dusk, watching the last play of light, high on the rim of the Kinder plateau, catching the craggy edge of Crookstone Knoll as the shadows gathered in the steep declivities of Blackden Brook, falling in folds and ripples among the knolls and hollows of Ashop Moor.

There was peace and silence in the little yard. A faint fragrance came to him from spikes of buddleia bending from a wall. A bat swooped in silent figures of eight over the washhouse roof.

He lingered over his wine while the first stars came out, and the night changed from dusk to dark.

Across the valley the owls had begun to call down in the Woodlands.

> An owl's cry, he remembered, *a most melancholy cry,*
> *Shaken out long and clear upon the hill..*

One August, not long after they were married, they'd pitched a tent up in the dark woods above Hollows Farm, and made love under a shower of shooting stars falling through the summer night, and fell asleep listening to the owls. That selfsame, shivering *vibrato.* Her life now was filled with busy-ness of one kind or another. Courses, lectures, book clubs, encounter groups, new diets, new therapies.. For all her activism she seemed to him like one of Plato's cave-dwellers, sitting with her back to the light, trying to figure out the significance of whatever shadows the flickering fire threw on the walls. Shadows were more satisfying than substance. Or else substance was all a shadow play to her.

Surely there must be, if only as a possibility, a place in each of our lives where we make contact with the world in which we really live. It might be a gritstone crag? A remote farm buried on a moor? Best of all, he thought, another human being..

Now, as the epidemic showed no sign of slackening, a kind of madness, as it seemed to many, ran riot through the land. As well as infected animals, and those on neighbouring farms, all those animals on holdings considered to have had close contact with infected premises were scheduled for slaughter.

A reservoir of blood flooded the fields and stockyards of the north country. Flock after flock, yet never flocks enough to stop the spread of the sickness. Naturally, it was not possible to take into account individual cases of hardship. The authorities, fearful of creating a precedent which might then be urged against them in a court of law, had set their faces against anything that might smack of favouritism, or special treatment. In all this carnage, perhaps only one change had taken place, and that was in the slaughterers themselves who, if they were ever conscious of a certain numbness stiffening around them as they went about their business, might have been glad of it, for it made their task less burdensome. Hardened now to tears, entreaties, they did what they had to do with a blankness that rendered them inaccessible even to the most heart-rending situations, as in the case of a widow who, with five pet sheep, had barricaded herself in the living room of her bungalow, cowering behind the furniture while they battered at her door. Within minutes, they had gained entry and the sheep lay dead.

Meanwhile, fuelled with tonnes of coal, diesel oil, straw and railway sleepers, the pyres continued to burn. An oily, foul-smelling smoke hung low upon over the land. These effluvia, the public was assured, though certainly unpleasant, were not in the least harmful to human health.

For many in the country districts their sense of utter help-lessness before whatever the future held in store had shaken them to the core. There were many like Jack Ashe who had, at the outset, given it six months, meanwhile suffering in anticipation the long ordeal, steeling themselves to endure the dread of what they might find on their daily round. There were times, though, watching TV, hearing someone on the radio, chatting to a neighbour over the phone, when it was borne in upon him that there was no reason why the epidemic shouldn't drag on for a year or more, with the autumn sales cancelled, no money coming in, having to buy in more and more food, borrowing to feed animals he couldn't sell. At such moments he could see no escape from the morass into which he was plunging deeper and deeper every day. Pointless to try to think of a way out, since there was no way out. Instead, he immersed himself as best he could in the tasks that had sustained him all his life, dipping, drenching, dehorning the new calves, making hay when it was possible to make hay. And he cut himself off from his wife.

Ellen Ashe, though, shivered at the change that had come over him.

"He's lost all interest," she told Hardman. "He doesn't watch the news. He couldn't tell you whether the number of cases is going up, or going down."

As he went silently to his work each day, she was haunted by thoughts of the farmer's wife who'd gone looking for her husband, and found him hanging in the barn. *He wasn't well,* a neighbour told the paper. *He'd not been well for a while. He needed to get out and see the family. But o' course, he couldn't..*

Something, anything, she saw, might tip a man like Jack over the edge.

In her anxiety she unburdened herself to Evelyn, her sister-in-law.

The voice that came back down the phone spoke the very words she longed to hear.

"I don't know why you don't sell up," said Evelyn, without hesitation. "You must be sitting on a small fortune, for the house alone."

"He says it's selling up your history."

"You can't eat history, Ellen. It's like May says. Times change, and folk have to change with 'em."

A breath of fresh air, it seemed, blowing through the musty barn of her marriage.

She felt encouraged enough to have another go at Jack. Surely, she thought, he must see sense at last. There were times when she convinced herself he was almost half-persuaded, when she sensed the relief dawning in him at the thought of throwing off the burden.

Then, at other times, he just dug in his heels.

"There's generations o' work gone into building up this farm," he told her irritably. "You can't let down your forebears."

Then there was friction as she flew at him.

"And what about us? What about letting down your family?"

Hardman arrived once at the kitchen door at the tail-end of a bitter exchange.

"*Poor!* We're not *poor*. If you've got a house – even if it's only four walls an' a roof – if you've got work to do, and enough food to put in your belly, you're not poor."

"Oh yes, work and stable, stable and work – that's you all over.."

As the days passed he became more and more concerned for what was happening at Dalehead. Often, now, with a foreboding, as if he were present at some sombre drama in the making. He saw that this calamity, which had destroyed so many others, brought more than ruin to its victims. It induced them to create their own suffering. The sickness was infecting human hearts.

*

There were members of Hardman's university for whom the Department of Humanities had acquired somewhat of a raffish character, the intellectual equivalent of a rather seedy drinking club or lap-dancing den. Engineers brought up on the nuts and bolts of their subject, whose professional competence had proved itself in the construction of bridges that had stood the test of time, and tunnels that met in the middle, were inclined to look askance at post-modernist colleagues who seemed unclear as to whether or not there was such a thing as truth, or a real world existing independently of human categories of thought and language.

But cross-cultural misconceptions are no strangers to academic life, a truth not infrequently observed by Professor Seton. Among the senior members of the university he was something of an isolated figure.

A beached whale, according to the Pro Vice-Chancellor. The waning of the leftist cause had left him stranded.

The fact that his department remained a breeding ground for ideas which failed to thrive at less rarefied altitudes attracted a fair share of uncomprehending ridicule. No one, though, would have questioned his achievements. If the truth were told, most of his colleagues were slightly in awe of Dr Seton. Prodigiously well-read, blessed with a phenomenal memory, he was beyond question the most distinguished member of his department. His list of publications far exceeded those of anyone else. His reputation in his own field was second to none. Moreover, he enjoyed that flourishing extramural career, writing for the papers, appearing regularly on the BBC, that most academics achieve only in their dreams.

He remained, for all that, a man not entirely sure within himself. The esteem of his colleagues, the respect in which he was held, had done little to relieve a certain dissatisfaction, reflected in the frown lines of a face seemingly at odds with a problem never quite resolved.

He waited now, working through the pages of a doctoral thesis, occasionally making notes on a pad at his side, every now and then glancing up at the clock on the wall above his desk. He was not looking forward to this interview. He was never at his ease with Hardman, could never be in the other's presence without that *frisson* of unease that passes between men who dislike one another for no particular reason.

The discomfort was entirely mutual. The man climbing the stair was remembering, with no great confidence as to his ability to fulfil it, his wife's instruction: *Do be nice to him..*

He found his professor sitting in an armchair, next to a low table stacked with books for review. He got to his feet on seeing Hardman.

"Tony," he exclaimed, with a show of brightness, indicating a chair.

He's as embarrassed as I am, thought Hardman.

Seton came straight to the point.

"As Lizzie has probably explained, we've managed to persuade the VC to agree to early retirement." His voice suggested a tricky negotiation skilfully handled. "On health grounds," he added. He didn't specify the details.

He didn't need to. Hardman pictured the scene with the VC, a vain, fussy little man dwarfed by his own horn-rimmed glasses, as Seton laid out the sorry facts of a valued colleague's breakdown – the growing isolation, the assault on an external examiner, the sexual harassment of a female member of staff – the horn-rimmed gaze growing more owlish by the minute.

Meanwhile, the Scots voice was droning on, explaining the terms of what he called 'the package'.

" ..though of course none of this can take effect until Christmas, for contractual reasons. Naturally, you'll be on sick leave until the actual date of your retirement."

He's enjoying this, thought Hardman, with a flash of the old resentment. *He always did enjoy the role of patron. Collections for cooks and cleaners, whip-rounds for this and that..*

He turned his head aside to stare out of the window, revolted by his own sourness. It was *true.* This place *had* damaged his health.

Meanwhile, Seton was obviously looking to bring the interview to a close.

So the two men came at last to a final exchange of courtesies.

"I hope we'll still see something of you, Tony."

They stood up to shake hands.

"Do keep in touch."

"I will."

Phoney to the last.

At the end of the month he returned to the university for the last time to clear his room. First, though, he paid a visit to the Finance Office. Dr Cross, the Bursar, had Hardman's file ready and waiting on the desk when he arrived. This disclosure of the glad tidings of the Universities Superannuation Scheme, the lump sum, the monthly income, the annual increment, was the part of his job he most enjoyed, and he performed it with the genial air of a family solicitor revealing the details of an agreeable bequest. A sharp-featured man with wings of white hair swept back behind each ear, he peered through his glasses at this latest beneficiary, before launching into an explanation of the figures printed on the sheet in front of him.

"You'll receive your full salary until the end of December," he explained, "so your pension will kick in at the end of January. And of course you'll get your lump sum. Naturally, it won't be what you would have received had you served the whole of your sentence."

Dr Cross grinned engagingly. A waggish fellow, he liked to affect envy of chaps who'd soon be living the life of Riley: the winter cruise, the holiday home in Spain, lots of golf..

Hardman smiled.

"I don't play golf."

"Pity. Never mind. I dare say you've got all sorts of plans."

"Not really."

It struck him suddenly, shouldn't he have plans? He hadn't got *any* plans.

He left the office with the Bursar's parting shot, following him through the door.

"Take up golf."

He found his room much as he'd left it, six months earlier. The shelves of books and box files. The board with its yellowing memos. His gown hanging behind the door. The graffiti, though, had been wiped, none too well, from the wall, leaving behind a smeary film of chalk.

Two or three plastic cups, left over from the last tutorial. Obviously someone had been using the room.

Motes of dust hung in the sunlight streaming through the windows. There was a fug of pipe tobacco. Fogg, presumably. He was forever scratching about inside his pipe.

Pulling open a drawer of his desk, he began turning out the contents: notebooks, old memo pads, pencil stubs, a penknife, a ballpoint pen, rubbers, boxes of paperclips, drawing pins, elastic bands, the detritus of office life.

He came across a postcard: *Don't you wish you were here? Love and hugs, Jenny*

Who was Jenny? Turning it over, he saw a picture of Corfu.

What, he wondered, would they make here of Jack and Ellen Ashe. What would they say, the colleagues? That they were gendered by patriarchy, constrained by kinship, fabricated by social class, possessed by property, uttered by the limits of their language, their lives scripted by historical necessity, the creatures of processes which stood over and against men and women, and pushed them around like so many matchsticks, no, not even continuing human selves, but merely bundles of local experiences and responses, of lights flashing in the brain.

Even now he could see, as if he were actually present, Perry Wiseman's puzzled expression: *No, I don't see why you should want to insist on the primacy of the individual human subject.*

He stared at the flaking breeze-blocks, smeared with the dust of old inscriptions.

Rotten and rotting others..

He saw then that the slogans were a projection of his own sickness, his own self-hatred. He'd projected that hatred on to his colleagues, who were, in their follies and delusions, their emptiness and trivia, no better and no worse than other human beings.

Sighing, he began the clear-out. He stripped the memos from the notice board. He emptied the filing cabinet, tipped the contents of the box-files into a bin bag. The books he packed into his rucksack. Opening the penknife he began picking at the screws to prize his nameplate from the door. Finally, he took his gown from behind the door, bundled it up, and slung it in the bin.

When all was done he looked around at the empty shelves, the filing cabinet with its yawning jaws, the smeary wall. He had been here for more than twenty years. He had spend his life in that which least concerned life, cooped up in this room, harbouring his sickness.

He sat for a while, surrounded by his bin bags, drawing in with each breath of stale air a sense of the chill, the darkness of a barren life, a sense of the void that had him reaching out instinctively for his wife.

EIGHT

It was a cold, grey day, with spits of rain appearing on the windscreen as the Ashes drove away from Heathy Lea. They'd Jackie and the twins at Alice Clarkson's. Alice never minded, she said, looking after the little ones. She was a good sort.

The boy, though, sat uneasily in the back of the car. He knew something was up, but he didn't know what.

"I've told you. We're going to your Auntie May's."

That was a shrewd idea of Evelyn's, thought Ellen Ashe. Meeting at May's. Jack was never at his ease with May. She could always get the better of him. Yes. And what was more, she was a survivor. Running that pub on her own after her Billy left her.

Yes, she thought, as she settled back in her seat. If anyone could take Jack by the scruff, it was May.

They trundled through Bamford, past the *Angler's* and the *Marquis*, rattling on along the wide Hope valley towards Hathersage. No one spoke. His dad hadn't spoken to anyone for days. But the boy turned his mind away as he always did when there was trouble. Besides, he was going to Eyam. He looked forward to that. He loved the *Eyre Arms*, the low, dark passages, the tiny bar where the big, easy-going quarrymen pulled his leg and spoilt him, the long lounge, full of swords and old long-barrelled guns. The lounge was where Jacky lived. *You put your fingers anywhere near that cage*, hissed his Auntie May, *an' 'e'll 'ave 'em.* While Jacky his head on one side, swivelling a yellow eye, as if to say, *I will an' all.. I will an' all.* He would, too.

Robert Eyre of Highlow built a house for each of his seven sons, he recited softly in his head. *Eyre* because the first of the Eyres had pulled off the king's helmet and given him the air he breathed. His whole leg got chopped off in the battle. That severed leg was still the crest of all the Eyres. It hung in the coat-of-arms above the door of the pub. An armoured leg chopped off at the hip. His mam had been an Eyre before she married his dad. Eyres were in his blood. Places he passed on days out grew darker, more resonant, for their presence: the grey lady of Highlow.. the shape that walked at Moorseats under the yews..

They kneel in brass in Hathersage church, Robert and Joan Eyre and their fourteen children, Jane Eyre, Elizabeth Eyre, born before Columbus sailed, still kneeling together.

That afternoon, the lounge at the *Eyre Arms* had been closed for the occasion. Lamps were lit at one end of the long, low room. A good fire burning in the grate. It was cold for the time of year. Cold or not, a good fire, in May's estimation, was an indispensible element of hospitality. The firelight, flickering in at shadowy nooks and corners, lit on armouries of rusty blades and glimmering barrels: Aladdin's Caves of brass and copper; fire-tongs, scuttles, ornamental plaques, trays and trinkets, as well as plates, toby jugs, china cottages and many other curiosities embellishing dressers, shelves and walls.

Fixed to the wall above the fireplace was a notice: EVERYTHING IN THIS ROOM IS FOR SALE. Everything, that was, except Jacky, a mynah bird on whom the gaunt Aunt May lavished her affection.

I'm a bugger I'm a bugger I'm a bugger, he boasted brassily, and swaggered on his perch.

"I wonder folk don't take offence at that bird," Evelyn told its owner.

"Oh, they do," said her sister dryly. "That's why they come."

She was the spitting-image of Jack Ashe. Dour, unsmiling, with the same thin ginger hair and bony masculine face, she might have been her brother's double. Yet the *Eyre Arms* was celebrated for the warmth of its welcome. In summer coachloads sat down to jumbo plates of cod and chips, or Aunt May's ham and eggs, with rings of pineapple and real field mushrooms.

Now, though, the room was empty, but for the family, gathered at two tables drawn together.

They had eaten a meal together, and the womenfolk, at least, were now ready to get down to business. The boy was stuck away in a corner with lemonade and a packet of crisps.

"Look at your book," Ellen Ashe instructed. She was a bag of nerves. It would be a crucial afternoon for her. *Grainfoot's been passed down from generation to generation*, she'd heard Jack's cousin Arthur saying to their Annie. *I wouldn't want to be the one as gives it all up.* At least she could count on Jack's sisters. Yes, she thought, thankful for those gaunt, capable women. Not much to look at, any of 'em. Three scrawny ginger toms. But they'd got all their chairs at home. Twenty years stuck up at Dalehead had seen to that. Not one of 'em had married a farmer.

It had to work. With four kids to bring up there were no two ways about it. And yet it frightened her beyond telling, the giant upheaval that was throwing them forward into some new form of life. And yet she knew she must put her trust in it, nourish it, help it on its way.

For a while the boy did some of the puzzles in his book, joining dots, and so forth. The men, under compulsion from their wives, now awkward, ill at ease, kicking around in sparse exchanges a desultory conversation about jobs and houses, had the air of relatives got together for a funeral.

"I dare say there'd be plenty of interest," Evelyn's Alan said eventually.

"Aye, well, it's a good time to buy," observed Arthur Greaves gloomily, filling his pipe. "The price o' land's less than three-quarters of what it were four year ago."

The conversation flagged a little after that. Gradually, though, the parties joined forces to present those rosier prospects a man contemplating the loss of his livelihood might wish to hear.

"A farm can be a good buy for someone in business," declared Evelyn. "They can use it to offset their tax problems," she added vaguely.

"Aye, to make a loss," put in her cousin Arthur.

Evelyn's Alan, though, ignored this sniping from the sidelines.

"That's right," he said supportively. "You might get someone from the south buying it as a single lot, turning the house into a holiday home, and letting the land to the Clarksons."

"We know Maurice Clarkson's looking to expand," said Ellen Ashe cautiously, climbing aboard the bandwagon. "He could take over the quotas and some of the stock."

Her husband, seemingly listening to what was being said, had withdrawn so far as to be spoken about as if he were no longer present.

"Aye, I dare say it'll put money in his pocket, but what will he do?"

"No reason why he shouldn't carry on doin' what's he doing now. As a journeyman."

Are y'all right, ma ducky, chipped in Jacky cheerfully from time to time.

The boy, intent on tracing his way out of a maze, heard only a murmur of voices in which that of his Auntie May grated harsher than the rest.

"You can't live off the scenery, Jack. And sheep won't pay the bills if the prices you're getting are less than what you got twenty years ago."

"We're not getting anything at present," grumbled Arthur. "And I don't know when we will. The wool's worth nothing. The Russians used to buy up all the sheepskins. Now that's gone."

Are y'all right ma ducky..

But the boy had slipped away to be with the quarrymen. Every day, after the shift, they came up with the dust thick on them to the pubs of Eyam. They climbed out of their roaring, blinding hole in the hill, filled with the din of crushers, mixers, drills, compressors, the revving din of heavy-engined trucks, to sink down in the cool dim bars, and slake lime-dusty throats, and talk. He loved to hear them talk. He'd hang about the passage, or if Mick took a turn behind the bar, slip in and hover there, half out of sight. He loved the rough, lively voices, the clink of glasses, the drugged, smoky air.

Mick drank a lot. *To wesh down t'dust*, he used to say, with a wink. He was a big, blond man with sharp blue eyes, and a rough blurry face. His working life had been a long affair with limestone. It had given him, as well as his mortary, roughcast looks, a kind of reverence for the rock. *It's nowhere thicker than it is here*, he liked to tell the boy. *Six thousand feet of it just under where you're standing now. There's limestone under your dad's place too. Aye, deep down under Blakelow.* He was a shot-firer. A prince of the quarries. The one who stemmed the holes for blasting, set in place the long, corded fuse packed round with gelignite and layers of powdered limestone. He preferred a fuse. You could use an electric starter to blast it off but Mick wouldn't touch 'em.

"Don't they work?" asked the boy.

"Oh aye, they work," the man said darkly. While the tiny bar rocked with a deep, grim laughter that was like the rumbling of falling rocks.

"They work too bloody well. Owt can set 'em off. A lad wi' one of them model aeroplanes. A mobile phone. Some bugger rings up his girl friend an' up she goes."

Mick had lost a mate once, killed like that.

"We picked up what we could find, like. Put it in a plastic sheet. Ah don't know to this day whether we picked up all on 'im."

The boy gazed in wonder at the big hand pulling a pint. *What would it weigh – a leg – a head?* But it was just an ordinary man's hand, with a fag clamped between thick, yellowy fingers, pulling a pint.

"Hey, you can do th' glasses. You like doin' that."

There was an automatic glass-washer below the bar. You pushed a glass down over the brush, and it swizzled round inside the glass. He did that for a while, collecting the glasses, emptying out the slops. Mick was wiping tables, emptying ashtrays into the fire.

After a while his Auntie May came along behind the bar.

"Here you are, don't go spoiling your tea," she said, as she put another packet of crisps down on the sink beside him. "And don't you break them glasses."

He knew Mick was fucking his Auntie May. It didn't interest him much. But from the way his mam and dad talked sometimes, he'd guessed that's what it was. He'd seen a couple doing it once not far from the road. He'd come over the ridge from Oyster Clough, and there they were, the man on top of the woman. He couldn't see *her* properly. Just the top of a head. Hair spread out over the rug. But he'd guessed that's what they were doing. Fucking. Just then the man had lifted up a hot, red face. Two glaring eyes.

He went away. Minutes later, he'd crept back through the bracken, soft as a fox, to watch. But they were gone.

Now, as he watched the bristly brush swirling round inside the glass, foaming in its mass of lather, he tried to imagine his Auntie May stretched out like that, with Mick on top of her. It didn't seem likely. But that's what it was. Mick was always here, when he wasn't down at the quarry, working behind the bar, looking after the cellar. But he didn't live here. He lived in Water Lane.

He lifted a glass, and the whirling noise subsided.

"Why don't you live here all t' time?" he said suddenly. He didn't look at the man.

"What, look after a pub?" said Mick scornfully. "Ah'm a

shot-firer, not an alehouse keeper. Besides, Ah'd drink all t' profits." And winked.

But the boy, repelled, had wandered off with his crisps, back along the bar to the lounge. He peered in surreptitiously. Tense, silent, Ashes and in-laws sat stiff, apart. Only smoke drifted in the air above them, drifting above the tables, cluttered now with pint pots, bottles, glasses of shorts. His eyes went to his mam and dad, but they looked no different from the other faces there. The aunts and uncles. Together, and yet somehow separate.

"We get by," his dad said. "We keep going."

There was in the man's voice a defensive note the boy had never heard before.

"An awful lot of folk just keep going," said his Aunt Evelyn. "They're struggling, and it's constantly on their minds. In the end it makes them ill. And the children suffer too."

In the bar behind him Mick's voice rang distantly above the babble of voices, the clatter of boots in the passage: "Come along now, lads, please.."

"Now just you listen to me, Jack. I won't say Time's a healer 'cause I don't believe it is. But life has to go on. You've got two choices. You can mope away as y'are doin' now, or you can mek th' best of a bad job and cut your losses."

May's voice, flat, final, stated what they all knew to be the truth.

In the hard, uncompromising silence that followed no one looked at Jack Ashe. They looked away, stared at their nails, studied their drinks or cigarettes. Only the boy stared at the closed, shut-off face of his dad, backed up against a wall.

"What's goin' on?" But no one seemed to hear.

"It's the children you have to think about, Jack," said his Auntie Anne. "What sort of a life will it be for them?"

He looked from one to the other. But no one paid him any attention.

"What's goin' on?"

Bewildered, he turned to find Mick standing behind him.

"Don't you worry. I reckon your dad'll get plenty o' work, shepherdin', wallin'. The Peak Park are allus lookin' for good wallers.."

Kindly, reassuring, the big man saw only the confusion written over the boy's face. The lad had no idea. He didn't know.

NINE

Now, with his bridges burnt behind him, Hardman felt exposed. He was missing Elizabeth. He'd had a couple of phone-calls, bright, impersonal. Leo was waiting for her at the airport. He sent his regards. She thought she might sign up for a course on Buddhist Psychotherapy when she'd finished teaching. He still dreamt about her. He didn't know what it meant, yet his heart told him that in it there was a truth to be embraced not rooted in his failures, or in the past. Yet it troubled him that he never saw her face.

Although he had his laptop with him, e-mail lacked the intimacy he felt in need of, the sense of physical connection that came with handwriting. He told her about his dream. They were going somewhere together. He was driving. She sat beside him, her hand on his thigh. Yet he never saw her clearly. All the same, he knew it was her. *You are always telling me there is a meaning in dreams. What do you make of mine?* Sometimes in his dream he was conscious of having an erection. He didn't tell her that. Sudden alarm as to what she might say made him hesitate. *Tread softly..* he added on impulse, *..for you tread on my dreams.*

Her answer, a shock of cold water thrown upon his fire, came by e-mail.

I'm not your analyst, Anthony. It's not fair of you to project your dreams on to me.

Even before his letter arrived Anthony had been an estranging presence. Oh, the Faculty were hospitable as ever. Old friends as welcoming. She did all the things she'd grown to look forward to, eating in the Oyster House, drinking serious coffee at the Spar, watching seals on the pier. She'd walked again in the dark woods dripping with moss, her senses feasting on wonders; the Olympic Mountains reflecting the pink light of morning, the great snow dome of Mt Rainier, apricot in the evening light.

There had been times when she'd wished she might have come to stay, not to visit. Here, in the company of like-minded colleagues, she felt at home as nowhere else. Her quiet room, with its view of the mountain. Her files and books waiting on the desk. Her seminars with little groups of students sitting under the trees. This was what mattered now, she told herself. This was her reality.

Yet the old satisfactions failed to sustain. She felt as if she was marking time, washed up on this Pacific shore, waiting on some rhythm in the strata of her life, coming from deep down, lifting her up and throwing her forward.

Sometimes she suffered what might have been the pain of a phantom limb. Pangs so acute she couldn't bear it. Sometimes she wept for the old loss come back in her.

She thought of Anthony a lot. She couldn't see him as friends here would have seen him if they were to come into her room to be confronted by that downturn at the corners of the mouth, the frown that had become engrained as the years passed. *You're beginning to look like one of those agonizing Polish intellectuals*, she'd mocked once, but tenderly, tracing with a finger the high jutting line of his cheek, the gloomy brow. *A youngish Party dissident*. It struck her then that perhaps those one has known from youth onwards, one never sees as they are. As they appear to others. Something lingers, an after-image, to perplex the heart, and confound the passing years.

Her friends, with that directness she'd come to accept in Americans, questioned why they were still together. She was attractive, intelligent. Why, if they'd drifted apart, hadn't she found someone else? It was entirely the wrong image. She and Anthony were like sole survivors of some disaster. Back to back on the same life-raft. Linked irredeemably. Linked for life.

Now, with the arrival of his letter, she felt as if he'd introduced a Trojan horse into her walled city. If Anthony's dream coloured his sleep, it haunted her waking hours. She would be working at her desk, and it would appear quite suddenly, in the middle of a sentence. She couldn't shake it loose. She found herself framing the questions she might have put to a client. The woman in his dream. Was she young? Old? Attractive? Unattractive? Active? Passive?

It was, of course, preposterous that she should even be considering it. Material selected at random from an unknown dream sequence. Considering it, moreover, without reference to the client, someone who couldn't, under any circumstances, have ever become a client of hers. She tried treating it professionally. To interpret dreams literally was always a mistake. In any case, an interpretation was only an hypothesis, never a statement of truth. Besides, treating it concretely failed to take into account the compensatory nature of dreams..

She looked again at the letter. *Tread softly, for you tread on my dreams..* When it came to special pleading, she reflected, Anthony was never lost for a quotation. She gazed from her window at the great snow dome of Mount Rainier. Sometimes, floating on the haze, it seemed itself like something seen in a dream. A mirage. Not a thing of earth. There were, she thought wryly, certain advantages to living at altitude. The years of her pregnancies had finally iced over. Those years of pain and loss. She had left them behind her. As sealed off as a ship in a bottle.

Freud thought that re-awakening memory would free the patient from the pain of loss. Well, she had found her own way of living with her loss. And was she now to come down from the clouds? From the snowfields? Had she not learnt to be still, and patient. To live for her work. She was what she was in herself, not relative to other people.

Besides, it was too late in the day for her to live again as a woman lives with a man.

Some of her seminars took place in the North American longhouse, on the edge of the forest. On either side of the entrance totemic figures, male and female, stretched out their hands in mute appeal. Raised on pillars, a kind of portico before the doors, a huge, carved thunderbird spread its wings, a symbol of the energies in nature. Each time she passed beneath it she was conscious of the summoning eye, the hooked, gaping beak. She wandered through the great hall staring up at hangings, woven of cedar bark, depicting mythic images of the creation. She seemed confronted, now, by images and symbols. After a morning of engrossing talk, they pointed her towards her inner life, a life beyond language, beyond the power of words to apprehend. Sitting among the rocks outside the longhouse, where water met the land, she was writing case notes she could make no sense of. *What does he feel about it,* she jotted on her pad. *What does he think it means?* Dream contents that were remnants of a client's own history were best interpreted by the client. But his dream seemed to be replaying part of *her* history. When they were first together, sitting, walking, she would have an arm around him, a hand on his thigh. Touching, holding, they lived, then, through one another's bodies.

Now, as suitor, lover, husband, he was a stranger to her. Now she knew him only as the man she'd married years before. Sometimes, abstracted from her book, she began to look back down the length of years. Sometimes, queer little gleams and shafts of light struck through to her deepest, most fugitive sense of self. Then her heart stirred suddenly, knocking at her ribs.

Celibate herself, she wondered if he had turned to other women.

She walked in the cool shade of the forest, up a trail lined by young cedar and dogwood, undergrown with chest-high ferns, thick cushions of moss. Overhead, Douglas fir, alder, maple reached towards the sun. There was in all life forms, even those which neither knew their own acts, nor reflected on them, an instinctual force pushing continuously towards some particular fulfilment. Then an old voice in her head seemed to be saying to her, *All are clear, I alone am clouded..*

She sat on a beach overlooking the waters of Puget Sound. Wreaths of smoke rose from the surface in the chilly dawn. It needed more life than had survived in her to start again. No, they had lived too long on separate shores.

An eerie expectancy hung over the sea. The mist stock-still, waiting. There was something unnerving in the thought of that *terra incognita*, all the more sinister because it looked so innocent on the surface. Strange and frightful creatures were said to lurk in the deeps of Puget Sound. They lurked, too, in other depths perhaps best left unvisited.

Powerless, as it seemed, to stir herself, she sat watching the writhing fingers of mist, assailed by images of shadowy things moving slowly through black, billowing silt. She seemed herself to be sinking helplessly, sinking down through swirling darkness, dissolving into darkness, until she touched on the nothingness beyond.

Her summer was marked by long, intense talks with Leo Goldman, sitting under the shade of trees, amid the sound of drums, the shouts of students throwing frisbees, sometimes downtown over coffee in a corner of his favourite speakeasy. Talks that seemed vitiated by her own ambivalence. What *was* it she was trying to clarify?

Sometimes they took place at his house, with Leo's wife, Miriam, a homely presence. Her old friend's probing served only to increase her anguish of mind. Discussions that began with Anthony's Tolstoyan flight swung, invariably as it seemed, to *her*.

"You saw him escaping into some safe, idyllic past, instead of confronting life in the present with all its problems, its uncertainties and risks? No doubt there may have been some truth in that. But have you considered what you might be running away from? What it is you are trying to avoid?"

His question dogged her for days afterwards. She took long walks through the solitary woods to hidden coves brooding on Leo's words. *Perhaps what you should be striving for is to reintegrate the rejected side of yourself. To take responsibility for it. To make it part of your total experience.*

Was that it? Some aspect of her own dark side from which she had taken refuge by projecting it on to Anthony? Sitting alone in a cove she began to wonder whether she ought not to resume analysis. Or was that, too, *a narcissistic regression. A flight into the past.*.

All she had done now seemed called into question. There was in every human being an instinctive urge for completion, for wholeness. Had she sought to thwart that by a punitive act? Was that what it was, her sterilization? When she was in analysis she'd been led to recognize it as a transformative force in re-establishing control over her life.

Yet Leo had turned that, too, on its head.

"Maybe that transformative force is urging you now to brave the dangers of self-discovery."

She shook her head. It was too late. She had lived too long alone.

Suddenly, what she yearned for, beyond all else, was the haven of her old, untroubled state before this turmoil, this tearing apart.

As her teaching stint came to an end, she enrolled for a course herself on *Buddhist Psychotherapy*. She had wanted to explore the possibilities of adopting an ancient Eastern tradition as a pathway toward mental and spiritual well-being. It was held at a farmhouse used for potlucks and cultural events, amid little plots of land where students grew organic produce. The instructor, a Buddhist priest of the Pure Land tradition, spoke of the ego as an egg, its shell a protection against the external world, of the need for the breaking of the shell of separateness, the opening of consciousness to reality outside the egg.

The course finished with a four-day retreat on the edge of the forest. There was talk of letting go. Of entering the darkness. Of self-emptying. When we were silent, the instructor said, with silent body and silent mind, we perceived something of this mystery. There followed hours of concentration, of silent meditation, sweating it out, hour after hour.

But however still her body, she couldn't achieve a silent mind.

On her last night Leo and Miriam took her out to dinner at a harbour restaurant. They sat at a table by the window, looking out beyond the Inlet. Across the water the Olympic mountains raised a jagged silhouette against the last of the light.

It was for her a miserable occasion. She barely toyed with her meal.

"What am I to do, Leo?" she said, eventually. She raised her eyes to his. "What am I to do?"

The question came from far away.

He looked at her gravely. She was, he saw, still shackled by her loss, back in the old, iced-over years of her pregnancies.

"Well, there are questions we have answers to, and questions whose echoes we must expand in order to contain."

He offered more wine. She shook her head.

"You know, sometimes," he added gently, "we can solve what appears to be an insoluble conflict by outgrowing it, by developing a new level of consciousness."

She quailed at the thought. She would sooner cling on to what she had, rather than be torn apart again.

"Look," said Leo, "I will tell you a story. A Jewish story."

"Ach, stories," said Miriam, fondly dismissive. "Always he tells stories. Ducks, rabbits you can't see, or touch, or smell.

Flies in bottles. Gardens no one visits.."

But the old man only smiled indulgently at his wife's mockery.

"There was once," he began, "a scholar who was taken by a demon to the top of a great rock, on which stood a high tower. On the plain far below he saw the whole of mankind scurrying here and there, bustling from group to group, absorbed in a vast network of activities. 'Below you,' said the demon, 'are the lives of men. For as long as you remain here you will be able to observe and understand all that they do. But you will be powerless to intervene in their affairs. No, not so as to assist a single man. You are too far away for them to understand you. And should you descend and go out on to the plain your wisdom would vanish as if it had never been. You would become even as they are.' "

For demons, he added gravely, *always talk like that*.

"But of course the scholar had no desire to intervene in the affairs of men, much less descend to their plain. And so, for many years, he enjoyed his bargain. (It was the usual bargain, by the way. Scholars have only the one thing to sell.) He remained in his tower absorbed in what he saw spread out far below him. Happy to observe, classify, analyse..

'The life of knowledge,' he told himself contentedly, 'is the life that's happy, despite the miseries of the world.'

"Centuries rolled by. Far below, life flourished on the plain. Generation followed upon generation, until the plain was black with bodies. The air rang with the clamour of their hopes, their failures, their joys and sorrows, their living and their dying. And the scholar, disturbed at last, threw open the great window and leaned out from his tower. 'The life of knowledge,' he cried, 'is the life that's happy, despite the miseries of the world.' He shouted. But his voice was drowned in the clamour. It was but a feeble voice. And besides, he was too far away to be heard. So, forgetting the warning the demon had given him, he descended from the tower, and tottered out on to the plain."

Leo finished his wine, and looked levelly at her across the table.

"Well?" asked Miriam. "What happened?"

"Ah. That I don't know. The story is unfinished."

His wife threw up her hands in disgust.

"Ach, now he tells sto ries with no ending."

"Look," he said. "Be patient. Give yourself time. We have both of us experienced the slow, methodical waiting of therapy to unfold. In what looks like absolute disorder there may be an evolving pattern, both in nature and in the self."

Ever kindly, reassuring, he was smiling at her.

Her eyes, though, were full of misgiving.

Autumn

For there is a dim glimmering of light yet un-put-out in men: let them walke, let them walke, that the darkness overtake them not.'

St Augustine *Confessions*

TEN

Summer passed, and still much of the north country remained devastated by the epidemic. A golden light lay over the purple moors. The rowans blazed again in the gills. And with the autumn mists came the first flocks of fieldfares and redwings to feed on the farmland. Up in the hills a shepherd, maybe, walking his walls, would pause to watch a pair of wild swans putting down on some quiet tarn. From Spitsbergen came flights of pale-bellied Brent and Barnacle geese to winter in the sandy bays of Northumberland, or the salt marshes of the Solway Firth. But for the men and women of the lonely farms there was no respite to be found in the customary autumn gatherings. There were no markets, no sales of produce, no harvest festivals. The shows were cancelled. The village halls stood empty. The pestilence had killed all pleasures.

Yet many members of the public, driving through the infected areas, were conscious of little out of the ordinary. It required an effort of recollection to recall that the sickness was still raging, for its presence was betrayed only by what was not: the empty fields, the absence of sheep and cattle, with here and there a strip of fluorescent tape stretched across stiles and bridle paths.

Meanwhile, those disposed to think ill of their fellow countrymen now found fuel for their prejudice in the disclosure of the vast sums paid out in compensation for slaughtered livestock. Hard on the heels of that revelation came an allegation by the authorities that farmers had been infecting their own flocks in order to claim public money. At the same time, the Minister now claimed that the sheep industry itself had actually contributed to the spread of the disease. The result was that the epidemic, which should have won sympathy and understanding for the stricken communities, now had the opposite effect as their detractors, with an appetite whetted by resentment and righteous indignation, feasted on stories of profiteers benefitting to the tune of millions of pounds.

Yet for the families in disease-free areas there was no compensation. In desperate straits due to the restrictions imposed upon them, and with no money coming in, they were staring ruin in the face.

"In the long run," declared the Minister, on the evening news, "a degree of wastage must be beneficial. For too many years now the industry as a whole has suffered from a surplus of small-scale farms."

Jack Ashe stared dully at the screen.

"They don't like us. They don't want us. They may as well cull th' shepherds with th' sheep, and be done wi' us."

"But it's true, Jack, love. Can't you see it's true?" For Ellen Ashe there was only one way forward. To get out, or go under.

They had to be out by Michaelmas. She was counting the days. Which, as the weeks went by, grew steadily darker. Man and wife scarcely spoke. Jack Ashe sank himself in what he had to do. Opened his mouth only when he had to.

Hardman watched him one day, slowly, patiently repairing a wall beyond the river. Intent, bent over his task, his eyes never left the stone. He was doing the things he had always done. Around him the newly weaned lambs were cropping the late flush of grass in the bottom land. It was like studying a man under sentence: a fit, capable man who, in a few short weeks, would be separated from his life.

There had been a change in the way they talked about the Ashes at the *Bridge*. From easy humour, directed at the lame dogs of the district, to that respectful awe accorded victims of some not-to-be-thought-of calamity.

"Ashes allus was unlucky," said Monty, shaking his head. No one contradicted him.

"It's happening all over," said George. "Folk selling up."

"That don't make it right. It's selling your birthright."

"Right's got nowt to do wi' it, Arthur. It's not economic. A part-time farm like that."

"Our Billy does all right." Malcolm's cousin ran some sheep at Upper Hey.

"Your Billy," a tart voice put in, "hasn't got four kids to feed and clothe. What'll *they* do for a living, eh? Stuck up there?"

"Does anyone know who bought the house?" asked Hardman.

"It weren't Maurice Clarkson. I do know that."

"No one knows. It was sold by tender."

"Well, they're not the first," sighed George. "And I don't suppose they`ll be the last either."

Hardman was thinking of the few whose directives, written in blood, had brought calamity upon so many. For them the land was simply a commodity, its creatures merely units of production, unconnected with the human enterprise. Small wonder, then, that they should claim their policy had brought success in the end, since it was founded on expediency alone. Yet it was without rectitude or decency. It was inhuman, and it had brought about a defeat of the spirit.

Meanwhile, he had begun preparations for his own departure. One afternoon he went up to Dalehead to return a chainsaw he had borrowed. He found Ellen Ashe coming out of the porch with a basket on her arm.

"I was hoping to find Jack," he said.

"He was at the pens with Maurice looking over some ewes.."

"Come on, then," she sighed. "Let's get this lot sorted."

They went out together, Hardman carrying the washing, she with the twins trailing at her skirts.

She began pegging out her line of little garments.

"They smell so much fresher when they've had a blow," she said cheerfully.

A certain brightness, registered in the voice, in the face turned suddenly towards him, transfigured her worn looks with a youthful vigour

She must have been pretty, it struck him, as a child.

"There's Jack," she said.

A short, stocky figure beside the burly, big-boned neighbour, he stood stoically by as one of the Clarkson lads bent over a ewe, inspecting another mouth. The Dalehead flock was passing out of his hands.

"It must be very hard for him.." he began.

Ellen Ashe kept a dogged silence. Hardman cursed himself for blundering in.

She, though, would have done anything to drag her husband back from whatever brink, if only she'd known where he was. There were nights when she lay awake, staring into the darkness, she on one side, he on the other. All her memories, now, of married life, were, as it seemed, of *not* loving Jack; of marrying him for the sake of the child, of escaping from a penniless, lonely life. She wondered what it really was, love, and whether it was still a possibility, loving him as he would need to be loved.

Meanwhile the boy, more feral than ever, roamed further and further afield. And would, if he could, have mingled with it, become the wild spirit of the place, flitting between hares and foxes, alive in trees and rocks, flowing with the dark, moorish waters of the Dale river. He lingered in the ruined fold, or in that corner of the dark plantation where the old man died, squeezing a handful of rotten wood, sniffing the dank mushroom smell, staring at the fibrous whorls coming away in stringy layers, filling himself with what he would soon be leaving.

It was the dogs, though, that finally brought things home to Tommy Ashe.

What would happen to the dogs?

It struck him like a thunderbolt. He came bursting into the kitchen with the worry of it written all over his face as if he'd hit on something everyone else seemed to have forgotten.

"What'll happen to the dogs?"

Jack Ashe was lacing up his boots. His mam was at the sink. The boy stared from one to the other.

"Gyp's going to your Uncle Arthur's," his dad said, stamping a boot squarely on the stone flag. "They want a young dog. Bob'll come with us."

Tight-lipped, Ellen Ashe said nothing. But the boy picked up, in the rattling of dishes, a note of sullen opposition. She didn't want dogs. Not in her new house.

"What about Meg?" They just couldn`t leave her. She was too old to fend for herself.

"I'll see to Meg," said his dad quietly.

"Where will she go?"

"I've told you," Jack Ashe repeated. "I'll see to Meg."

But the man's voice, firm and yet evasive, alarmed him.

"She's all right," he said uneasily. "She's just old, that`s all."

Suddenly solicitous, he went out to look for her.

"Meg," he called. "Meg.. come by, Meg.."

"You see," hissed Ellen Ashe. "You should ha' put her down months ago. But you wouldn't."

He'd been hoping he wouldn't have to. Thinking she mightn't last the summer. But she'd lingered on. Aye, he thought, with grudging admiration. She'd cling till she dropped, though it was as much as she could do to drag herself from her stall to the sunny wall of the rubbish pit.

Well, one day was as good as another, he told himself more than once. And still he put it off, until it couldn't be put off any longer.

The boy had not been told. It'd only have caused an upset. Jack Ashe could see no sense in that. He preferred to do what had to be done in his own time, and with as little fuss as possible.

First off he dug a good deep hole. He wasn't sure he'd feel up to doing it after. He dug it a little way behind the house, below the bankside. At the foot of the forest ride that ran up steeply between the larches.

Aye, he thought. *I'll put her there.*

And dug, sweating in the autumn sun, breathing in the scents of fresh turned earth, and severed roots, and the dry piney smell of the plantation. What filled his mind, though, was that black wet night with the men slipping, staggering, and the collie whining round them, and the boy snivelling as he dragged her away.

She'd been fed. Jack Ashe had seen to that.

She didn't bark at the familiar tread, but looked up, as if surprised to see him back. Her tail thumped lethargically once or twice.

She showed no alarm as Jack Ashe put the barrel to her head.

For days the boy went about in a kind of shock. Silent, withdrawn, he was discovering for the first time how the worst can happen.

Ellen Ashe came across him once, moping in his bedroom.

"It was kindest, really," she told him. "She was old. She couldn't get about. She didn't enjoy life any more."

But he wasn't thinking of that. He was thinking of her whining, getting between the men's feet, the night he found his grandad, and the hot, wet, stink of her as he'd clutched her to his chest.

Her mother's heart was torn open by the tears filling his eyes.

Jack found him once, up by the forest edge, in the very spot where the old man died, crying his heart out. And brought him home.

"He'll get over it," he said.

It was all very well for him, she thought. It was all in a day's work to him, shooting a dog. But she was alarmed. He'd always been so bound up in himself. In a dream-world, his teachers said. She flinched at the thought of bombs falling on that world. For the first time a shadow of fear fell over the future she was counting on. The dream she'd planned for them all.

"He'll come round," said Jack, unmoved. Who'd seen distracted animals. And knew.

But still it went on, the weeping. It was like the bleeding in him of some dreadful wound. The welling up of an inconsolable grief. Nothing she said could staunch it.

Hardman came across him one afternoon on his way home from school.

The boy looked round at the man's approach.

"We've got to leave here," he said suddenly.

Hardman felt a stab of pain. At the dead voice.

They went on together down the track in silence.

Suddenly, it flared up again, the pain of his own powerlessness wrenching at him, tearing him out of connection with all he knew and loved. Lost, nowhere, he tramped on, close to tears. But he didn't cry. With the man there he wouldn't cry.

"Me mam wants us to go and live in Glossop."

Hardman, on the point of churning out some stuff about towns, exciting things to do, bit back the stream of lies in time. Even so, he could see she was absolutely right. There was no future for them at Dalehead. He saw the months, years maybe, stretching ahead, working themselves to exhaustion, with nothing to show for it, the debts mounting, no money coming in, no hope of a better future.

He thought of those despairing evenings at home, with less and less to say, losing sight of one another, failing to keep alive the feeling that he or she was loved. What chance had any marriage of surviving such a future? No, it was the sensible thing to do. Sell up, take the money and make a new life.

Yet at the thought of Jack Ashe in Glossop, Hardman felt a shiver of unease. In his bones, his flesh, in the strings of his nerves and sinews, the shepherd carried centuries of experience. It was his human essence. It made him what he was. To expect a man like that to change his way of life was like asking him to step outside himself. Like asking him to disappear.

*

Hardman was going home. He'd had a series of bland e-mails from non-Elizabeth, bustling with activity. She'd hiked in the rain forest, watched elks on the slopes of Mount St Helens, fed wolves in a wolf sanctuary, seen a whale, the course was wonderful, the students were wonderful..

He'd responded with equally anodyne replies. Neither of them made any further mention of his dream. She was due back at the end of the month, and he was wondering who or what he would be picking up at the airport, and how long the analgesia would last.

He spent his last afternoon at Moor House generally clearing up. Then he chopped a fresh supply of logs, stacking them neatly in the washhouse and thinking, as he swept the cobbles, that at least the next asylum seeker shouldn't lack for warmth.

That evening he went up to Dalehead to say goodbye. He found Ellen Ashe sitting by the kitchen fire. She wore her long hair loose. He'd not seen her with it loose before. She had fine, straight hair. Freshly washed and spread in a lustrous fan across her shoulders, it shimmered as she turned her head. She was nursing the girl, the little blonde one, on her lap while the twin boy, grizzling, buried his face between her knees. Absently she stroked his head. The girl, too, put out a tiny hand. Patted her brother's carroty tufts.

Hardman smiled to see it.

"Oh, she'll do that for him", said the mother drily. "You watch her bat him one if he tries to climb up here."

"I've come to say goodbye," he said.

"Oh aye. Off, are you?" Jack Ashe was washing his hands at the sink.

He'd lapsed from the brief intimacy shared while the other worked beside him.

"That's right. First thing tomorrow." He looked round, but the boy was nowhere to be seen.

"The lad's in the stable, feedin' t' dogs."

This parting had the awkwardness of all farewells. A self-conscious shaking of hands, of wishing each other well. It was as if they'd already become strangers again.

Hardman went out to the stable to look for the boy. He found him sitting on a box, watching the dogs wolfing down their dinner.

"Gyp's grown a bit since I first saw him. Do you remember me bringing him back that day?"

Receiving no reply, the man said simply what he'd come for.

"I've come to say good-bye."

He saw then that the boy's mind was on quite another leave-taking.

"It'll be OK," he told encouragingly. "You'll see. I'm sure it will"

At a loss, he cast about for something else to say.

"Hey," he tried. "Remember that card you sent me, the fox with the huntsmen? You'll have to do the same. Lose yourself in the crowd. Keep quiet, keep your head down. To start with, anyway. Just keep thinking of your fox."

But the boy's eyes knew better. They'd seen what happened to foxes.

That night Hardman lit his fire for the last time under the monumental chimney breast. He did so with a sense of regret. This room, so alien when he first arrived, had become a home, however shabby and old-fashioned. He would miss it, even the funerary dresser with its row of plates, grimier now with wood smoke than when he arrived.

As the fire burned up, he opened a last bottle of wine and prepared his supper, an assortment of leftovers from the fridge. He ate it, looking out across Blackden to the high line of the encircling hills, pitch-black against the pale night sky.

Why had he come here? Perhaps, subconsciously, he'd been hoping for some kind of *metanoia*, some truth issuing in a simple, single command that would release the part of him locked up in darkness, change his life from what it was. He'd looked to find it in the scenes and memories of youth. He'd come back to where he'd started, only to discover he'd become a different person. The effect had been to leave him more than ever a stranger to himself?

He sighed..

Jack, at least, knew where he belonged, what he should be doing. Jack, and the boy.

He felt a pang of dismay at the thought of the boy. Things cut off at the root withered and died. Could anything of child-hood survive that dislocation? Could it? Oh, he hoped so. He wished for Tommy Ashe what, he knew, he would have wished for his own son, had he lived. Joy. A continual becoming. Gladness, spreading like a tide through all his days. A man in whom the child's heart and mind had died was little more than a dead man.

Next morning he completed the last of his tasks before leaving. He cleaned the fridge and cooker. He cleared out the grate, replacing the electric fire in the hearth. He made a final check of the house, opening drawers and cupboards. In the orange bathroom he flushed the loo for the last time. He took a look round the bedroom, then picked up his bag and set off down the stairs, past the farmers, the country lawyers, along the hall, and out through the front door.

As he was about to set off, the quad bike came roaring past him, turning off the track and onto the grassy verge beside the entrance. Jack Ashe swung open the gate, and stood aside to let the Rover pass. Then, as the car drew level, he lowered his face to the open window.

"And did you find what you came for?" The blue eyes reflecting something of their old candour.

"No, Jack. I'm still looking."

Yet in his own mind he was in no doubt that he had reached a turning point, that something in himself was spent.

ELEVEN

They went away together, the Hardmans. A colleague at one of the clinics where she practised had offered Elizabeth his house in the south of France.

"It's an old water-mill," she said to Hardman. "In the Vaucluse."

She'd thought a lot about Leo's story. It was, as much as anything, a parable about the knower and the known, life as a flux, a process. Why wasn't it finished? Because, of course, the outcome couldn't be known in advance. It was the last thing he'd said to her at the airport. *Healing can't be willed into existence. It must be borne along on the stream of time.* She could free herself from the past only by leaping into the stream. She thought, with aversion, of that maelstrom of bodies, the clamour, the harsh cries. *Submit yourself,* was what he was saying. Yes, run the risk of being swallowed up in the chaos, of sinking without trace.

Was that really what she wanted? Could she really trust herself to that?

They hired a car in Paris, and set off south early the next morning, Hardman driving, not saying much to each other, for the uncertainty of their undertaking was weighing heavily. Each was feeling the withdrawn edginess of an agent embarked on a mission, the details of which were not yet specified, the location undisclosed, the outcome impossible to predict.

South of Lyon, tiring at last of interminable miles and the soulless road, at her suggestion they turned aside from the autoroute, and headed into western Vercors.

They went by sinuous valleys cutting through the limestone plateau. Here were forests of beech and walnut, and winding roads carved into cavernous crags, climbing over passes, dropping down to genial valleys, graced with tumbling streams. It was a country blessed by an ever-present spurting of water, spouting from crevices in rocks, rampaging over cliffs, cascading down the narrowing jaws of river beds.

A natural delight in all they saw lifted them into the larger world around. In a village rising out of the rocks they bought *eau minérale*, fresh bread and cheese, which they ate while watching the slow swirl of a green pool under a bushy bank.

Then, sweeping down a narrow canyon filled with waterfalls to yet another hairpin bend, she spied a bell-tower emerging from a cluster of walls clinging to a craggy cliff.

"Let's stop," she said.

So, towards evening, they entered a crumbling village of ochre walls, and rusty terracotta tiles. Here, in a courtyard off a little square, they came upon, of all things, an Italian inn. *Albergo Vittorio Emanuele*. Baskets of flowers hung from the low eaves.

Yes, there was a room. It was small, dwarfed by a vast bed, with clean white walls, and a window overlooking the square.

Downstairs, the lamps were not yet lit in the inn, where a long table was laid with cutlery and glasses, as if for a family party. Shafts of late sunlight, streaming through a window, glittered like gold enamelling on the patina of crusty loaves. The room was empty, but for some old men playing cards.

He ordered a *risotto*. She, a salad of pungent little black olives with sweet ripe tomatoes, hard-boiled eggs and anchovies.

"Oh, this is good," she said.

The dinner party began to arrive. All male, it seemed. Swarthy men, dressed formally. A sodality, or a masonic gathering. They stared curiously at the foreigners, the blonde woman and the man. Massive in black, *la Signora* moved between the tables with a great pot of coffee. Her grave eyes rested on them a moment. Elizabeth Hardman smiled. Shook her head.

They sat contentedly amid the smells of cooking and coffee,

while rich, warm voices rose and fell around them like an exotic sea. A fat white cat leaped up into her lap. Now and then from the card players came cries of triumph or disgust. From time to time a voice called out, amid laughter from the kitchen.

"O! é bruto!" it cried protestingly, " é bruto!"

Next day they set off south, following the narrow, winding road along steep valleys lined with oaks and sweet chestnuts. Midday found them descending a hillside to a plain of olive groves, and small fields broken by cypress hedges. Here, entering the Vaucluse, they slid back the roof of the car to let in the sun. All around them now, as far as the eye could see, the silvery-green of olive groves. Westward, the distant slopes of a massif gleamed with the same silvery-green.

They came at last to a town set amid a corrie of wooded hills, with a castle set on a rock. They crossed the river by an old stone bridge and drove on, mile upon mile, past hillside villages and grassy river-banks. On their left hand, growing ever closer, a bald hump of limestone rose, isolated and severe, above the orchards and the vineyards and the slender pyramids of slim, green cypresses planted in parallel ranks to fend off the Mistral.

"That must be Mont Ventoux," he said, craning to look.

A fringe of dark trees clustered about the lower slopes of the mountain. Above the trees a vast field of glittering white scree rose and disappeared behind the curtain of cloud drawn about the summit.

On they went, through vineyards, orange and gold with the tints of autumn. Beyond the fields and farms, lifted above a periphery of pines and oaks, a long succession of spires and turrets cut a jagged silhouette against an azure sky.

"It might be the Cuillin ridge," said Hardman happily, "but for the sun."

They began to feel detached from their ordinary, lesser selves, so drawn up were they into the light, the spacious air, of this land of lavender and melons, of vineyards and olive groves.

Ever south they went, past ancient towns and baked villages where crumbling stucco and flaking shutters testified to the re-lentless onslaught of sun and wind.

So, at length, they reached the fringes of the Plateau de Vaucluse, a wild, empty land pitted with chasms, where isolated umbrella pines, and scraggy trees bent by violent mountain winds, clung to the living rock. The twisting road carried them up through the gorges to a pass in the hills, then down again in a series of swoops and lunges, when, plunging suddenly into a rift in the plateau, they saw, perched on a hill, a village of beige stone, glowing orange in the afternoon sun.

"This is it," she said.

'Le Moulin' took some finding.

"He did say it was off the beaten track," she murmured, as he drove slowly down the narrow lane that ran under the base of the cliff.

"Well, it has to be by the river."

They found it eventually, deep in the woods at the end of the track, a grey stone house, with bright blue shutters, and a curious door at the top of a stair of stone flags.

While he hauled the bags from the boot, she juggled with the keys to the door. Inside, more steps led to an upper level, and the accommodation, a large single room arranged into sepa-rate areas, whether for cooking, eating or lounging by the fire. A huge arched window, let into a gable end, filled the whole area with light.

He was humping the luggage up a wooden staircase to a mezzanine bedroom slotted under the roof. There was a bed be-low a skylight, next to a long, low table. He laid the cases on the table, under a colourful poster of lavender fields.

She flung open a French window, and stepped out on to a little terrace, with a low wall at one end, and a wild, wooded garden of oleander, still in blossom, and ferns and mossy boulders.

A plank bridge led across the river to the further bank, where a vague trail began through the woods.

They were blessed with the weather. An Indian summer, she would have called it back in England, these long, slow, cloudless days of sun and light. They breakfasted out on the terrace, with the sound of water swirling through the mill race below the wall. They wandered about the labyrinth of cobbled streets, shopped in the market, ate at the cafés. As tourists do. But the tourists had all gone. And the absence of others like themselves contributed to a feeling of unreality about their presence in this place. They were at a loss to know what they were doing here. She, especially, felt a stranger to herself. Stopping somewhere was not to have arrived.

So, abandoning the village, they began to look elsewhere for a destination. In the woods the arbutus was in blossom. White clusters of bell-shaped flowers hung suspended above their heads, with orange berries, left over from the previous year. Here, within a tracery of light and shade, they opened to the silence and seclusion.

They said little in these solitary wanderings. Indeed, each might have been alone, except that they were alone together. Sometimes their hands would touch, fingers clasp. She came to see it was the present moment which alone was real.

One evening, deep in the woods, the path divided, the left-hand branch slanting up to where a shrine, cut in the rock, sheltered a statue of the Virgin. A few withered flowers told of a recent *fête*. She, a little way in front, looked back at him uncertainly.

Two roads diverged in a wood.. The poet, he remembered, had taken the one less travelled by. For Frost, it made all the difference..

"Keep going," he said.

The path, narrowing now, ran on along the bed of the stream. Silent but for a trickle of water. Among the shady rocks, a dense carpet of ferny foliage, studded with starry flowers of bright blue bugloss. On each side trees sprang up steeply.

They came at length to a widening of the valley floor, where dry sticks of reeds bordered a hollow. Here, in this bowl of the hills, the river, dammed centuries ago, had created a peaceful tarn filled with water-lilies. Rocky hillocks of tussocky grass stood up like islands in the water. Beyond the tarn, in a sunny hollow sheltered by cypress and wild olive tees, the path petered out amid the tumbled stones of a monastery. All around were wooded hills of pine and oak, and dry rocky slopes ablaze with patches of fiery vegetation.

They passed under a ruined, ivy-covered doorway through which the sun fell on a tangle of wild thyme and lavender. Somewhere, a sound of falling water intensified the silence of a place seemingly closed to the material world, as if bodies were to be left at the gate, and only souls allowed inside.

A faded board told of the suffering which is history. Sacked by the Gascons, ravaged by the Black Death, put to the torch by the Waldensians during the Wars of Religion, it had been abandoned and refounded many times before it was finally suppressed in the Revolution. Now, all but forgotten, it mouldered in the heart of its forest wilderness.

In a space beyond the cloister garth, they found the remains of four slender columns. Under one wall, a cracked grave slab incised with a crozier. A stone bench running round.

"This must have been the chapter house," he said.

Though whatever faults and failings were admitted here had found absolution long ago.

They sat side by side on the stone bench. Solitude, she was discovering, was different from loneliness. When you were lonely you became acutely conscious of your separation.

"I wish I knew what went wrong," she said. And took his hand.

"I always loved you," he said.

Little clumps of purplish flowers were springing up among the fallen stones. Self-heal, she thought. Where the light struck the walls, the dressed stone was white, white as ivory.

"But I couldn't see what was happening," he went on. "I assumed your pain was the same as mine. I never allowed you your own pain. With me you were never free to be yourself, not even to suffer."

No, she was thinking. Men don't have babies.

"Then for years," the man went on, "I could not accept what had happened. I felt my life should have been richer than it was. That I should be living it differently."

"There was no need for you to have stopped," she murmured. "But you did. You had to punish yourself. And you blamed me for it ever after." But she spoke absently, as if it were old history she was repeating. Something burnt out long ago.

"I lived in the hope of moving on. Finding whatever it was I'd lost."

For the woman, too, reality had been incomplete.

"Running away," her husband added, "has not cured me of my shame. Of not being what I should have been."

Suddenly, he was outsized by his own anguish as he contemplated the failures without number, appearing everywhere, like holes in the tattered garment of their life together.

"Where has it gone," he asked. "Our life?"

She took his hand, which she had released in order to brush away some flying thing.

So they sat, held together in the knowledge that a loveless world is a dead world, that eventually the hour comes when the soul wearies alike of the mountain and the tower, and longs once more for the mansion of loving kindness.

As day followed day they came to accept one another's strangeness. Still something remained unresolved. Sometimes, one or other would wake under the skylight, and lie staring up at the night, and wonder. Neither knew whither they were travelling. Only that there is a wisdom which knows when to question, and when to stay silent. Meanwhile, they were content to let the days come and go, more at ease with one another than they'd been for years.

There was a market every Thursday, held in the village square. She sent him off for the day.

"Be a tourist," she said brightly. "Go and find something to look at."

Yet, as she watched the Rover bumping down the track, she felt the first quiver of misgiving about this scheme of hers. Then, climbing the steep road that wound between the tiers of houses, looking up at the village, she saw, scattered here and there among the buttressed walls and rocky outcrops, the chimney pots and ugly storage tanks, little patches of colour, protected by a balustrade or painted railing. Boxes of bright flowers. Geraniums in tubs. Trellises of climbing plants. Here and there a cat, sunning itself on a balcony. Secret terraces for the tender life to cling to. They survive, she saw, these gardens of the heart. In spite of everything, they survive.

She wandered through the market, between rows of sprawling ripe tomatoes, beans, green almonds, shiny new white onions. There were pizzas and pâtés, sausages and salamis, hams, capons, towering monoliths of creamy butter, cheeses wrapped in leaves. At one stall she bought wild mushrooms (all tested, she was assured, at the *pharmacie*). At the *boulangerie* she bought olive bread and *roquefort* bread, and tiny pastries freshly baked that morning. She bought peppers and olives. She bought radishes and watercress. At the *épicerie*, shrimps and yoghourt from the freezer. She bought so much she had to hire a taxi. And then, with all her shopping safely stored inside the ancient

Citroen, and the engine ticking over, she simply had to go back for an armful of madonna lilies, long stems topped with green, creamy cones ripening to vanilla.

She spent the whole day preparing the meal. She peeled shrimps, crushed garlic, scrubbed sticks of celery, with music from a French radio station playing beside her as she worked. She mixed, chopped, sliced, pounded, with the sun streaming in at the gable to exalt her spirits with a gaiety, an excitement that bubbled up now and then in little snatches of song as she moved lightly about the kitchen.

Facing her across the table hung an Art Nouveau mirror. A young girl from a Mucha poster offering a bunch of grapes. *Le Festival de Champagne*. From time to time the woman gazed at the girl, and felt a *frisson* of pleasure at the thought of the dishes set out beside the bed, an indulgence that evoked the early days of their life together.

She was stripping the charred skin from some peppers, slicing them into quarters, when, slithering into this dream, came a serpent voice:

> *Si tu t'imagines, fillette, fillette,*
> *qu' ça va, qu' ça va,*
> *durer toujours*
> *la saison des amours..*

It was a nursery rhyme for foolish virgins. A cautionary tale for the wasp-waisted, the rosy-cheeked.

She knew it instantly, from the first stabbing syllables to the final mocking lullaby. Oh, and the singer too, that smoky voice feasting on its words, swooping, soaring, crooning, caressing, the throat closing like a nutcracker about those guttural *g*'s and *r*'s, gagging – *quelle horreur* – at the offence of age. The slack flesh, the sagging breasts..

Elizabeth Hardman pictured all too clearly the slight figure, always in black, the pale face with its jutting cheekbones, the tangle of raven hair, the lemur eyes, ringed with *kohl*. That *rose noire* of the *rive gauche* no wistful English rose of twenty-one could ever hope to resemble. Nor did she dream then that song could ever fall like a sword on her.

Chastened, she looked down at the bowl of warm oil waiting for the fleshy peppers. What was she thinking of? This rolling back of the years. This meal for lovers. This folly.

Then, in the mirror, beyond the Mucha girl offering her grapes, she saw what she was. A worn Englishwoman of a certain age. A woman, moreover, who'd stood off from life as from a leprosy. Could she love again, she, with a past haunted by something that never happened, a yearning that had washed away her life like sea water through sand?

Elizabeth Hardman stared dully at her reflection in the glass while, in the background, the radio continued to transmit the last bars of the song, the lesson of one who had lived a woman's life with a passion, an intensity, she herself had never known.

> *Allons, cueille, cueille,*
> *les roses de la vie..*

She stared at the lilies, now unfolding under the sun's caress, filling the room with their pungent, heavy scent. The petals, peeling back to uncover a corolla of rose pink, studded with blood-red spots, had the sheen of youthful flesh.

It was too late. She had withdrawn too far into herself, lived too long in the old indifference.

Unable to love herself, how could she expect to receive love?

She went on with her preparations. In a cupboard she found a collection of little earthenware dishes of a deep glowing yellow. She took them down, washed them, and laid them on the draining board. As cheerful as sunshine, they were. Simple, and bright. As simple, she saw in a moment of self-forgetfulness, as the crisp, appealing freshness of lettuce hearts, the rosy firmness of radishes, the lush spillage of fresh watercress across the table top.

And when at last all was done, the food set out in the little yellow dishes, she gazed with wistful pleasure at the fruits of her labours: as many shapes, colours, textures as there were salty, smoky, spicy flavours. To go with the radishes, the watercress, the hearts of lettuce, raw heads of celery, were mushrooms marinating in oil with lemon and garlic, cucumber sliced paper-thin, mingled with chopped mint in a dish of vinegar and yoghurt, a salad of salted chick peas with sliced onion, tomatoes sliced and opened out like little concertinas, interleaved with slices of hard-boiled eggs, thin slices of *saucisson*, studded with peppercorns, a *terrine* of smoked salmon, little cheeses of goat's milk, speckled with herbs. There were dishes of sweet peppers glistening in oil. There were bowls of olives, of stuffed eggs, of garlic mayonnaise. There were shrimps swimming in little ramekins of melted butter. There was brown, nutty bread, and a salty flat bread made with olive oil, cut into squares and spread with a *tapénade* of olives and anchovies.

Finally, on an oval yellow platter, she arranged a little pyramid of small green figs.

Nervously, they undressed together under the pitched roof, turning away from one another, not sure what they were advancing towards, nor what wounds might be inflicted. They were used to one another's naked bodies, but not to this joined, vulnerable nakedness. The man, taking off the last of his clothes, was thinking he didn't know if he was up to this. The sun, streaming through the skylight, left their exposed flesh nowhere to hide. She felt useless and desolate, standing there.

"I don't know what you're expecting," he said uncertainly.

"I'm not expecting anything," she said, looking at him steadily.

"Only it's been a long time," he added.

She was afflicted by the pathos of bodies, and put her arms around him.

"All you have to do," she said, "is eat."

So they did eat, and talked together, spurred by memories of the companionable character of a bed when there were two of you. What was once a narrow cell for solitary dreams become suddenly a grassy bank, a forest glade, a picnic spot for delightful meals and playful conversations, where you could eat, make love, sleep, eat some more, and talk of all things under the sun.

He was discovering that what he'd always wanted was this return to the garden.

For her, seemingly, an old song had lost its terrors.

At length, drowsy with food and wine, she drew her fingers idly along his side as he sprawled sleepily, half-turned from her. She was startled by the change in him. Gone, the fleshy pads above his hips. He was lean-ribbed now, hollow of flank as a farmyard cat.

"You're thinner," she murmured.

He only grunted.

She swept her hand idly along his thigh, over his buttocks. She preferred the firm compact curve of male bottoms. Hard. Round. So much more satisfying than a woman's.

"Like an apple," she said.

"An apple!" he scoffed. "Why not a cabbage? A cauliflower?"

"No," her fingers judicious. "An apple."

"I see. I have an arse like Granny Smith's."

"No, no.. a *cooking* apple. Hard. Chunky."

"Or sometimes," she added softly, touching him as he lay beside her, touching him so lightly as to send shivers through his body, quivers she felt herself, "sometimes fuzzy, like a peach."

Afterwards, unmoved, she lay awake, conscious of the sleeping body in her bed. The rise and fall of its breath. The moon streamed in at the window. Fell across the stranger sprawled on top of the quilt. Tentative at first, he had eventually coupled with the god. Now he lay on his side, milky in the moonlight, an arm flung up above his head.

There was something infinitely remote about the still, male body lying as if cast aside by whatever had made use of it, a chilly luminescence repudiating all connection.

If you escape yourself, she wondered, what life do you step into?

Then the moon passed behind a cloud.

Yet there were moments when fragments of their former selves clung together, seeming to merge in recognition. Once, with a gasp, he came softly, involuntarily. Flat against her breast, and yet she sensed him poised unsurely, hanging over her.

"You didn't expect that," she whispered.

He shifted slightly. She knew he was looking down at her through the darkness, searching for her.

"Nor did I," she murmured, tightening her arms around him.

And they dissolved in laughter, hugging one another in the bed.

He was the first to stir, waking to the sun streaming through the skylight. He got up and went downstairs, coming back eventually with a pot of coffee on a tray.

They breakfasted on bread and olives, and creamy butter from the table beside the bed.

Suddenly hungry again, he was helping himself to what was left of their supper. She lay propped up on pillows to sip at her coffee.

"You hear about people coming through years of unhappiness," he said abruptly. "Do you think it's true?"

She hesitated. She was weighing her words.

"In my experience," she began, "a damaged child continues to hold itself responsible for the calamity of its life."

She sipped at her coffee. Once again, he saw, she was keeping him at a distance.

"If it's fostered, or adopted," she went on, "it will strive constantly to confirm what it fears most. That the offer of love is false. Even though love is what it is most in need of."

In the room nothing moved but the sun, which had begun to creep towards the poster of lavender pickers on the wall above the bed. They were listening to each other's silence. The woman had begun to think of the creature, what was it called, the man-beast who haunted the labyrinth of love.

"The best those who try to care for it can hope for is somehow to outlast the worst it can inflict, caring for it come what may. Sometimes they can't. They end up abusing it too. Then the child knows it was right. About the world, and about itself. No one can love it."

He would have to make do, he saw, with riddles.

"So you're telling me that love can fail."

He was at a loss in this tangle of strange truths which she had thrown around him.

"Not as an aspiration." She put out a hand to reach for a fig. "As an aspiration it never fails, since it 'hangs in there', as they say. Its power lies in the faith that somehow it must get through in the end. But in specific circumstances – yes, it will fail."

She spoke calmly, dispassionately, her fingers busy with the fig. It was as well for him to know these things.

"So it's all hopeless. A damaged child stays damaged."

She was a stranger, the woman was thinking, even to those who knew her best.

"No, not hopeless. Or else I wouldn't do the work I do. But it's true, I think that a damaged child stays damaged."

She offered him the fig. He shook his head. She closed her eyes, wrapped in the great dark of her own estrangement.

The man stared up at the wall. He could have been contemplating a line on some big face, not known before, which had to be worked out on the rock, a series of precarious moves, poised always on the brink of failure.

He seemed to have fallen asleep again, curled up beside her, his head on her breast. She kept her arm around him, which was now quite numb. She would have to move it before long.

The sun, streaming in at the window, lit on the poster on the wall above the bed. It picked out the low farmhouse of yellow stone. Behind the farm a line of long, low hills. In the foreground were rows and rows of grey-green mounds topped with blue flowers. Women in broad-brimmed hats and loose, black garments were picking the flowers. Time seemed suspended. So clear the air, so intense the light, she could almost smell the lavender. A blessed land, it seemed to her. So close she might have stepped across, and pulled him with her.

It may be, she wanted to say, that we are marred beyond redemption. Yet always there is the possibility that powers hitherto unknown will prove adequate to our coming right.

And maybe the ability to receive was also something given.

So she lay, still with her arm around the sleeping body of her husband, hoping for release. Yet always, in her heart, the child who died. Everything was marked and judged by the silence of her heart.

TWELVE

A bright day would be best to bring a stranger over the Snake and down the long winding hill into Glossopdale. Bright and glittering. Not that the gaunt mills put on majesty. Nothing so soft. Nor could you ever come across it as it was, the dark handsome town where Ellen Ashe was born, with its noises rising to meet you as you descended, that steady humming, with now and then a hollow *clank*, of the life that used to be. Though some, at least, of the grey stone terraces are still in place, the wet roofs glinting like gun metal as they step up the hillsides: and the brook, cutting a long, lazy half moon from Howard Town to Wren Nest.

It was no accident that a town should have sprung up in that damp, narrow dale between the hills, or that manufacturing fortunes flourished so amid the wet clinging air, so favourable for the spinning of cotton. In Glossop they say it rains two days out of three. It rains sulphuric acid. Sulphur dioxide drifting up from the smelting works dissolves in the warm, wet westerlies that come scowling out of Manchester. The cloud backs up in a dense bank to the north and west, settling lower and lower, then a rain falls that poisons grass, they say, for miles around. Kills cows, according to farmers. Melts the lead flashing round chimney stacks.

Two hundred years of technological innovation have bred, as a by-product, a wry humorous folk well adapted to the fluctuating fortunes of their industrial heritage. Some years ago a ninety-metre chimney was erected to disperse the fumes into higher, colder air. A tall, tapering finger of molybdenum steel, it dominates the dale for miles around. *Does it work?*, you ask the man in the pub. *Oh aye, it works*, he tells you. *They're gerrin it in New Mills now as well as us.*

Just such a man, it might have been, who'd lived all his life

250

directly in the track of depressions moving in from the Atlantic, gazing at the pinched face staring from the front page of the *Manchester Evening News*:

MOOR BOY: SEARCH RESUMES

Police and mountain rescue teams today resumed their search of the bleak Derbyshire moorland for runaway Tommy Ashe. Tommy, aged eleven, is believed to have been spotted yesterday on a hill farm above Glossop. With weather conditions over the high moors worsening, fears are mounting for the boy's safety.

Who shook his head, and asked himself what was he thinking of, a little lad like that.

The boy, though, could no longer settle for the alarming poverty that had now become the condition of his life.

On Friday they had an inset day. Then, on the Monday, Mr Cramp was away. A man they didn't know came to take them. He didn't look too pleased about it, either. He gave everyone a piece of paper, then wrote on the board: *My day off.*

"Right," he growled. "Get on with it." He was a ratty-looking man with glasses, and bristly hair that stuck out of his ears.

We had Friday off, wrote Tommy Ashe, *and all other classes off and we play hide and sek and my brother hide his eys and count up to and I had to hide I and behind the bins and I was I was of fox in the fores and stars in the nigt and the blak sky and the moon.*

He could not describe his own world as it was, nor fit it into any system of knowledge such as was taught to him at school. It was nowhere like a town. A place of roads and streets, where things stood in rows. Even to the boy, who knew it best, it remained in the deepest sense unknown. Yet when he stood again among the stones of the track he began to recognize, in the wind soughing through the thorns, in the vast beckoning sky, that otherness which entered into him, and made him other.

Having no home he cared to go to, he'd not gone back there after school, but slept that night buried in the hay of a barn at Mossy Lea. You forgot your troubles in the snug warmth of the hay. He dozed, and woke, and dozed again, fitfully, for hours. It was broad daylight when, stiff and hungry, he dropped from the loft and set off along Doctor's Gate. A thin drizzling rain was falling.

In his head Dalehead stood fast, just as it always was. So he was puzzled, every now and then, as he passed large stones, painted white, set out at intervals on either side of the track. And at the end of the track, new gateposts and a new wooden gate, and the cobbles of the yard, not covered in muck any more but washed clean. A lamp-post stood at the corner of the garden wall. And a gleaming car.

As he halted at the gate a fat, floppy-eared dog, ambling out from the old dairy, began to bark at the stranger.

"Hel-lo?" A tall, smiling woman had followed the dog out of the dairy. "Be quiet, Toby," she said to the yapping dog.

Just then a lank cat slid out of the barn. It fixed its eyes on the aliens a moment, then trotted swiftly across the yard.

"Tip," he called to her. "Tip."

"He's very wild, I'm afraid," began the woman, apologetically.

"It's a she," mumbled Tommy Ashe.

They stared at one another, the woman still smiling, puzzled, so evidently waiting for an explanation: *Who was he? What was he doing here?*

"I've gotta go," he blurted suddenly, then turned and ran for all he was worth, running back along the track, before darting down the bank to the footbridge across the river.

He didn't stop till he'd put a good quarter mile between himself and the house.

It was midday on the Tuesday before the police received a reliable sighting from a quarry worker who'd seen a boy crossing Shire Hill on the edge of the moors the night before. His wife had heard the appeal put out over the local radio.

"Do you think you should tell the police," she said, "about that lad?"

He said perhaps he'd give 'em a ring later, when he'd had his dinner.

The police called in the mountain rescue team. By early afternoon they'd begun a search of the woods and quarry workings on Shire Hill. Some examined the underworld of flowing water along the Shelf Brook and Shittern Clough, scrutinizing the pale shapes of old feed bags pinned under the drooping branches of trees, that might have been a dead face dissolving in the current. Others were combing through the plantation along the Moorside, the local barns and farm buildings.

The search went on long after dusk closed over the short winter day, gathering the moor, and with it the missing boy, into the darkness.

In the dale the thin drizzle had turned to steady rain. Up in the steep woods under the rim of Rowlee a small wooden hut stood in a clearing. An old abandoned shooting cabin, it was used as a base by various troops of scouts. The boy hung back in the trees, watching it for several minutes. But he saw and heard nothing. Only the pattering of rain among the branches, pattering in the bracken.

Far below he could see the lights of Dalehead, as he'd seen them many times, coming down through the wood with his grandad. Only he couldn't go there now. He thought of the old man going up the steep bankside between the trees. He seemed very near. All around, up in the dark trees, even the damp air, filled with presence. Then, so close he near jumped out his skin, an owl went, *Hoo-hoo-hooo.. Hoo-oo-oo-oo-ooo..* That slurry, shivery call sent shivers down his spine. *You try*, the old man whispered. Showed him how. Put his hands together for him. But he never could. Though he'd tried and tried, he never could.

Cautiously, he advanced into the clearing, tried the door of the hut. It was locked. He peered through the small window but it was too gloomy to see inside. He broke the glass with a stone and, gingerly, reached a hand inside. The catch was stiff. He couldn't get a proper grip of it. At last he got it to move, cutting his thumb as he did so. But he got the window open, and scrambled in.

Feeling along a shelf beside the window he found a candle and a box of matches. The box was damp, and it took several goes before he got a match to light. He saw just a bare room with bunk-beds at one end, benches and a table. A cupboard, though, held some tins of food: beans, spaghetti, some rice pudding. He hooked a finger through the ring-pull on a can and yanked. He ate the cold beans with his fingers, then licked them clean, licking away tomato sauce salted with the taste of blood. It was stinging, his cut thumb. But he felt better when he'd eaten.

Meanwhile the search had switched to the dale. Men with heavy duty torches were working their way through the barns and outbuildings, starting with Moor House and Heathy Lea.

At Dalehead the blonde woman, switching on the radio at six o'clock, had put two and two together.

"I didn't realise till I heard the news," she was saying again, pouring a cup of tea for Maurice Clarkson. "I thought he must be one of yours."

*

The rain was general over southern England. It grew heavier as Hardman got further north, drumming on the windscreen faster than the wiper blades could push it aside. He felt the past sucking him back.

What does anyone run from? Whatever overwhelms, seeks to consume. Fire had set him running once. At a party long ago in an old house in Cambridge. A room lit by candlelight. He must have leant back against a candle, for his shirt had flared up suddenly. And he ran. He ran from the flame searing his flesh. Out of the room he ran, tumbling down a stair, where someone caught up with him, draped a coat over the flames. Then he was lying face down at Addenbrooke's, while a nurse picked fragments of charred shirt out of his flesh.

Hardman drove. Shut up in his steel box he began to suffer that isolated, cutoff feeling driving at night sometimes induced. Trees and bushes reeling past. Solitary lorries looming up and disappearing, their lights receding in his mirror. He switched on the radio, flicking through the bands for another human presence. Hardman drove.

After the ribbon sprawl of Chapel-en-le-Frith he took the old Sheffield road. Up ahead, a thousand feet above the road, loomed the long line of the Pennine moors, a vast, brooding darkness. Now and then lights came down towards him from that darkness, and swished past on the wet road.

If they haven't found him yet..

He thought of the ewe the dogs had found that day in the snow. Crouching in a hole it had scraped for itself, with its lamb huddled up to its chest. A hissing wind so bitter it seemed to burn. What was it the old man had called him? *A winter lamb..*

He was assailed by a sudden memory of the boy dipping his boots in disinfectant before trudging up the track. He flinched at the thought of those gatherings in front of the TV for the nightly chapter of horrors, scenes no child should have to look upon, sights that outraged the natural order of things. *Why were the lambs separated from their mothers?*

But it is not possible to take upon oneself injuries which are not one's own. The boy's wounds were not susceptible to operations of the mind.

In the dale the slanting rain fell in spears. The owls weren't calling any more. No sounds. Only the hammering of the rain. Far below, the lights of Dalehead seemed as distant as stars across the vastness of space. There were other lights too, glimmering along the track.

For a while he warmed his shrunken hands over the candle flame. Perhaps, though, he ought to save a bit of candle. He blew it out. There was no bedding in the hut. Only the bare boards of the bunk-bed. He lay on his side, his legs drawn up, with the fur-trimmed hood of his parka pulled over his head.

It was after closing time when Hardman arrived at the *Bridge*. George was just putting the towel over the pumps as he walked into the bar. Most of the lights were off. The bar was empty but for Malcolm collecting glasses, and a handful of local men lingering over their drinks. No one seemed surprised to see him.

"Scotch, is it?" The landlord pushed a glass under the optic.

"You'der thought they'der bought a house round here," Norman was saying.

"She'd get more for her money in Glossop, that's for sure," said the landlord, waving away Hardman's note.

"How much *did* they get, d'you reckon?" Monty was filling a roll-up.

"Now you're askin'," grinned Malcolm, coming back with the tray.

It was a question the newcomer, sitting around the edges of the conversation, had wanted to ask. He sipped at his Scotch, content to listen, while others picked over the bones.

"Not as much as she was expecting, I'll be bound."

"I don't suppose the farm sale fetched in much."

"I do believe," said Norman, "the land was leased back from the bank."

"They do say if the farm was ever sold the proceeds 'ad to be shared out between Jack and the sisters. It were in owd Tom's will. So I've 'eard."

"They'der done better to put it up for auction." Eric was stacking glasses on the bar.

"There were so much wanted doing."

"The woodwork wanted seein' to, I do know that," said Norman, who was a joiner.

"Does anyone know who's bought it?" put in Hardman.

"Some big Sheffield builder." George began rinsing glasses in the sink. "He hadn't bought it a week before he'd got a gang o' men in there, workin' on it."

"*They* spent nothin' on it." Beryl poked at her slice of lemon.

"Owd Tom had nowt to spend. What they couldn't do themselves didn't get done." Monty drained the last of his pint. "Are you right, then?"

"Aye, best get off," sighed Norman.

"I don't suppose there's any news of the boy," asked Hardman, when they'd gone.

George shook his head.

"The Glossop team were up there today. Eric's lads will be turning out tomorrow. Edale too, I shouldn't wonder."

"I hope to God they find him."

"Aye, let's hope so."

Hardman swallowed his Scotch. Was about to go.

"Where are you stopping?"

He shrugged. "I expect I'll sleep in the car."

"You can kip down in the snug if you like," the landlord offered. "It'll be a sight warmer than your car."

*

As soon as it was light Tommy Ashe left the hut. A part of him wanted to stay, to let them find him: not to go down to the farm, or even out into the dale, just stay until he was found. Yet another, wilder part, knew it had to get away from the dale as soon as possible. So, at first light, he was on his way. He took the candle, matches, and some of the tins of food in a carrier bag he'd found in the hut.

The rain had stopped. A glance at the grey cloud settling lower over the moor told him it would start again before long. His wet clothes had dried overnight to a damp warmth that was not uncomfortable. But the spiteful wind soon had him shivering.

He went up through the trees, heading for the rim of the moor. He was surprised at the effort it cost him, the steep bouldery slope. He was soon gasping, sweating. At the top of the slope, where the remains of an old boundary fence ran up against an outcrop, he stopped for a pee. The bitter air was shuddering on his skin.

A scrap of dark hair snagged on a wire caught his eye. He looked, first at the wire, then at the channel scraped in the damp earth underneath. No fox that moved in the dale did so at random. Each travelled a highway carried in the head, full of twists, tunnels, in and out of rocks, under roots and fences, that took it away to safety whenever danger threatened. The boy, though, felt blind to what he stared at, a place where two worlds met a moment, then parted.

Up on the open moor he met the wind again, a strong wind, gusting into his face. As he headed south-east over Rowlee, battling against it, he began to feel the first drops of rain.

Rain was in the air when Hardman got to the dale. A spitting wind from the west. The high moors cloaked in mist. Only the grass gleamed improbably in the gloom. As he opened the gate he glanced up at his former home, looming under the dripping trees. Dark patches staining the wet stone walls. The gaunt house had never looked more grudging.

He left the Rover at the end of a long line of vehicles parked along the track, and went on foot to the farm. The bottom land was dotted with the first of the ewes brought off the hill ready for tupping. Further down the track he fell in with a familiar figure, lifting a sac out of his boot.

"It's a bad do, is this," said Eric Smith.

They found the yard thronged with volunteers. Hardman spotted the tall spare figure of Maurice Clarkson, with several of his lads.

"I thought we'd got shut of you," said a voice at his shoulder. It was Jack Ashe. He was gazing at his tups, grazing in the paddock. Bareheaded, in the same shabby donkey jacket he used to wear for lambing, he seemed an unlikely figure in all that mass of bright wet weather gear.

"Looks a bit different now." He didn't offer to shake hands.

Hardman was made aware, for the first time, of the lamp-post, the fresh paint.

A woman, clutching a steaming jug and stack of paper cups, was bustling here and there. Cheerful, capable, she had a smile, a word, for every one.

"This place has changed a bit," he heard someone say.

"Well, there was an awful lot wanted doing." A rueful laugh hinted at generations of peasant squalor that had to be scraped away.

The next moment she was coming up to Hardman, jug at the ready.

"This," he told her harshly, helping himself to a cup, holding it as she poured, "is Mr Ashe. This used to be his home."

Among the volunteers waiting for instructions there was that speculation as to likely developments that is found among participants at any looming tragedy.

"They won't send a chopper up," a man informed a friend

he had just made, "not in this."

The mountain rescue teams pored over maps. They looked up at the sky, knowing in their bones what the elements were telling them, asking one another if he could survive another night in the open.

"It's this raw, wet cold is the killer," said Eric Rhodes.

Hardman, though, had spotted someone else. A singular figure in old-fashioned breeches and grey flecked sweater, he stood apart from the rest. At his side was a tall, tapering alpine sac.

"That man," he said to Eric. "I've seen him somewhere."

"Him? Aye, he turns up sometimes. We see him now and then."

Standing with folded arms, eyes at a distance in the blank, leather face, he might have been awaiting a summons, waiting for his time to come.

The boy was scarcely more than a mile away, stiff with cold as he went stumbling down the Derwent side of Rowlee towards the woods of Lockerbrook. The rain had soaked through his jeans and the wind, gusting against his sodden parka, was battering the heat from his body. He was getting colder by the minute.

At Dalehead, in the lee of the hills, the cloud condensed as a fine steady drizzle, borne on a blustery wind. The worsening weather and failing visibility were giving cause for grave concern. But the search was getting under way. The first wave of volunteers, each man no more than a dozen yards from the next, had set out at last on the tedious, painstaking sweep of the dale bottom. A second wave was climbing the hill across the valley to scour the forestry. A third, led by the Derwent team, had taken the fellside beyond the river and would sweep back to the Snake road. Hardman and Jack Ashe were going with them.

"Where d'*you* reckon he'll be?" asked Eric bluntly.

Jack Ashe shook his head.

"I was hoping he'd be here," he said wearily. "The only other place I can think of is Arthur's over in Derwent. Mabel always made a lot of him. He might be heading for Grainfoot."

Stiff, stumbling awkwardly over the rough pasture, the boy was now losing heat faster than his body could produce it. At Lockerbrook he had to stop for another pee. He found it diffi-cult to get himself moving again, and when he did so he was halfway down the track towards Ashton Clough before it struck him this wasn't where he should be going. Turning, he stum-bled back up the slope. He was stumbling a good deal now.

Warmer air, condensing over the waters of the Derwent valley, fell as flurries of sleet, swirling on a rising wind that set the branches of the trees in motion, and sent little wavelets streaming over the Derwent dam. As he set off down the steep fellside Tommy Ashe could scarcely feel the toes in his wellies. The carrier bag had slipped from his grasp, the tins tumbling down the slope. He couldn't rouse himself to bring them back. He was shivering violently, even on the move. A fox that by day haunted rocks close to the path saw him staggering, falling, as he came down through the forest. The boy's veins had begun to stream with ice.

At Dalehead, now the search headquarters, they were still in the process of re-deploying a team to drive round to Grainfoot, when news came of the discovery of the broken window at the hut. Of course, as Eric said, anybody might have broken in, a rambler looking for a night's shelter, anyone.

They were still discussing when Jack got a call on his mobile.

"It's Arthur. No, he's not there. Though they'll carry on looking. Of course he might still be on his way."

Then news came in of a boy seen near Lockerbrook two hours before. Acting on the assumption that the boy was some-where between Lockerbrook and Derwent, they planned their sweeps accordingly. One party would head east over Rowlee, another would drive round to Fairholme and sweep up through the forestry towards Lockerbrook. A third team would head for Arthur's, and work back from there.

It was a gamble, but they had to take the risk. All agreed the lad was most likely heading for Grainfoot.

But for the boy, somewhere beyond the body signalling its desperation, a cold wind of dreaming was carrying him away, so that it seemed he might escape them after all. Already it had lifted him onto a different plane. He was discovering a deep calm that lay hidden beyond the wind's turbulence, and the lashing rain. Yes, you crawled through a hole and came out in a place wholly unexpected. Too small for a man yet big enough for a boy to stand up straight in, with ledgy walls where you could stick a candle, and some tins. You could watch a man passing within ten yards yet not be seen yourself.

So he went on, looking out from his refuge over the folded Howden moors to the strange mushroom rocks of Back Tor to the north and, a pinpoint in the distance, the lonely cairn of Lost Lad.

*

They drove the eight or nine miles round to Derwent in meagre, drizzling half-light. Cloud cover, and the densely-wooded slopes climbing into the mist on either side gave to the deep, narrow dale an oppressive, shut-in feeling.

Jack Ashe stared fixedly ahead, huddled in his sodden jacket, wiry hair plastered to his skull. All day he'd plodded his patient, shepherd's stride. Hardman, trudging at his side to make a kind of company, remembered him in the same tattered donkey jacket, driving a fence-post, tireless, under a downpour. No yielding till the job was done.

"He were like a sick beast," he said at last. He was remembering how the old man used to talk of real wild sheep, fetched off the moor in heavy snow, who'd starve sooner than eat the cereal blocks he'd fed 'em. "He just fretted all the time."

Then, somewhere in the car, a mobile phone began to ring. Jack Ashe took the call, his face expressionless. Hardman peered through the screen, hearing only the monotonous *whirr.. whirr..* of the wiper blades. The call seemed to go on and on.

"That were Arthur. They've combed every inch of the barns and outbuildings. He's not there."

Hardman could think of nothing to say. His eyes were fixed on the road, winding interminably beside the grey, gloomy waters of the reservoir. What he saw, though, was a houseless fugitive floundering through marsh and grey rain-smoke, trekking towards a final bolt-hole.

Suddenly he tumbled to it.

"I think I know where he might be heading," he said quietly.

Deep buried in a clough furnished with a few stunted thorn trees, the boy was indeed flogging up the steep, left bank of Mill Brook, making for the bivouac cave on Dovestone Tor, though by now no more than a shadowy destination. Sheep huddled under the thorns turned towards him eyes full of misgiving as, gasping, slithering, he floundered up the sodden fellside, grabbing with hands that wouldn't seem to clutch. He was slipping gradually beyond the sinking instrument of his body. He could scarcely feel his feet any more. If he still managed to put one boot in front of another it was becoming a haphazard manoeuvre. Sometimes the boots collided, pitching him forward. Getting up took longer every time.

The rim of the horizon had begun to loom as a dark, misty wall above the curving bank of the clough, towering close, yet still a long way off, a strange crest of rock, startling in its jagged crenellations. Most hospitable to his weary legs, what appeared to be a level sward of plushy green. He'd stopped shivering. He no longer felt the cold. Quite drowsy now, reduced to such a state of numbness, he might have tumbled into sleep. But carried on nonetheless. The green carpet upon which he floated was as soft as eiderdown, and quivering, so that he was most grateful to be sinking down at last, next to the stile, in that dark corner by the fence..

Grainfoot was crammed with vehicles, choking the yard about the huddle of stone buildings. An ambulance, turned and ready to leave, waited at the end of the lane. Police and ambulance men stood about, some talking into radios. Jack Ashe stood with them, waiting with his cousin Arthur, waiting for news. He seemed dazed, bewildered by what was shaping up around him.

Mabel Greaves, coming out to them with mugs of tea, saw he was in need of mothering.

"You're soaking wet, Jack. You'll catch your death. Come along with me into the dry."

Unprotesting, he let himself be led into the farm kitchen.

Mist shrouded the fell. The line of searchers, red and blue and yellow, tailed away into the mist, the men set-faced as they toiled uphill. Since the last message, hours earlier (*No.. not at the cave..*), they'd been combing the lower slopes either side of the dale. To eyes alerted at every turn, the boy seemed present everywhere. Yet what confronted them, the whole, vast, complex organism of stones, water, earth and vegetation, seemed barely accessible to human vision.

Now re-grouped, and with the light failing fast, they were making one last sweep of the great hollow below the Tor. Here were puddingy parts where a dark thick moss like tiny palm trees grew. Though boots sank in a bit, a grown man could walk safely there. And wetter places, streaked with oily patches of slimy green and clotted white stuff, where sticks, pushed in, came out with a bubbling gurgle, and a stink like shit. And level bits of bright green, like a soft green sward which, if poked, wobbled for yards around.

If he's up here, thought Hardman, he must have collapsed. He thought of that, the last warm vestiges of life leaching into the sodden earth, sinking without trace.

"They've found him."

A blowing of whistles, coming down through the gloom, passed the news swiftly along the line of volunteers straggling the fell above Millbrook.

It was the medical officer, one of the fittest of the Derwent team, who spotted the pale orange glow of a shelter tent against the sleety gloom of the moor. He got there seconds ahead of his mate. His first glimpse, as he lifted up the side of the tent, was of a spare, leathery face. A solitary man was clutching the boy to his chest, it might have been to give him warmth.

Another member of the team, arriving with oxygen, heard a mutter of voices.

"I can't find a pulse."

"Is he breathing?"

"Just about."

Gently they laid the boy on an insulating mat. Laid him on his side.

"Tommy! Tommy, lad. Are you with us?"

But the boy's mouth and eyelids would not open for them. It might have been a piece of marble they'd laid hold of. The hands, hard, colourless, were marbly cold. They covered them with thermal mittens, pulled a woollen balaclava over his head, and put him in a bag.

Then, when the rest of the team arrived, slowly, carefully, they began to carry him down.

Hardman, halted on the misty fellsides, heard rather than saw them looming: the soft thud of boots, laboured breathing, a muffled clink of metal. Then, as they came suddenly from the mist, he recognized in the faces as they passed, not relief, but the strange lull that signifies a search still unresolved, a life hanging in the balance.

As they reached the wall above the Mill Brook the stretcher party stopped for another change-over of carriers. The boy's face was indistinguishable under the oxygen mask. The man at his side checked the neck for a pulse, glanced at the mask, fogging with some vestiges of breath.

Then the stretcher party moved on again.

Hardman fell in beside the medic.

"What chance has he got?"

"Touch and go, I'd say. He's still breathing. If we can get him down without his heart stopping he's got a chance."

He found Jack Ashe waiting with the ambulance. If neither of them spoke it might have been because they didn't know what to say. Or else there are times and places when words fail altogether.

Together they watched the stretcher lifted gently into the back.

"You the father?" said the ambulance man.

Hardman shook his head. "You want Mr Ashe here," he said.

Jack, though, seemed not to have heard.

The ambulance-man looked at him enquiringly

"Shall you go with him," he prompted. It was, as respectfully as it could be put, an instruction.

"Aye.. aye. I'd best go with him."

He climbed inside. The doors closed. Seconds later the ambulance was on its way, its blue light flashing, flashing between the trees.

It was over. Yet groups of men still lingered in the road, standing behind their cigarettes, talking in quiet voices. "Is he alive.." the voices murmured. "Is he still alive.."

"You're not going back to George's, are you?" someone called.

Hardman turned to see Eric Smith fastening a sac.

"Could you do us a favour? Could you give these lads a lift?"

*

That night hot soup was served to all who wanted it at the *Bridge*. Though many of the rescuers had far to go, few were leaving. Some lingered to exchange anecdotes, to be released back into the flow of life again. If others were silent, it was because they did not have anything to say. Or else they were waiting for something which had yet to happen.

Eric came over to Hardman with a mug of soup.

"Have you thought about it, then?"

Hardman looked questioningly.

"Stanage," said the blunt man. "It's green now, and damp. Come back in the spring when the rock's warmed up, and the days are stretching out a bit."

"I'd like that," said Hardman.

The cold shell of his body had found a place around the fire, and was cupping its hands around the mug of soup, but his deeper self flowed out into the night, and over the wet road.

It entered the porch, and went into the kitchen where Ellen Ashe was brushing the children's hair. Or else it was Jack, stamping the snow from his boots on the stone flags. He would like to have spoken words of encouragement to the faces that looked at him expectantly, but he could not. He would like to have gone through to the sitting room, where the boy might have been waiting to be read to. Only he was not.

So he returned to waiting at the *Bridge*, waiting with the rest.

At long last came news that what they were expecting had come to pass. For a second or two a tense silence held. Then, slowly, quietly, the talk began again, as the living returned to themselves out of the great emptiness of death. Some were standing up to take their leave. Men and women, drawn together for a while, beginning to disperse, slipping back into their separate lives.

Hardman went out into the car park to ring Elizabeth.

"You know?" she asked.

He flinched at the pain in her voice, the old distress at the tragedy of dead children.

"Yes. We just heard."

"Why?" she whispered. "What was he thinking of?"

"Who knows," he said wearily.

The first of the departing volunteers began to pass him in the car park. Looking up, he saw in their faces the imprint of arduous aching toil, and the long trudge back, with the sense of nothing saved.

"Maybe he was trying to get back to the source," he added obscurely. "To recover what was lost. I don't know."

*

Flakes of wet snow were falling as he turned the Rover down the slip-road on to the motorway. He peered through the screen, straining to see beyond the ceaseless snowflakes dashed aside by the wiper blades. Yet his mind remained with the boy, perishing at the last like any other creature of the moor. He saw again the eyes fixed anxiously on him, heard again the halting voice. *Would it have hurt, dyin' like that.* And his own careful answer. *They must have been very frightened, and alone.* He thought of their winter walk together, tramping back over the darkening moor, and the strange light blazing out, and the boy enfolded in the light.

Wrenched out of his life, Tommy Ashe had run back towards it. Yet he could not have said what drove him, any more than the man, groping for whatever instinct, arising out of what was most primitive and forgotten, sought to return the boy to where he belonged. No, he could not account for the mysteries of existence.

Once or twice he caught himself nodding, the Rover veering towards the central barrier of the motorway. Or else the road was bending to the left. He switched off the heater, turning the temperature to 'Cold'. He switched on the fan. Then, opening a vent, directing a draught of cold air directly at his face, he set about the task of getting himself back safely to his wife.

The snow brought widespread chaos to the south of England. Over Bleaklow the cloud hung low, above a long bar of purple light. But the last of the snow was clearing from the dale. The track was empty again. Only the marks of the tyres remained along the verges of the thorns, and in the soft ground down by the ford.

At Dalehead the newly installed central heating boiler had broken down again. The woman, sweeping up the last of the litter from the yard, shivered at the thought of no hot water. How the moor seemed to close about the house on these short dark days.

High on the hillside above the dale the eldest of the Clarkson lads, 'young Maurice', was whistling his dogs between the banks and hollows. He was bringing the Dalehead ewes down to the tups.